Treating Children with Autistic Spectrum Disorder

Treating Children with Autistic Spectrum Disorder: A Psychoanalytic and Developmental Approach outlines a unique model for working with young children with autistic spectrum disorder, which has been adopted by many day care facilities in Israel, and is now arousing interest in the US and UK.

Drawing on psychoanalytic and developmental psychology, this model offers guidance on multi-professional working with the difficulties arising out of administering treatment to young children in day care and other non-residential settings.

With contributions from professionals, all with many years of clinical experience working with ASD children, this book provides a comprehensive overview of this model and depicts an integrated therapeutic network, which encompasses every aspect of the child's development within an educational day care facility. Each of the book's chapters is devoted to the daily problems that arise when working with ASD children, such as weaning and toilet training, as well as the effects of ASD on wider family functioning.

Treating Children with Autistic Spectrum Disorder offers an essential, practical guide, which will be an asset to any clinician working with young children on the autistic spectrum, as well as the parents and siblings of these children.

Tami Pollak is a therapist and supervisor in a day care unit for ASD children, and teaches in the Psychotherapy Program at the Sackler School of Medicine, Tel Aviv University and in Winnicott Center, Israel. She also has a private practice in Tel Aviv.

Treating Children with Autistic Spectrum Disorder

A Psychoanalytic and Developmental Approach

Edited by Tami Pollak

Routledge
Taylor & Francis Group
LONDON AND NEW YORK

First published 2018
by Routledge
2 Park Square, Milton Park, Abingdon, Oxon OX14 4RN

and by Routledge
711 Third Avenue, New York, NY 10017

Routledge is an imprint of the Taylor & Francis Group, an informa business

British Library Cataloguing-in-Publication Data
A catalogue record for this book is available from the British Library

Library of Congress Cataloging-in-Publication Data
Names: Pollak, Tami, author.
Title: Treating children with autistic spectrum disorder : a psychoanalytic and developmental approach / Tami Pollak.
Description: Milton Park, Abingdon, Oxon ; New York, NY : Routledge, 2018.
Identifiers: LCCN 2017029589| ISBN 9781138308206 (hbk) | ISBN 9781138308565 (pbk) | ISBN 9781351389976 (ebk) | ISBN 9781351389969 (mobipocket)
Subjects: LCSH: Children with autism spectrum disorders—Treatment. | Autism in children—Psychological aspects.
Classification: LCC RJ506.A9 P66 2018 | DDC 618.92/85882—dc23
LC record available at https://lccn.loc.gov/2017029589

ISBN: 978-1-138-30820-6 (hbk)
ISBN: 978-1-138-30856-5 (pbk)
ISBN: 978-1-315-14300-2 (ebk)

Typeset in Times New Roman and Gill Sans
by Florence Production Ltd, Stoodleigh, Devon, UK

Contents

Contributors

Tami Pollak – Clinical social worker. Ph.D. in Philosophy. Therapist and clinical supervisor in Shaked day care unit for ASD children, and in a private clinic. Teaches in the primitive mental state track in the Psychotherapy Program, Tel Aviv University, Israel, and in Winnicott Center.

Pam Yogev-Platek – Clinical psychologist and supervisor. Head of the multi-disciplinary clinical unit adjacent to kindergartens for ASD children in Holon, Israel.

Orly Shalev – Dance and movement therapist and psychotherapist. Therapist and clinical supervisor in Shaked day care unit for ASD children and in a private clinic.

Joshua Durban – a training and supervising child and adult psychoanalyst at the Israeli Psychoanalytic Society and Institute, Jerusalem where he also teaches. Teaches in the primitive mental state track in the Psychotherapy Program, Tel Aviv University. Works in private practice in Tel Aviv, Israel.

Tamar Meidan – Dance movement therapist. DMT. M.A. treatment coordinator, therapist and clinical supervisor in Shaked day unit for ASD children and in a private clinic.

Karen Peleg – Clinical psychologist. Therapist and clinical supervisor in Shaked day care unit for ASD children and in a private clinic.

Limor Montal – Clinical psychologist. Therapist and clinical supervisor in Shaked day care unit for ASD children and in a private clinic.

Yael Eitan – Clinical psychologist. Therapist and clinical supervisor in Shaked day care unit for ASD children and in a private clinic.

Hilit Bechor Cohen – Clinical psychologist. Therapist and clinical supervisor in Shaked day care unit for ASD children and in a private clinic.

Hadas Benari Livny – Clinical psychologist. Therapist and clinical supervisor in Shaked day care unit for ASD children and in a private clinic.

Tamar Assal – Clinical social worker. Therapist and clinical supervisor in Shaked day care unit for ASD children and in a private clinic.

Pazit Gur – Speech–language pathologist – certified instructor. Therapist and supervisor in Shaked day unit for ASD children and in a private practice.

Edna Lahav – Clinical psychologist. A candidate in the Psychoanylitic Institute – Human Spirit.

Nechama Faber Ben Pazi – Clinical psychologist. Head of 'In School' – a therapeutic multi-professional support system in primary and secondary schools. Teaches in the primitive mental state track in the Psychotherapy Program, Tel Aviv University, Israel.

Preface

This multi-author book is the end-result of twenty years of work at the Shaked kindergartens, a therapeutic-pedagogic framework for young Autistic Spectrum Disorder (ASD) children, located in Holon, Israel. Through years of integrative work with these children, which is theoretically informed by a psychoanalytic-developmental approach, our senior staff had amassed a great deal of clinical experience in the relevant therapeutic and pedagogic fields.

Diving to the depths of such a severe, enigmatic, and multi-faceted disorder, many of the staff members began developing a unique way of thinking and a language and a form of learning and growing while holding the integrated fabric of theory and clinical practice. We gained a deeper understanding of the importance of multi-professional integration in working with these children. We conceptualized a psychoanalytic-developmental model for therapeutic response, which includes the kindergarten-pedagogic space as a therapeutic environment and developed our own theoretical thinking.

The human developmental potential is realized in external reality, the inner world and the potential space between them, in light of the organizing and generative reference point of relatedness and communication with significant caretakers. ASD children encounter difficulties in each and every one of these aspects. One witnesses difficulties concerning the ability to separate and connect in simultaneous stimuli processing, in body organization, in the 'me'/'not-me' distinction, in the decoding of emotions and their expression, in establishing relatedness, in the ability to link sensation and meaning for the creation of language and more. This book focuses on describing and conceptualizing these difficulties as well as addressing them through multi-professional care. The various chapters include the personal experiences of the therapists, the inter-professional dialogue, the everyday function of the kindergarten as a therapeutic environment and more.

The book's pregnancy – which included many fetuses – was very complex and may reflect the essence of our work at the kindergarten. It began with therapeutic distress that 'pushed' us to a phantasy about professional pregnancy, in the guise of a conference whose revenues could fund additional therapy sessions. Unsurprisingly, these unfunded sessions were devoted to play and communication groups (DIR)[1] in pairs – child and educational assistant – under the supervision of therapists specializing in this area. As a new feature, 'The Assistants Project' was designed to reinforce the years-long integration of educational assistants in paramedical and psychoanalytic supervision and instruction: designed to make them more professional, to help them acquire a conceptual language, but also to simply let them take a break, for their own education and well-being.

Being accustomed to long, slow processes, the pregnancy took quite a few years. Its beginning was fragile and miscarriage was a very clear danger. How does one enlist the entire staff to support a phantasy about a new baby? Who does the phantasy belong to? Who has the strength to take on more tasks when the resources of our extended family are sparse to begin with? Who can guarantee that our imaginary fetus would survive, develop and come out into the world? And once out – will it be given its due place? All these desires and anxieties, all the envy, aggression, and ambivalence evoked by these and similar questions had to be worked through in long discussions between the various staff members. Gradually, the conference began taking shape: the groups came together, the subjects became clearer and each group began its search for equilibrium on the tightrope between theory and clinical practice. Finally, with diligent slowness, we toiled over the maturation of those lectures presented at the conference, so that they could go out to wander the world on their own – in book form. The authors whose ideas are presented herein are only a small part of a much larger team, who shared the indispensable preliminary thinking.

The book is divided into eleven chapters.

Chapter 1, **Theoretical background: the experience of the autistic child and the transition towards a post-autistic organization** (Tami Pollak) serves as an antechamber, leading into the unique and strange space of autism – which is not particularly welcoming, where one's intuition is a poor guide and where one requires a special survival kit. The chapter applies different theoretical and clinical perspectives in illuminating the various gates that will open, one after the other, in the following chapters. The author presents a primary map of autistic space and lays down the fundamental coordinates for psychoanalytic-developmental contemplation of this modality of 'being' in the world.

Chapter 2, **The structure of the multi-professional therapeutic response for preschool-age children with autism** (Pam Yogev-Platek) presents the practical application of the psychoanalytic-developmental perspective – the foundation of the densely woven therapeutic net required, in our view, to address the needs of these children. The chapter discusses the pedagogic-therapeutic array as a living organism, which entails feedback loops and mutual-enrichment between distinct yet related therapeutic approaches as a feature of the everyday holding environment.

Chapter 3, **'I'm not moving, don't you move!': treating a child with an organic disorder and autistic defenses – an integrative case study** (Orly Shalev) represents the combined efforts of a team of therapists treating a child named Elay. It offers a multi-professional depiction, which expresses the child's unique course of development, while also shedding light on common developmental characteristics in other ASD children. The case study moves between acknowledging the child's extensive deficiencies and difficulties and recognizing his potential for development. It raises crucial therapeutic questions and sheds light on the structure of the kindergarten's clinical practice.

Chapter 4, **Case discussion: in the beginning was the Word?** (Joshua Durban) observes the clinical material from outside the kindergarten routine, offering a foundation for enriching the psychoanalytic understanding of autism.

Chapter 5, **The body-schema and the development of the self** (Tamar Meidan and Karen Peleg) focuses on cases where children are preoccupied with their concrete body functions as a key issue in their psychotherapy. The authors trace the integration of the 'body-schema' in normal development as well as the theoretical and technical dilemmas raised by disruptions typical to ASD children.

Chapter 6, **Thoughts on diaper weaning and its contribution to the development of the self in ASD children** (Limor Montal and Yael Eitan) uses an elaborate clinical vignette to trace the overwhelming impact of primary anxieties of psycho-physical breakdown and the horror evoked by change and adaptation to external demands – as these are heightened throughout the weaning process. The authors present dilemmas that arise for parents and members of the pedagogic and therapeutic environment in this potential window of opportunity for self-organization.

Chapter 7, **The autistic constitution and its impact on the disruption of parental functioning** (Hilit Bechor Cohen and Hadas Benari Livny) discusses the manner in which a baby with a deficient innate constitution might cause 'an extensive parental disruption' in unconscious phantaphantasy, in communication, in thinking processes and in actual parental functions. Functions associated with the parent-infant relationship – container/contained relations, object-use, absolute dependence, the mirror role, aggression and others – are distorted and parenthood is inevitably damaged in a way that requires rehabilitation.

Chapter 8, **In spite of and because of words** (Tamar Assal and Pazit Gur) discusses the intriguing and challenging presentation of ASD patients who have acquired language, but still fall short of the full sense of linguistic functioning. The authors trace the contribution of the combination of educational goals, the multi-professional approach and the psychoanalytic perspectives on the child's autistic use of speech.

Chapter 9, **The consulting room – the structure, texture and beauty of the object as a path for the development of primal psycho-physical space** (Tami Pollak) discusses extreme cases in which the child's psychic mechanisms are so diminished that transference relations are precluded. The only dimension of the child's experience that remains available for therapeutic intervention is their physical action in the consulting room, which is seemingly devoid of communicative intent. The consulting room is discovered as a place where body and space function as subjective objects birthing phantasy from matter.

Chapter 10, **Dimensions of (non-)space and the autistic state** (Edna Lahav) presents the autistic state as a unique spatial modality, which effaces the distance between distinct points of reference and limits the motion this distance may generate. The author portrays the therapist as a 'space-object' facilitating the very gradual and piecemeal formation of the patient's inner space.

Chapter 11, **The multi-aged child** (Nechama Faber Ben Pazi) concludes the book by turning its gaze to a developmental and therapeutic dilemma that emerges in treating older children, given the vast developmental gaps characteristic of post-autistic children. The author distinguishes between age-appropriate, multi-aged and non-aged psychic organization, suggesting that one should offer a distinct emotional-existential response to each developmental level, without abandoning the child's healthy mental functioning that would enable an age-appropriate response.

Tami Pollak
Jaffa, 2014

Note

1 DIR (Developmental, Individual, Relationship-based) is a method for treating ASD children, based on S. Greenspan's developmental model for expanding circles of spontaneous communication.

Constitutional history

In 1992, several parents living in Holon asked the Association for Children at Risk, a group of professionals focused on helping young children with autistic spectrum disorders, to establish a kindergarten setting for their children. The Association's professional advisors – Prof. Nati Laor, head of the Ramat-Hen Mental Health Center, Dr. Abigail Golomb, head of the Tel Aviv area Infant Care Unit, and Ms. Yemima Halfon, the chief clinical psychologist at both the Unit and the Association – had joined hands in forming the first ASD kindergartens in Tel Aviv. From this framework and with its close professional guidance, clinical psychologist Pam Yogev-Paltek set out to establish the first ASD kindergarten in Holon. For about a decade, three kindergartens sharing the same physical space and the same psychoanalytic-developmental mindset operated in Holon; this is where the professional core of this book came into being. Since then, Holon saw the establishment of more kindergartens, all with the support of the Ministry of Education, the Ministry of Health, the municipal authority and the Association; today, a unit comprised of fourteen therapeutic kindergartens is operating in the city. Each kindergarten relies on the pedagogic administration of a kindergarten teacher and all are supported by an extensive professional team, headed by Yogev-Paltek, the unit's chief clinical psychologist, with psychiatric assistance from Dr. Golomb. During these years, the Association established some 200 kindergartens nation-wide, whose therapeutic work is informed by diverse professional approaches (psychoanalytic-developmental, integrative-developmental, cognitive and behavioral).

The vast increase in number and distribution of the Association's kindergartens is indicative of the sharp increase in ASD diagnoses in children, a phenomenon which, in our view, requires considerable investment in planning, training, resource allocation and establishment of new settings – processes which are headed at the Association by Adv. Tzipi Nagel-Edelstein, the Association's CEO and her professional teams. But there is a need for more: in our opinion, it is imperative we strive to achieve a theoretical understanding of both the phenomenon and the best ways for dealing with it.

Chapter 1

Theoretical background

The experience of the autistic child and the transition towards a post-autistic organization

Tami Pollak

This opening chapter will serve as a sort of antechamber accommodating the reader as we draw a primary map of autistic space, which will be explored in greater depth throughout the following chapters. I shall outline the basic coordinates orienting psychoanalytic-developmental thinking about autism, relating to central theoretical and clinical dilemmas.

The initial conception of autism as a distinct pathology merited its differentiation from other pathologies by the assumption that the difficulty is derived from the child's external environment. The child's strange behavior was understood as a particularly massive display of familiar defense mechanisms vis-à-vis a cold and lethal maternal environment (Bettelheim, 1967). The developmental prism had made it possible for us to step out of this judgmental mire, by assuming that the difficulty lies in the child himself and that autism manifested a halt at a particular stage of universal human development, one which Mahler called 'normal infantile autism' (Mahler, Pine, and Bergman, 1975). Both conceptualizations pointed to an extreme manifestation of familiar mechanisms, rather than a unique psychic organization.

Although these two initial positions are no longer accepted today, when autistic organization is construed according to its own distinct theoretical prism, their traces are still common in our countertransference. Even today, it is quite surprising to discover the extent of the unconscious difficulty to leave behind this premature splitting, which constantly raises its head, alongside the decisive conscious negation of both approaches. Even today, it is hard to withstand the temptation to believe that the child's difficulty is merely a product of damaged parenting or, alternately, that as time goes by, 'the obstruction will relieve itself' and the child will resume his normal development. It might be dangerous to sweep such nonintegrated thinking under the rug, since its very existence obliges us to keep minding our responses. These outdated approaches are not secluded in some historical domain, but are rather right here with us, and we must turn our gaze to face them in order to diminish their influence.

How, then, are we to extricate ourselves from the binary division between inside and outside, child and environment? Even Tustin, one of the pillars of the psychodynamic approach to autism, unburdened herself of Mahlerian dogma only late in life, after decades of work. Infant observation, as well as some help from Ann Alvarez, had finally led Tustin to acknowledge a third path – the one which guides our work in the kindergartens. Tustin encouraged us not to conceive of autism as a reaction, an arrest, a regression or a disruption of some particular function. In her final paper, she referred to autism as a unique congenital structure, dictating an obstruction of the developmental potential for separateness (Tustin, 1981). In her understanding, we are dealing with a baby which exhibits an extreme predisposition for sensual-fusion, a baby whose acknowledgement of bodily separateness is always traumatically premature. As a defence against this traumatic separateness, the tendency for self-oriented sensuality develops excessively, eclipsing normal infantile sensuality, which is capable of acknowledging the dynamic relationship between self-originating and external stimuli. This brings about the distortion which replaces dependency with detachment and openness with seclusion, inducing disruption at every subsequent developmental junction. This tragic distortion hinders the convergence of the various developmental functions into a unified structure – the self – which enables both subjectivity and communication.

This split-off constellation constitutes a primary and crude level of organization (Klein, 1952), in terms of both internal organization and the evolution of thinking. Dividing the focal point of difficulty between inside and outside, the rigid and dichotomous etiological split I have presented is, in itself, highly characteristic of autistic organizations. It is unsurprising, therefore, that it should prove so difficult to dispose of when thinking of autism. The complexity of autism gives rise to a tendency to entertain fragmented notions of it. Each perspective excludes all others and fosters a type of therapy which fails to correspond to other kinds of treatment. Some view autism as a pathology in terms of defensive organization, stemming from a massive disruption of sensory regulation. Some view it as a reaction to 'bad' chemical agents, such as those found in vaccines or various food ingredients. Others indicate that the root of the problem is a cognitive difficulty in integrating different perspectives (Lantz, 2002). Others emphasize the communicative aspect, the capacity for play, acute behavioral disorders, difficulties in attaining a personality structure and so on and so forth. This abundance creates an imaginary reality, in which these various theoretical and practical perspectives exclude each other.

Although autism has been studied from multiple angles for the past several decades, we still do not fully understand the cause of this phenomenon. Nevertheless, we are indeed capable of describing it and conceptualizing its particular inherent difficulties, in hopes of achieving a more effective therapeutic response. Our work in the kindergartens embodies the constant effort to avoid a fragmentary 'either/or' position in favor of a more inclusive holding, containing within our minds the profound interrelation of the various functional aspects accompanying the course of development. Focusing exclusively on any isolated professional perspective undermines the ability to provide a 'good-enough' response to the developmental needs of the child. Faced with the danger of fragmentation, our work in the kindergartens seeks to address the child's developmental needs by means of a comprehensive approach, which links these various aspects together. This position is elaborated in the following chapter, which outlines the depth-structure of the therapeutic response offered in the kindergartens. I now wish to present a view which broadens the scope of understanding, as far as our limitations allow.

In order to discuss the link Tustin made between autism, the difficulty in bearing separation and the non-functional use of the bodily-sensual foundation, I will begin with an example of the simultaneous maturation of motion-sensation-affect-cognition-relation and separation in normal development. Imagine a baby crawling up to the living-room table and trying to pull herself up to a standing position. Although her motivation for exploring the space around her is at its peak and despite various motoric, cognitive and communication skills, which have been providing her with 'I can' experiences, this time, she did not plan her movement adequately and bumped her head. Her mother responded by making a face, tapping herself lightly on her head and saying 'ach' (the Hebrew expression for 'ouch'). The expression 'ach' thus serves as a warning code, shared by the heedlessly explorative baby and her attentive parents, indicating a manoeuvre that may end in pain. Several weeks later, when she was brought to the window to wave goodbye to her father, this baby tapped herself on the head and said 'ach'. The mother made a sad face, saying: 'ach, aba halach' (Hebrew: 'ouch . . . daddy went away'). She used this same gesture to help her baby link the familiar sensation of physical pain with emotional meaning, encompassing representation, relatedness and separateness. Some months later, during the similar goodbye ritual, the baby tapped herself on the head, saying 'lach' (a short version of 'halach' – 'went away'). 'Ach' has become 'halach' and by now the baby is capable of linking physical space and the pain of separateness in a way which maintains continuity – relating to both sound and word. Soon enough, the baby learned the word 'went away' ('halach'). At first, she used it to describe any kind of motion in space – for example, when her pacifier fell down, she exclaimed: 'went away'. Later on, this expression became specifically associated with voluntary movement. In this manner, spontaneous bodily and emotional experiences within relatedness facilitate the birth of words, which, in turn, resonate within a space spanning interpersonal meaning and subjective creativity.

The psychic motion between the benign and painful aspects of separateness is thus made possible by the simultaneous maturation of these various functions. In ASD children, studies have shown gaps of varying degrees between functions that are still attainable in development and those that have been frozen in time. In addition, they exhibited an active attack on the congenital tendency to integrate the various functions in a way that is conducive to the creation of a personality structure. Therefore, we must look for ways of understanding and working with the disruptions stemming from this kind of grossly discontinuous development.

In the world of psychodynamic psychotherapy, the object-relations school, concerned with the most primary organizations of human experience, is the central psychoanalytic approach preoccupied with the study of autism – and one of the dominant sources influencing our work. Those treating autistic children are exposed to the tangibility of the archaic psyche in a way which surpasses treatment of any other pathology. This exposure enables us to perform a unique clinical investigation into the subject's origins and the initial emergence of psychic functions. For these reasons, the study of autism appeals even to those who are not involved in treating autistic children and has become a cardinal element of the broader discourse regarding primary psychic states.

According to the meta-theoretical mythology of object-relations, found in the writings of Gaddinni (1992) or Tustin (1972, 1981), for example, the subject begins to form in the homogenous mother-infant space, in which separateness, form, structure and time do not yet exist. This hypothesis is not some peculiar psychoanalytic concoction; religion, myth, and philosophy suggest similar existential origins. Let us take, for example, the French philosopher Emmanuel Levinas, whose thinking matured during the same years as that of Tustin and Gaddinni, just 'across the channel'. Levinas presupposes a state, which precedes the birth of the subject, a state of affairs he calls the 'there is' ('*il-y-a*'). He claims that in order to approach this state we must divest any subjectivity, identity, and unity from the subject, as we traditionally conceive of it, thus approaching an anonymous and a-personal existence, sheer 'being' (Levinas, 1978, 53–62). This sheer being has no 'I' and no objects, but it still resounds, according to Levinas, with a 'rumbling silence', as that emitted by an empty seashell (1985, 48). This is the paradox of the presence of absence. Rings a bell? I suppose it does: Tustin herself had used the image of the empty seashell to describe her encounter with autism.

How, then, does the subject emerge from this unsettling rumbling of undisturbed silence? For Levinas, the primal rupture in the 'there is' occurs through an act of finding a place, made possible by the deviation from the inertia of an infinite continuum. From the perspective of object-relations, we might say that this primary 'placement' can only occur in the mother's lap, as the holding it entails is a precondition for the more mature face-to-face encounter.

I believe that, as therapists in our day and age, after having weaned ourselves from the habits of the split perspective, we may gain access to a field of thought whose core is a paradoxical organization: the encounter with autism is inhuman, unbearable and deeply unsettling as well as highly relevant to any human subject. Perhaps for the observer (unlike the child, who is unfamiliar with the oscillation of paradox), autistic rawness is the most archaic root of the 'uncanny', which, as Freud (1919) conceived of it, is always an existential paradox. In the spirit of this paradox, it is important to stress that accepting the notion of an impersonal infrastructure preceding the subject as one of the roots of its existence is in no contradiction with the teachings of Trevarthen (1977), Beebe, Jaffe and Lachmann (1993, 1994, 1997), Stern (1985) and others – who elaborated on what any observant person knows: that the human baby is active and relating and thereby also communicative and inter-subjective from the moment it is born. In the paradoxical scheme I am proposing, the link between the personal and the a-personal binds together two elements that both exclude and create one another. In autism, the roughness of impersonal materiality is exposed as the lack of motion toward the personal and the subjective, bringing us in contact with a 'being', which the psyche experiences as intolerable. Autistic psychic space is often depicted as dead, hollow, two-dimensional, void of meaning and so forth, and the encounter with it is often dubbed deadening, numbing, draining, as a kind of black hole which bars all resonance. I think that anyone willing to step into the Styx, that mythological river joining and separating the living and the dead, to suspend their soul in autistic space, will find in it something of the wonder of creation, something that cannot be felt in any other encounter. For me, at least, this serves as one reason for my years-long addiction to autism.

This primary, homogenous space, bereft of separateness, form, structure and time, has been described by Tustin in aquatic terms. Following in her footsteps, we may argue that water and liquidity, arising as a countertransference image, are derived from an identification with the actual watery sensations characteristic of the infantile environment – the amniotic fluid, urine, milk, tears, and others. We may also claim that alongside such bodily concreteness, which is essential for thinking about these layers of experience, liquidity is also a rather astute metaphor for describing 'oneness' – at the resolution of our experience of liquid flow, water is a unified, contiguous, and unstructured substance: we have no way of telling one drop from another, the original from the newly introduced – much like Levinas's notion of origin. In this state of uninhibited admixture, we cannot apply the distinctions and links characteristic of psychic functioning. Autistic children in this state wander around in space, hovering indistinctly from object to object, moving between activities without any change in affect; they are utterly unaware of the importance of the Other and they run like water from any attempt to hold their attention. Without the experience of dependency, one cannot feel the sorrow of lack; in this context, we can fathom Meltzer's claim that autism is a state void of all anxiety. While it may be free of anxiety for them, it provokes much anxiety and agitation in those around them. Those Others shoulder alone the responsibility for any 'twoness', for acts of creation designed to 'divide the waters'. Eventually, however, we cannot help but come up against the anxiety of separateness. This maneuver both overwhelms the autistic child with primal anxieties and ignites the processes of mentalization, resulting in a huge challenge for him and those around him.

Another important fact suggested by the metaphor of a 'liquid' state is the realization that in order to make use of a liquid, we must resort to an external factor that would determine its accumulation. It makes no difference if this accumulation occurs naturally (in a riverbed or a gully), voluntarily by using our body (in our mouth or our hands) or culturally, in artificial containers (such as drainage basins, vases, glasses, etc.). Nature, our body and our culture all constitute frameworks for a transition – from formlessness to form – and are all equally necessary for the creation and aggregation of the subject. The utter dependency of the liquid on a form-giving object is associatively conducive to the depiction of the absolute dependency of the baby on maternal holding, and that of the autistic child, who regardless of age still manifests a liquid organization, on the psychic mechanisms of those caring for him.

In order to step into this *experience* of complete dependency and contemplate its relation to autism, I wish to invite the reader to an excursion at sea, to embrace a hypothetical situation that I have devised, inspired by one of my favorite artists, Jenny Holzer:

> At a random spot on the beach, a post is fixed in the sand, on top of it is a metal box, holding a spotlight which emits a beam of light. The spotlight is constantly projecting its light and when the sea is calm, it is aimed just over the horizon, so that the beam of light and the surface of the sea form two parallel lines that will never meet. Most visits to the beach reveal nothing – the spotlight projecting into infinity and the indifferent sea are completely alien to each other. Why then bother observing these apathetic neighbors? Why have I dragged you all the way to the beach? Because things, nevertheless, change when these basic conditions are radically altered – when the wind is blowing and the sea becomes wavy, the rising waves create a surface which encounters the beam of light, which now has something to refract on. This refraction causes a sentence to emerge. A corny lover's line such as 'I love you, Johnny'. Now, the sentence that only existed in potential is revealed, existing in a shared space: alienation and indifference are transformed into a gesture of love and communication. And then. . . . As the wind subsides, it all vanishes once more. And one can remain standing there. . . . Just waiting for the wind . . .

I think that the frustration over a state of affairs in which no object will appear and no space will open is all too familiar to those spending time with an autistic child. Why did I invite him into my clinic? How can this be called therapy? The most potent experience is that of helplessness – we are powerless to cause the sea to swell with waves! But the extent of our helplessness equals that of our sense of wonder, as I mentioned before, in the moment of revelation. The elusive eco-system I have depicted is both private, intimate and essentially unique – miraculously addressing a person named 'Johnny' – and present in an a-personal space, pertinent to each of us, as we are all, like Johnny, simply waiting for the wind, as we all become realized only through an encounter that uncovers a loving sentence that was already there, preceding us. Is this eco-system not a manifestation of the same primary materiality that we witness, so intolerably and wonderfully, in our encounter with autistic children? Naturally, the more common experience with these children is that of parallel lines that are never to meet; but let us remember that the miracle of revelation – in our case, that of the renewal of the course of development – is nevertheless an inherent part of this universe. The heart of therapeutic work beats with the faith – held only by the therapist – that our world contains the possibility of encounters and revelations and that even if these tarry, they will surely come! Vanishing and reappearing. Who knows how or when? And what if the wind is merely a possibility and, unlikely as that may seem, it refused to blow?

This utter dependency on the wind is reminiscent of the existential dependency of the emergence of the subject on the mysterious workings of the α-function (Bion, 1962), which transforms raw sensory perception into representations. And, having mentioned the α-function, could it be that this psychic function serves as the answer to the attempt to find what could 'contain' that unstructured infantile liquidity? Bion had offered us the 'container-contained' relationship as an expression of the innate tendency of our relation to objects to manifest as a psychic structure through this function. This function is not part of some pure abstract consciousness, roaming through possible worlds; it is acutely dependent on β-elements, that is, on the raw sense-perceptions related to the actual materiality of the body and the world. Therefore, we must take into account the complete dependency of this psychic function on the normal or abnormal state of bodily materiality or, in other words, on the organic foundation.

While the organic foundation is, indeed, congenital, in a more meaningful way, it is more than a mere deterministic given, it is also a potential. Normally, the first layer of raw impressions that form the container entails the double-lining of many essentially psycho-physical mechanisms: autonomous,[1] sensual,[2] and affective regulation; transition between sensory modalities; the primary capacities for planning and intention; the potential for organization through a matrix of sequence and causality. At first, none of these systems are matured or regulated; their respective maturation occurs through their mutual regulation, which facilitates the relationship with the mother. At the same time, successful perceptual processing creates a background of security for the baby, that is necessary for the reduction of the anxiety of experience in general and that of addressing an object in particular (Sandler, 1960). In normal development, this forms a benign circle, in which object-relations facilitate maturation, while the realization of the maturational potential enables the consummation of object-relations. In autism, since the psycho-physical matrix is congenitally distorted, the same cyclic pattern gains a destructive momentum. Psyche and soma are thrown off track in a way which imperils even the emergence of the hyphen that serves to link and differentiate them (Winnicott, 1954a): the course of development is distorted from its very beginning.

In many cases, the starting position for ASD children entails difficulties in regulation, as well as in each of the physical aspects and the capacity for linking them. Tustin made a strong connection between the kind of bodily and sensory system these children possess and their emotional development (Tustin, 1981). She stated that in cases of extreme fusion with the mother, the acknowledgment of bodily separateness becomes intolerable and traumatic, experienced as a bombardment of painful sensory impressions and overwhelmingly violent emotions, for which the psycho-physical equipment is not yet ready (Tustin, 1994). These children develop an overactive and powerful sensuality, meaning that primary sensuality is diverted away from caretaking figures and thus from relating to them. As a result, deficient autistic responses proliferate. We often see the children plugging their ears, reacting anxiously to changes in the touch of clothes on their skin or producing a constant sensory stimulus as a buffer against stimuli they cannot control. As the roots of the self are so clearly embedded in the normalcy of physical experience, as it matures within the framework of relatedness, occupational therapy – the allied health professions designed to enable the development and maturation of the bodily foundation required for higher functioning – is vital for them. While the absolute interdependence of the various functions requires therapists unfamiliar with this field to mind difficulties in terms of sensation or regulation, the occupational therapist possesses the unique tools for distinguishing one disturbance from another and for planning informed responses. In addition, guidance or counsel from an occupational therapist is indispensable for parents, psychotherapists, clinicians, and kindergarten teachers who wish to become familiar with the child's physical profile and select activities or interventions that the child could benefit from.

In order to highlight the organic foundation of the container-function, I will shortly describe the particular deformations of the container as manifest in the autistic child's psychic space. In order to do so, I must elaborate on Bion's container function – an idea both abstract and intricate – which utilizes a simple and intuitively accessible image. What is a container? It is an object with some manner of enveloping which defines an interior and an opening which allows for insertion and extraction. We do not conceive of a strainer as a container, nor would we define as such any hollow object whose envelope is sealed (a ball, for instance). This image entails several basic assumptions about the psyche which, in the course of normal development, emerge and are experienced in a natural and unconscious manner:

1 The intuitive notion of psychic space as a three-dimensional space, that is, as possessed of depth or interiority.
2 The existence of boundaries that are clear enough to allow the experience of envelopment and the distinction between inside and outside.
3 An intuitive and *subjective* acquaintance with the container's openings – the body's orifices – which embody the subject's openness to the world and to the Other.
4 As derived from these three assumptions, the potential for taking in external material and excreting internal material.

All these stages of existential structuring are made possible for the baby by its dependency on the mother's containing function, a function that is not spontaneously or intuitively available to ASD children. They exhibit each of these container-functions in a highly distorted manner, making them one of the most significant focal points of the therapeutic process, which is always long and difficult. In this context, the word 'material' has two layers of meaning: a concrete-physical layer (food, sense impressions, etc.) and a metaphoric-psychic layer (information, emotion, affect, etc.). One of the essential difficulties in ASD children is that the a-symbolic character of their thinking keeps them from distinguishing between these two layers. As far as taking in is concerned, we encounter massive difficulties in eating as well as in the willingness to take in the presence of the Other and its significance; as for outward openness, we find difficulties in toilet-training, emotional expression, and communication. This is why their affliction is so encompassing, requiring such a multi-faceted therapeutic response.

Donald Meltzer conceptualized the autistic spectrum in relation to the deviation of the organization of psychic space, from the normal, three-dimensional organization of the container. He describes autism as a state of total failure of mentalization, as a one-dimensional experience. In this state, there is no sense in discussing experience or learning from experience as any data perceived is strictly sensory, detached from any other aspects of experience and precluding any sense of continuity of self or of external objects. This definition is somewhat rhetorical, as even the most extremely autistic child has layers of depth, to which we may appeal, and states to which Ann Alvarez' notion of 'reclaiming' is still applicable.

The two-dimensional experience is an apt depiction of a psychic reality which already entails the fragile acknowledgment of external objects, although the encounter with them still does not seem to resonate with any depth of subjective meaning. In this kind of organization, the psychic mechanism acquires its objects by gluing their surface to the surface of the self. Initially, this act is performed through sensual practices, such as stereotypical motor-sensual motions or phonic echolalia. As the development of this organization utilizes the psychic mechanism of adhesive identification, we often encounter children who have acquired the use of language as well as other functional skills, but these are all void of any subjective tint, have a bizarre air to them and are employed rigidly, in a patterned and repetitive manner.

The three-dimensional experience portrays the psychic space of post-autistic children, a space which can house a depth of meaning, albeit for short periods of time. We often witness, in these children, a thick and intricate shell of information, speech and thought; yet it is important to recall that we often face pseudo-thinking, void of any subjectivity – the essential component of thought as an emotional event – and that the accumulation of information serves as a substitute envelope for the normal skin-Ego (Anzieu, 1989), which remains unattainable for them. The motion between various aspects of space in post-autistic children is fragile and prone to be overwhelmed by anxiety and distortions caused by psychotic or perverse mechanisms, that emerge from beneath the autistic shell.

But there is also a fourth dimension – time. In normal development, time is first and foremost the spontaneous and unconscious process of change embedded in growth. In the one-dimensional organization, time is frozen still, but the initial establishment of the capacity for separateness and the emergence of psychic mechanisms open up the possibility of relating to the succession of time as well as the changes and distortions it entails.

In autistic children, psychic motion requires great flexibility from the therapist's notions of time and space. Motion along these two parameters may occur outside our normal range of perception: at the speed of light, with several twists and turns in the course of a single session, or with glacial slowness, which bars any neurological impression intelligible enough to serve as a mental representation. As mentioned before, our work as therapists relies on the possibility of motion, which exists, to a certain extent, even in autistic space. In order to trace, in a perceptible level of detail, changes in the child's use of objects as expressing the qualities of his psychic space, I now wish to tell you of *Adam* and his button.

Adam came to our kindergarten when he was about three years old, with extremely autistic functioning. He would hold, in a fixed and unalterable manner, a small shell button, taken from a man's shirt. He would place it at the center of his field of vision, as a kind of blind spot, serving to block his openness to the world and his perception of the world as possessed of depth, both literally and metaphorically. Obsessively, he would try to find the perfect way of holding his button, so as to hypnotize himself with the light glittering off its surface. Usually, objects serve our psyche in an integrative manner, that is, when they are structured through the active link our psyche makes between their various aspects – sensual, functional, communicational, inter-personal, social-cultural, and others. This plurality of aspects makes it possible for us to use each object in a flexible manner, according to its different qualities. The autistic object is the exact opposite: more often than not, only one of its qualities is significant – one of its sensual aspects, evidently peripheral to others who consider this object – and the autistic child holds on to it as a barrier against everything else. This behavior corresponds to the protective sensual addiction Meltzer depicted as characteristic of one-dimensional space. Tustin referred to these hard objects, used obsessively and non-functionally, as Adam used his button, as 'autistic objects'. She conceived of them as constituting a particularly primitive 'patch' for the anxiety of rupture and leakage evoked by primary separateness. Tustin recommended that we avoid letting the autistic child disappear into his 'auto-sensuality' for long. She argued that altering the use of the autistic object proves a decisive moment regarding further changes in psychic space, functionality and communication. All well and good, but how are we to pinpoint the right moment – a moment that is not lethal, reinforcing the mechanisms of seclusion, but rather conducive to triggering processes of adaptation?

For Adam, the difficulty was enormous, giving rise to a paralyzing anxiety among the therapeutic and pedagogic staff as well. His separation from the button began to gain momentum only in his second year at kindergarten. At this stage, he gradually began shifting it away from the center of his field of vision and started looking around himself, at the surface of a world inhabited by objects, both human and inanimate. This is, in itself, a characteristic of two-dimensional psychic space. He safely deposited the button in the fold of his little finger and began making minimal use of his hands for functional purposes. Those who did not know him could never have noticed that his pinkie was reserved for such an act of holding.

I believe that this holding had created a unique environment for the button, one which may be considered a significant step – as awkward as it may be – on the path toward internalization and a post-autistic organization. True, the rolled-up finger was a substitute for the mouth, and the button for the nipple and the milk; holding something does not quite constitute taking it in; the button was not transformable as an object; and, above all, there was no trace of any human object-relation. Still, despite all these essential distortions, the button was no longer a buffer or a shield. Quite the opposite, it was now a personal, semi-internal companion, with the pinkie allowing for a kind of incorporation. Adam grew more and more involved with what was happening in the kindergarten and soon acquired the ability to point with the button grasped in his knuckle.

Stepping away for a moment from this particular case, I wish to discuss the distinction, in developmental terms, between 'grasping' and 'pointing' as two essentially different types of 'motor intent'. The primary organization of the infantile hand is the fist and grasping is the instinctual potential, enabled by the fist, for a direct link *between two*, with no need for any further communication or mediating reflection. As this organization is the counterpart to the innate relation between the nipple and the mouth, I term it the '*maternal*-prototype'. Pointing, however, is a communicative intention involving *three*: it requires the joint attention of two, who are observing a third. This act relies on a separation from the tactility of grasping, and the acknowledgment of a space endowed with depth. I refer to this phallic gesture of pointing as the motor '*paternal*-prototype'.

Adam's button was making the journey from an experience of one, to two and three, as a pre-symbolic foundation for the Oedipal organization and the threshold of the post-autistic path. Several months later, in the psychotherapy room, Adam placed the button on a sheet of paper and used a marker to make a circle around it. For a long period of time, he only made countless identical circles. However, at one critical moment, he picked up the button, looked at it from a distance and added two dots to his circle, matching the two sewing holes. This entailed deeper familiarity with his related object, as he could now link touch to sight and bear the knowledge that this object was heterogeneous, that it was structured as a circle with two holes. Several sessions later, I sensed intense preoccupation with these two internal dots, which were growing thicker. I shared my thoughts with Adam: 'are these eyes?' Expressionless, Adam added a horizontal line at the bottom, where the mouth would be and looked at me. He had now made the transition from form to representation. The button had run the entire gamut from being an autistic object to a representation of a human face. Who knows how long it had nested as a transitional object at the fold of Adam's pinkie, without us knowing?

One day, Adam pushed the button through the crevice under the door of the psychotherapy room, looked at me and then opened the door to bring the button back into the room. This activity became a game, involving much communication and enjoyment. The button was no longer confined to its secret lair. It now became a channel for exploring the room's opening as a space of meaning – as the threshold to a whole new level of questions: where is something that is not here? What happens to it over there? What do things look like when they are concealed? These questions are the very crux of the aesthetic conflict discussed by Meltzer – a conflict between two complementary modalities of exploring and knowing: one that is positive, grounded in sense-impressions and seeking to uncover what is; and one that is rooted in the imagination, establishing an aesthetic space of possible objects, similar to the mother's internal objects. Adam was there already!

The transformations of a button – from an autistic object to a transitional object and a representation – have allowed us to sense the clinical actuality of the abstract conceptualizations regarding the various organizations of psychic space. Now, I wish to take up Adam's play involving the room's door in order to argue about the difference between two-dimensional and three-dimensional organizations, by highlighting the essential distinction between holes and openings.

The literal definition of a hole is an unexpected discontinuity in a surface that should, in reality or phantasy, be uniformly continuous. Therefore, this lack of continuity is experienced as a rupture or an injury. An opening, however, is an area that is predictably and structurally designed to organize the possibility of desired motion between inside and outside. No one would live in a room that had no windows or doors. Even our own physical make up includes the skin, marking the distinction between interior and exterior, alongside the orifices – mouth, eyes, ears, and others – which undermine this distinction. Therefore, the subject's normal envelope, whose prototype is the skin, is not perforated or breached, but neither is it continuous and closed – its structure must manifest the subject's cohesion *and* its existential openness *as well as* the tension between the two. In autism, what is normally experienced as necessary and desired openings in the psycho-physical make up are instead experienced as holes,[3] which may bring about the catastrophe of annihilation. In these states, the therapeutic goal is to attain an experience of cohesive existence in spite of the rupture, so as to eventually create the emotional meaning of 'opening'. In the above vignette, we may notice how Adam's ability to relate to the room's door marked a new organization in terms of psychic space.

I now wish to share with you, with the help of *Ben*, a more primary clinical manifestation: a change in the experience of the mouth, from being a hole to being an opening. This transition will allow us to shed more light on other matters as well.

Ben was alarmingly thin. He almost completely avoided any foods that required biting or chewing, that is, he avoided any use of the hard parts of the mouth. His diet was composed, almost exclusively, of dairy products, namely – a generic brand of chocolate pudding. Ben also salivated excessively and his shirt was constantly wet.

In the session I am about to describe, Ben lay curled up inside the inner tube of a truck's tire[4] in the corner of the room and had covered himself up with a blanket. I was glad to hear deep, rhythmical breathing coming from under it and I sat down on the carpet, next to the inner tube. Suddenly, he reached out from under the blanket, grabbed my hand, put one of my fingers in his bellybutton and squeezed my hand down to keep it there. I was stunned, confused and before my wits were gathered, he had grabbed my other hand and started licking my fingertips. It felt awful! Disgusting! I started pulling my hand back. He reacted by allowing me to separate the finger that was in his bellybutton, while changing his use of my other hand: he now placed all of my fingers in his mouth and was sucking hard. I used the freed hand to lift up the blanket and saw him looking at me as he sucked, with his huge, black, and painfully beautiful eyes. The intolerable was now made possible. I took back my hand and he stayed on his back, looking at me. Eventually, it turned out to be a one-time experience and he made no attempts to repeat it.

Let's stop for a moment and think about what happened there. Two pestering questions arise: one involving the understanding of the psychic dynamic, the other involving technique. While this situation may evoke countless theoretical considerations, in reality, it gave rise to a difficult technical dilemma regarding touch. Technique in such borderline cases is a fascinating field, which merits an entire book. For our present purposes, I will only touch upon it lightly. It is crystal clear that, for many important and inherent reasons – to which I am profoundly committed, physical touch is not our therapeutic instrument, even if the patient is a child and even if he is autistic. However, the encounter with children in general and autistic children in particular often unsettles the professional platform upon which we sit comfortably, obliging us – when faced with certain acts – to turn our gaze to the darker areas of our practice. Physical coercion, as that which took place between me and Ben, is a situation that the psyche cries out against. Often, in our counter-transference it is this very experience that colors those moments when the actual encounter thrusts us, unwilling, to a state that places us in domains of experience we have never dreamed of visiting voluntarily. These are places where the unifying rationale of technique is applicable only in a partial and limited way, yet the urgency of the actual encounter summons us to tackle them. If we decide to open the subject for contemplation – as we are often compelled to engage in touch with the children – this deliberation must be founded on a dynamic understanding.

The network of primary integration linking the various senses and connecting them with motor communication and motion is a potential network, which is spontaneously set in motion as a space of meaning, by the relation to the object in actual experience. In the reality of Ben's life, his mouth, as a primary integrating instrument, could not have been available to him as a constitutive experience and, in order to take this primary step, he required the conditions present in the therapeutic incubator. In a child whose vitality is manifest in concrete, a-symbolic and pre-verbal areas, the search and the realization cannot become displaced, represented or metaphoric – such distance is already too far. As the therapeutic framework is, nevertheless, designed to enable development for such a patient, we must address the issue of the relation between wish and need. It is the common belief that in normal cases the frustration of the wish is conducive to psychic work, leading to a significant developmental step. Nevertheless, we must keep in mind that turning our back on a primary developmental need, especially an existential one, whose expression is so feeble and fragile that it is already at risk of being annihilated, is a different matter altogether; it may be a fatal mistake. Winnicott viewed such situations as a matter of psychic life and death. Are we, however, facing such a need here?

If, in thinking of Ben, we hold on to the notion of the 'container', we cannot help but consider his sucking on my fingers as an expression of the constitutive relation between the mouth and the nipple. Concealed in the blanket, Ben set out from this intra-uterine twilight zone, which served as a platform for exploring the container-contained relation. The possibility of umbilical nourishment rids one of the need to distinguish inside from outside, holes from openings – but this solution becomes obsolete at birth. We may say, with clinical certainty, that since his birth, Ben's mouth had functioned as a hole, making the full meaning of nourishment unavailable to him. Saliva leaked out just as chocolate pudding slid in, without any mechanism that could distinguish or link hard-soft, in-out, 'me-not me'. Anxiety was massive. By sucking my fingers, so saturated with transference, Ben had, for the first time, created a situation that held great meaning for him. He substituted his autistic habit of licking metallic surfaces – such as the kindergarten's set of keys, his favored object – with an experiential acquaintance with his bellybutton and mouth as related to an object. His mouth no longer functioned as a leaking hole, but as an opening, as part of the multi-dimensional structure of phantasy, inherently linked to the desire for an object. This had enabled the link between motor action, sensation, gaze, relatedness and dependency, arousal, and calmness. This kind of integration is vital to the effort to bring Ben closer to the lovely healthy baby I described in the beginning of this chapter.

In the present case, I think I had the exceptional fortune to encounter need in its most basic form and respond appropriately. Working in the kindergartens, we therapists often find it hard to decide what kind of actual physical holding to offer, if any. Should we allow the child to place his finger in our mouth, as a primary exploratory movement, sit in our lap, and so on? Once we agree to consider the possibility that these questions have no objective or predetermined answer, we may keep contemplating them, each in his or in her own way, in accordance with our own subjective boundaries.

Throughout our next sessions, Ben had explored the potential, both realizable and unrealizable, of the encounter between his hands and feet and my body. I had to engage in very intricate working through in order to distinguish between a touch that I could recognize as a developmentally significant *need*, which I would then allow – as when his feet pushed hard against mine – and what I experienced as a *wish*, which I therefore refused. Bodily separateness was established gradually and through mediation. Eventually, Ben left his inner tube, sat down by the table and pointed at sheets of paper that were in the room. For a minute, this created the impression of a tremendous developmental leap, but then he began salivating on the paper. He was leaking again, evoking strong feelings of disgust in me. After a while, pulling myself together, it entered my mind that he might be drawing. Admittedly, this was not a representation, but simply an expulsion of his liquid interior onto an external two-dimensional surface – but it created a third that we could both see. At some point, the liquid had dissolved the sheet, making a hole. Ben went wild: 'no hole! . . .' But in the following sessions he began making holes on purpose. I pointed at the hole and said, 'this is Ben's', establishing it not as a fault, but as his own subjective trace. He labored over the hole with great intent for about half a minute, until the mechanisms that attack all structures, especially subjective ones, began to surge and he crumpled up the sheet and flew into a rage. As time passed, he went from drawing with saliva to drawing with markers and a certain 'congestion' began to appear around the hole, which I considered to be the focal point of his composition. He no longer crumpled the paper, but instead folded the sheet so that it partially covered the hole. He had gained control over revealing and concealing, opening and closing. The hole became an opening, the real became a representation.

In conclusion, we cannot neglect addressing the issue of language, a major difficulty for children on the autistic spectrum. It is no coincidence that I have saved this issue for last, as the development of language from communication is founded on the preconditions I have mentioned above. As the subject of language in autistic children has been widely addressed in various contexts and is thoroughly discussed in two of the following chapters – the one presenting the case study and the one devoted to language and separateness – I will only mention that a certain degree of distance and separateness from concrete sensuality is necessary for the creation of symbols and that for children on the autistic spectrum, this loss is often beyond their ability to bear. In many cases, even when words are formed, they do not represent a complete network of signification-relations, but various shades of transition between the subjective capacity for symbolization and the shell of sense-speech, which always remains stiff and hollow to some extent. When the possibility of speech is gained, this often accentuates developmental gaps. As a child who had reached a developmental stage in which he himself began feeling the confusion created by these gaps once asked me: 'Tami, am I a midget child or a giant baby?'

In closing, therefore, I wish to share with you the joy and sadness of my encounter with *Eitan*, a child who is still in therapy with me, although he had long since finished kindergarten. This encounter highlights the problem of gaps in psychic organization and post-autistic speech – a problem that will accompany these children, to a certain degree, throughout their entire lives.

Throughout all the years that I have been treating Eitan, he has repeatedly asked 'to see my boobies'. When I had first met him, he was under four years old and incapable of communication or speech. Today he is ten, speaking incessantly and full to the brim with countless suggestions and ideas for realizing his wish (this is a fine example of the essential difference between wish and need). As expected, the torrent of ideas he proposes does nothing to advance the plot in the direction he desires. At one point, during parent guidance, I learned that at home, Eitan employs various violent tactics to force upon his family the delusional solution stating that he is a girl with 'big boobies'.

He came to our next session with a hair clip and was talking non-stop: 'Tami, I am simply crazy,[5] crazy, Tami – say crazy . . . I am totally crazy . . . Tami, I have boobies'. I stopped his ranting and told him about a boy who made himself into a 'crazy girl' so that he could have boobies that were always his. Eitan lay on the couch, fiddling with the edge of the covering, smelled his fingers and asked me to tell him again and again about this boy who went 'crazy'. I repeated this story in various ways until suddenly, in some unclear leap of thought, he asked me: 'Tami, where do you live? Tami, I'm from Holon . . . Tami . . . What is Tel-Aviv-Jaffa?'

Me:	'We're from two different places. Are you asking about my city?'
Eitan:	'Is your city two?'
Me (still searching):	'Two, like me and you?'
Eitan:	'Tel-Aviv . . . and Jaffa.'
Me:	'Yes, now my city is two . . . At first there was a city called Jaffa, and then they built a new city – Tel-Aviv'.
Eitan:	'So Jaffa is Tel-Aviv's mommy?'

He leaps off the couch and starts running around the room, screaming: 'Jaffatelaviv, Jaffatelaviv, Jaffatelaviv!' I tell him that he's gluing together mother Jaffa and her boy Tel-Aviv; just like the way he is using his imagination to glue boobies on Eitan. Eitan runs even faster and then stops: 'NeveTzedek[6] that's not Jaffa and not Tel Aviv? No! It's not! It's both Jaffa and Tel Aviv? Yes, it is, it's true! It's a very special place!'

Narcissistic gratification aside, the special place is neither the neighborhood of Neve-Tzedek nor the particular location of my office, but our shared space, in which the transitional organization of 'both at once' begins to dawn, the space where separateness is no longer traumatic, because it is held as a paradox. I feel like hugging him, the 'crazy boy'; even language itself shudders at his inability to reconcile between his wish and his developmental needs. One can witness his roller-coaster, running wildly between the primary-sensual organization and more elaborate ones, the motion between the ability to bear separateness and being terrified of it, the oscillation between the various mechanisms of coping and communication and the struggle between the psychotic-delusional parts and those reaching for – and attaining – knowledge. One can also note the gap between the level of organization and material that can be held in the session and the unbearable and impossible expression of the same material at home. In spite of such comprehensive difficulties, many of these children take very significant steps forward in development and acquire the use of language, functionality and inter-personal relations on a level that corresponds to their abilities. Those who are able to take enough essential steps move on to small classes in regular schools and, wherever they may go, they will keep coping – using the tools they have at their disposal – with a course of development that always entails the art of bridging gaps.

This, as mentioned, was but the antechamber. The following chapters will elaborate, deepen and elucidate the various subjects I have presented here so briefly, adding many more aspects of the intricate work required in order to facilitate development in ASD children. Moreover, these chapters will also substantiate certain assumptions regarding primary psychic states that are being explored in contemporary psychoanalytic discourse.

Notes

1 Hunger-fullness, sleep-wakefulness.
2 The normal organization, which enables receiving and processing sensory data from each of the senses as well as their convergence into an experiential totality.
3 Tustin (1981) discussed the clinical significance of the experience of the mouth as a hole in autistic children.
4 The rationale of this unique feature in the therapeutic setting is elaborated in Chapter 9.
5 Using the feminine form of the adjective.
6 The neighborhood in which we meet, right on the border between Tel Aviv and Jaffa.

Chapter 2

The structure of the multi-professional therapeutic response for preschool-age children with autism

Pam Yogev-Platek

Discussion group:

Pam Yogev-Platek – clinical psychologist; Tami Pollak – clinical social worker; Galit Gampel – clinical psychologist; Smadar Sherf – dance therapist.

This chapter presents the psychoanalytic-developmental multi-professional therapeutic structure developed throughout the two decades since the establishment of the Shaked kindergartens.[1] In order to allow a clinical consideration of the kindergartens at the structural level, the discussion will trace my thoughts regarding two children, who embody the essential difference between individual children on the autistic spectrum. My observations regarding the first child, whom I will call *Yoni*, will serve as an example that could be generalized to apply to other children. I will share with you the model we have developed, which is grounded in psychoanalytic-developmental thinking, in order to outline our conception of the various therapeutic responses the child requires as well as the vital link between them. I will emphasize the possibility of viewing the therapeutic response as a living organism, regularly applying distinct therapeutic methods that are interrelated through systems of reciprocal feedback and inspiration on a daily basis. Thus, each professional perspective functions as a single thread within a *densely woven therapeutic fabric*. In our understanding, this kind of fabric is necessary for providing the quality of holding that would facilitate the development of a young ASD child.

I will progress along a timeline beginning with the moment immediately after the 'bomb' of the initial diagnosis was 'dropped': throughout these days or weeks, the parents are just beginning to grapple with the question of their child's future – what will it look like? What kind of professional care should they seek – both pedagogically and therapeutically? Should they comply with the recommendation to place him in a regular kindergarten, with the required assistance? Or should they follow the recommendation advocating special-needs education programs? Both these options entail great difficulties and choosing one over the other is a formidable task.

The loss of the phantasmatic 'perfect child' is traumatic for the parents, distorting their sense of time, as a representation of the potential for change and development. In the child's experience, time is manifest as frozen or utterly non-existent; in that of the adult, it is present as the disruption of the notions of growth, change, and development in the child. Eventually, most parents oscillate between a stern, demanding and uncompromising attitude, wishing to make their child 'just like everyone else', and an approach that denies time, hinders the setting of boundaries and avoids confronting the child with age-appropriate demands. This doubles the responsibility of the kindergarten staff for finding a proper position for addressing the child's actual developmental needs. It is very difficult to sustain the tension between the child's chronological age – which fuels the desire to push him forward and bring him closer to the standards of society – and the developmental locus the child actually inhabits. We also harbor the wish to see the child as younger than his actual age, thus ostensibly allowing greater hope for his eventual development, while nourishing our own sense of potency. However, as time goes by, reality comes knocking at our door and we must, as a team, conduct age-appropriate evaluations, which we too find daunting. We often face very difficult feelings regarding our self-esteem as professionals, doubting our ability to help the child and questioning our professional tools. In the attempt to maintain this tension, friction may arise between the two parents, between them and the extended family as well as between the parents and the various professionals and between the latter and the family. Beyond the various roles or professions, these differences of opinion are also rooted in personality and transference: for some, reality is first and foremost; for others, it is the child's internal organization and subjective experience, which are pre-eminent.

Yoni's family chose not to face the difficult period immediately following the diagnosis alone and had sought private consultation with a psychologist specializing in the treatment of autism in preschoolers, at one of the special-needs education kindergartens in their city.[2] They asked her to support them in their critical deliberations preceding their choice of a preschool program. She held sessions with the parents, with the parents and Yoni together and with Yoni alone. Her impression of the parents was that they were so invested in the child as to ignore their personal needs and those of their other children; that they were anxious about him in a way, which distorts their parental judgment; that his condition was painful for them and that they were having a hard time dealing with him. They were still shocked by the diagnosis, struggling with the knowledge that their child, as they believed they had known him, was lost, and insisting that 'everything must be done in order to make him normal again'.

The mother, who was at an advanced stage of pregnancy at the time, had seemed depressed and withdrawn. The father was experienced as the dominant functioning parent and as the one holding on to the hope of finding a 'solution' for the child, which he relentlessly pursued. The mother found herself having difficulties thinking independent thoughts, which did not coincide with the father's overwhelming confidence that 'Yoni can make it'. They hoped to have him integrated into a regular private kindergarten and provide him with all the necessary treatments privately. They believed that, as Yoni had begun acquiring the use of language, he needed to be able to imitate normally developed children in order to keep developing. The psychologist had helped them see other aspects of his functioning which may make it very difficult for him to be integrated. The most significant occurrence in this period was the process by which the parents came to realize the intensity of their wish, which had become an 'adhesive' equation,[3] stating that 'if Yoni went to a regular kindergarten, Yoni would become a regular child'.

By seeking consultation, it was possible for the parents to begin an initial working-through of their anxiety, confusion, and narcissistic injury as well as a crude mapping of the developmental distortions governing Yoni's functioning. The gaps in his functioning were enormous. In many ways, he was like a little baby, in need of primary maternal preoccupation (Winnicott, 1956), of an object that could create for him the experience of a regulated and held 'going-on-being', through which he could gradually and delicately feel the transition between 'me' and 'not-me'. It was apparent that his physical constitution was damaged: his arms and legs were unrelated and he, naturally, had no capacity for positioning them in space. His motor planning was deficient and he also seemed to be suffering from decreased sensation. Verbally, he commanded a wide vocabulary consisting of nouns, with no verbs, pronouns or prepositions. He would only express one word at a time, which then seemed to hang in mid-air for a second before evaporating. No communicative intentions were evident. It was clear that Yoni needed psychotherapy, occupational therapy and speech therapy and even more than these. The diversity of these treatments was vital, but it was still insufficient – in order to begin his existence, Yoni needed a much more continuous, close-knit and containing environment.

Thinking together with the parents, the psychologist used 'new words' and a novel perspective to portray Yoni's more intricate difficulties: his impaired relatedness and communication, his intolerable anxiety, his overwhelming sensations and his difficulty in holding on to a single thought, let alone link several thoughts together. The parents also became aware that even with his own assistant, Yoni would be 'lost' in the kindergarten environment, which is essentially vibrant, fast-paced and unregulated. Being so fragmented, Yoni's daily reality required the presence of professionals who could see and experience him, in order to create an environment that would be suitable to his needs and significant in his experience. The psychologist reached a mutual understanding with the parents that Yoni's levels of anxiety and sensory overstimulation will prevent him from being integrated into a regular kindergarten, even if accompanied by an assistant – in fact, his needs required a smaller, more adaptive framework. The difficulty in choosing a special education program was great but, as the process drew to a close, the parents were ready to try this solution.

In most cases, children are enrolled in our kindergarten for three years. Admission and departure are the most prominent markers along this continuum. We arrange for admission to be slow and gradual, in order to create an environment of 'going-on-being' that is optimally adapted to the child (Winnicott, 1965). In the year leading up to departure, the kindergarten framework, as part of the gradual process spanning the entire three-year period, sets more social and pedagogic demands as well as additional boundaries, in preparation for the transition into first grade.

The timing of the admission diagnosis (the 'intake') is highly significant. In the summer months, the transition between leaving the previous program and entering a new one creates a void, which may evoke intense anxiety, especially in the parents. They had just been through the ordeal of the placement committee and had received written approval of their entitlement to a special-needs education program as well as their kindergarten designation. Now, they were required to admit their child into a special-needs program, with all that this entails. As we are well aware of their anxiety, their deliberations regarding the different programs, the immense gap between the child's needs and their heartfelt wishes, their fear of stigmatization and the overwhelming information they have to deal with, we are well prepared to help them through the admission process. This help is tantamount to creating a space for parents to deliberate out loud, to come to the conclusion that there is no such thing as a perfect solution, that their choice for their child can be 'good-enough', thus turning their split position into a dynamic spectrum, their time into a continuum and their decision into something less fateful. We attempt to lay out the child's special needs along an axis of varying urgencies, in order to distinguish the necessary from the desired. By building such initial trust with the staff and even by becoming physically acquainted with the kindergarten, parents are able to reduce the level of anxiety characteristic of this period and allow a safer entry into the kindergarten framework.

For us, the process of admission sets in motion our thinking about the child and his family, emotionally prepares us for taking on a new child and brings to mind the coming separation from children about to leave our program. Prior to admission, we conduct the diagnostic process, involving some five sessions and including a primary diagnosis in all areas of functioning and treatment (independently conducted by a teacher, a psychotherapist, an occupational therapist and a speech therapist), as well as a house call, allowing us to meet the child and his parents in their familiar environment. A psychodynamic therapist acts as the 'intake coordinator', in charge of the practical aspect of this entire process: she is responsible for gathering the information from the various diagnostic sessions in order to prepare the child's initial multi-professional profile. She also serves as a liaison for the parents' questions and inquiries, until the child is admitted. In most cases, she will then become the child's psychotherapist, provide guidance for his parents and coordinate the child's therapy file, in order to allow continuous holding.

Throughout the last week of August, just before the school year starts, we hold staff preparation days for our two teachers (morning and afternoon), assistants, the therapy-coordinator and the regular allied health professionals. While this preparation also entails the readying of our physical environment, its main focus is team-building and holding meetings in which we develop our shared thinking about each child, the group of children as a whole and the kindergarten space. While such meetings are only based on a brief acquaintance with the children, their goal is to establish, alongside each child's initial developmental profile, a conception of the eight children who will comprise the kindergarten group. We find it important to pinpoint both the needs that are common to all the children and those that are particular to each child, to note their individual abilities and plan ways to use these to create a group experience. These meetings are highly significant to our process of creating a space that is actual and public, while being optimally adapted to the eight children, both as a group and as individuals.

Alongside their practical and pragmatic purposes, these meetings also serve another, less explicit, goal: through the staff's psychic intent, we hope to begin establishing our 'nest' – clearing up the psychic space hitherto reserved for children already in the program, in order to make room for assimilating newcomers. This psychic activity is tantamount to a new organization, much like that of parents during their second or third pregnancy: thoughts and fancies, excitement, the pain of separation, and phantasies about what is ahead. It is always interesting to hear staff members, anxious before the year starts, perform psychic splits and experience what is about to happen as difficult and impossible: their fears of intolerable gaps, taxing children or not having anything to found the group on resurface once more, with alarming intensity. Nevertheless, within a few days, things start to look different. Having worked through their initial anxiety, the staff is able to encounter reality in a more regulated manner. Clearly it is an ongoing process, requiring additional work, thought it is clear that the next wave is coming and will require still more work, until the next cycle begins. . . .

The kindergarten director and her staff have taken on a task both arduous and intricate. The teacher aspires – note the use of the word 'aspire' – to create a secure and continuous 'environment-mother' (Winnicott, 1958) that will enable the children to experience their 'going-on-being'. This environment will take into account all their sensory sensitivities, their misunderstandings, their difficulty in linking and giving meaning to experiences and their need for a clear schedule that will allow some degree of predictability. All these factors constitute the actual foundation of the experience of 'going-on-being'. It is vital to remember that, for some children, the very presence of other children in the same space disrupts this experience. Atop this primary foundation and through constant thinking about the children, relatedness and communication between children and staff members are gradually established. The teacher will attempt to transform every actual kindergarten experience – entering its premises in the morning, finding one's personal drawer, sitting down to eat, etc. – into a meaningful and rich event that could facilitate further development. She will remind the team of assistants that tidying up and setting things in order, ostensibly irrelevant to the needs or wishes expressed by the children, may become rigid and mechanical activities, as an inverted reaction to the children's senseless chaos.

Autistic mechanisms are so powerfully present in the kindergarten's daily routine that the staff's conceptual flexibility and emotional liveliness, which represent separateness and change, are constantly on the brink of collapse. As I have mentioned before, the children oppose any change in schedule and to that we may add their difficulty with changes in space. Every alteration in terms of activity or place, such as finishing a session and moving on to eating lunch, creates an intolerable gap – a gap of separation, a terrifying hole in their protective shell. In such situations, we witness the fragmentation of external attention, withdrawal into states of over-sensuality and increased use of autistic mechanisms. For non-professional eyes, this environment seems bizarre: each child is on his own, the group appears dismantled. The staff may become repeatedly 'infected' by the children's patterned and rigid behavior, even to the extent that their internal thinking space sometimes collapses. Despite all this, the teacher aspires to maintain a balance between stasis and change, familiarity, and novelty, the pleasure

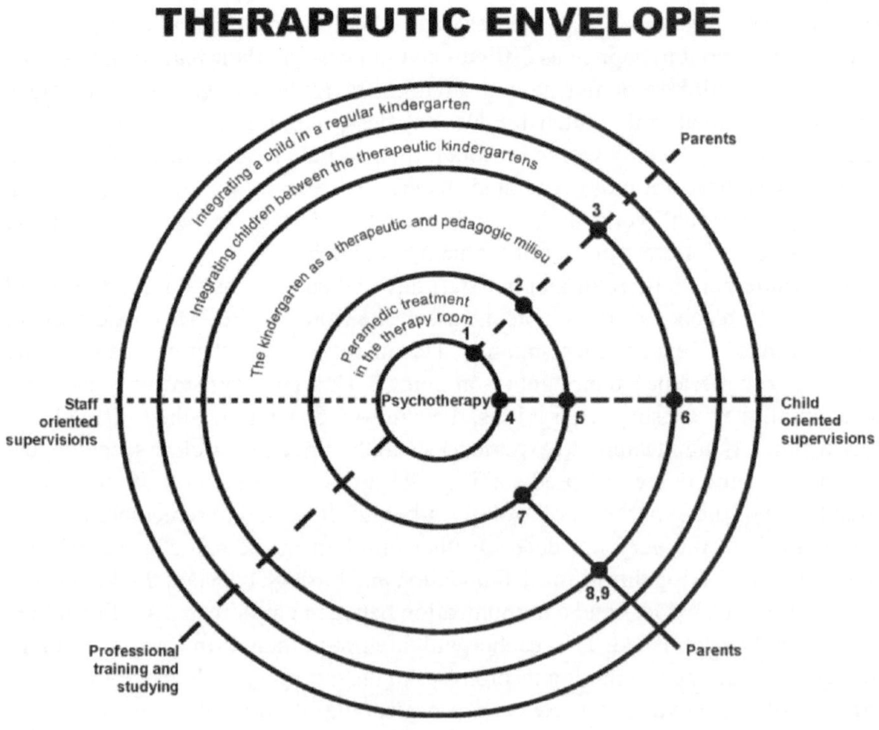

of soothing repetition and the challenge and ordeal of learning and development. You may have expected me to use the word 'plan' or 'aim', instead of 'aspire'. Plans and aims have their rightful place, but it is aspiration that I wish to emphasize, because it is essentially dynamic. It may not always be fulfilled – the wish may sometimes become narrowed, making everything pointless and contrived. The word 'aspiration' also holds the hope that things may change, a little at a time.

You may ask – how is all this possible? I will now present a graphic model of the network of links and containing circles, which demonstrates our way of thinking about the proper therapeutic-pedagogic response for these children.

1 Parent guidance with psychodynamic therapist
2 Parent guidance with allied health professionals (speech, occupational, physical therapist)
3 Meeting of parent with teacher or/and therapeutic coordinator to process the kindergarten reality
4 Weekly professional supervision for the psychotherapist
5 Weekly professional supervision for the paramedic therapists
6 Weekly psychodynamic supervision for the teacher and educational staff
7 Three times a year, the teacher, therapy-coordinator and all the therapists meet to discuss each child
8 Weekly meeting of teachers, therapy-coordinator and educational staff to think about the kindergarten

At this point, the model is much like a map of uncharted territory, without a legend, so that it still does not provide the desired orientation and understanding. I hope that it is clear enough that it is depicting a series of expanding concentric circles that are not merely parallel but also share a common center, around which they are ordered. The different membranes are all interrelated through functional radiuses and their intersections are of utmost importance.

I will now describe each of the different membranes and points of intersection in turn, in order to endow the entire territory with meaning. The concentric circles all revolve around the center – the child – representing the various holding membranes of the child and his family from the most internal to the most external, from subjectivity to reality, from optimal adaptation to the child's needs to the space that is most public, where adaptation is minimal and reality reigns unmitigated. The expansion begins at the first internal circle, that is closest to the child's experience as it is manifest in the psychotherapy session; the second circle refers to the intimate familiarity with the child's developmental position, as manifest in the various allied health treatments (occupational therapy, speech therapy, physiotherapy, couples therapy) held in the consultation rooms; the third circle refers to those allied health treatments carried out in the kindergarten's open space and targeting the child's everyday functions; the fourth circle indicates the holding of the child by the kindergarten as a therapeutic-pedagogic setting, in which functional and social reality plays a more significant role; finally, the fifth circle relates to the parental membrane, which is integrative and continuous to those of the kindergarten. In order to enliven the integration of the various membranes, which the child himself is incapable of linking, we have founded the role of therapy-coordinator, which holds sway over the entire map.

The therapy-coordinator is always proficient in psychodynamic thinking. In addition to the professional qualities required for conducting psychotherapy with children, the coordinator must possess considerable experience, as well as a multi-professional understanding of the disorder. In order to allow her to observe from a greater distance than the rest of the staff, it is preferable that she does not treat any children in the particular kindergarten in which she holds the position of therapy-coordinator. In containing the staff, she works together with the teachers, functioning as a transitional-figure: belonging to the kindergarten's internal setting, while also watching it from without. For some two hours a week, she comes in to observe both the children and the staff. This observation is not intended for inspection purposes, but rather for the establishment of a linking perspective, encompassing both her professional knowledge and the information she gathers from the respective therapists regarding each child and the actual comportment of the environment. In addition, she encounters the children through the eyes of their parents, in the parent groups, and through the prism provided by the staff, in meetings and supervision sessions. She is the one who weaves together the various functional and professional elements into the therapeutic membrane particular to each child, as well as the conceptual membrane containing the staff and the parents. As a figure related both to occurrences in the child's inner world and to his actual external surrounding, she is capable of performing acts of integration for the staff, preserving their thinking space and sustaining it when it collapses. Through actual and conceptual accumulation and linking, she integrates external and internal reality, encouraging communication between everyone at the kindergarten. She is the one holding the aspiration that all adult professionals in the kindergarten will join together to create the accommodating, gathering and linking environment, which is designed to facilitate mentalization and signification processes in the children. Similar to Bion's notion of maternal 'reverie' – the maternal function vital to the infant as it experiences emotions and endows these experiences with meaning – the role of the coordinator is to use this remarkable psychic activity to digest the children's raw and unintelligible elements, as these were gathered by the staff – as well as those of the staff members themselves. This role is carried out in close collaboration with the teacher, supporting her – and the rest of the staff – in performing this exacting task.

Having depicted the intricate task the teacher is charged with as well as the essential role performed by the coordinator for the teachers and the kindergarten staff, I now wish to return to Yoni, in order to demonstrate the work of the staff.

Because the staff included a psychotherapist that was already somewhat familiar with Yoni and his parents who, on their part, had already established a certain degree of trust in and dependence on her, we chose her to function as his psychotherapist at the kindergarten, to guide his parents and coordinate his therapy file. The first meeting we held concerning Yoni included all the members of the pedagogic staff involved in his care – the two teachers (morning and afternoon), the coordinator, the psychotherapist, the speech therapist and the occupational therapist. We focused our thinking on his needs and those of his parents. This meeting was held at the beginning of the second month of the school-year, after the psychotherapist had already met with the parents several times.[4] She shared with me her impression – that they were interested in results, finding it difficult to contain a more process-oriented approach. Moreover, she sensed that the gap between the two of them as well as their fear of missing out on a chance to 'fix' Yoni, were preventing either of them from finding any solace or expressing their individual pain. She was still shaken by the father's intensity and the mother's absence. She felt a strong urge to meet each parent separately, in hopes of creating a more comfortable and intimate space. Working privately, she may have acted on this hope, but together with the staff and the coordinator's insight, this approach was found lacking: her wish was fueled by an adhesive identification with Yoni's experience, which only had room for one – either himself or one of his parents, mostly the father. In the future, we may be able to offer each parent to join a different therapist for a dyadic guidance session with Yoni. For now, we had to wait, contain our anxiety and try to make room for both of them in the guidance sessions.

The teacher said that the staff was having difficulties relating to Yoni. When the school-year began, he had charmed the staff with his wide vocabulary and his ability to separate from his parents so easily. These gave rise to the hope that he would adjust quickly and make use of the new program. Soon enough, however, they began experiencing the hollowness of his speech, that was void of any reference to objects. They experienced themselves as mere instruments for him and found it difficult to be empathic toward him. The staff described how Yoni was wreaking havoc running around the kindergarten, how nothing stayed in its place: he ripped the drawings off the blackboard, threw about chairs, toys and so forth. During meals, he dropped his utensils to the floor, refusing to eat anything other than cornflakes, which he ate only with his hands and straight off the table. In the daily gatherings, he was attentive to the songs but was otherwise incapable of sitting still. Only one assistant formed a relationship with him and she accompanied him throughout most of the day's activities. He enjoyed being cuddled in her arms for brief periods of time. The general experience was that of difficulty and helplessness. The occupational therapist suggested that during particularly difficult episodes, the assistant could playfully roll him about inside a thin mattress, 'squishing' him. The deep touch involved in this activity, which nevertheless does not entail detachment from the kindergarten space, had indeed calmed him down and made him less frantic.

Thinking more generally, we turned to contemplate Yoni's therapeutic plan – its composition and the best ways to apply it. From the experience we have amassed, we know that it is ill-advised to begin all treatments at once and right away, as that may overwhelm the child. One must take into account that entering an unfamiliar program involves an overload of information and the difficulty in meeting a large number of new people for a child exhibiting undifferentiated relatedness. We also needed to manage the number of times he leaves the kindergarten to attend a treatment, thus disrupting his 'going-on-being' at the kindergarten. How are we to build a therapeutic plan, then? How can we gradually introduce the various treatments?

The therapeutic-pedagogic plan is tentatively outlined at the beginning of each year and is then reconsidered, adapted and modified throughout the child's entire stay at the kindergarten. The therapeutic plan has a predetermined aspect, prescribed by the child's institutional rights (according to the criteria and budgets provided by the Ministries of Health and Education) and a variable aspect, which is decided in light of our best judgment and according to our evaluation of the child's developmental needs. The institutional aspect dictates a certain number of hours to be divided between psychotherapy, occupational therapy and speech and communication therapy. Our judgment concerns the manner in which each of these therapeutic fields is applied in practice. We ask ourselves whether two weekly psychotherapy sessions are enough, or should we allocate three weekly hours to this particular course of therapy. Should we add dyadic therapy sessions – and if so, which kind (one parent, two parents together, two taking turns)? How should we conduct the occupational and speech therapy sessions? These can be conducted privately in a consultation room or focus on more functional matters in the kindergarten space. Perhaps we should choose to work in pairs or groups? The various therapeutic options are considered through the personal prism of each child and that of the needs of the group of children as a whole.

Our thinking about the therapeutic plan becomes clearer and clearer throughout several fixed meetings that are built into our program. Graphically, the 'meeting axis' determines those points of convergence in which our professional thinking encounters the various circles of therapeutic holding – these encounters all include both the teacher and the coordinator:

1 *Therapists meeting*: every week, this meeting is devoted to a particular child, in a fixed rotation. Taking part are all the therapists treating that child, the kindergarten director (the morning teacher) and the coordinator. It is designed to interrupt the daily functional-therapeutic routine and establish a fixed window of time for thinking and for dialogue between the different therapists. This meeting is concerned less with any actual constraints and more with fine-tuning each child's personality profile, as it is manifest in the consultation

rooms. This is achieved by understanding the gaps between the various professional perspectives concerning the particular child and elucidating the relation – as well as the distinction – between the individual treatments.

2 *Kindergarten meeting*: this meeting includes the head teacher (the kindergarten director), the afternoon teacher, the coordinator, the speech therapist, and the occupational therapist. Its chief focus is the personal and collective aspects, as these are expressed in the shared space, rather than the individual consultation rooms. The meeting is intended for contemplating the kindergarten space, which is essentially pedagogic, but also therapeutic. We take the time to think about the children as a group and consider a different pedagogic and therapeutic activity each time.

3 *Pedagogic staff supervision meeting*: this meeting is highly important as it is the only holding forum available for the assistants. The assistants perform a crucial role in accompanying the children throughout their everyday activities in the kindergarten – it is their presence which is most continuously felt by the children. The teacher is in charge of giving them their daily assignments – they may be asked to conduct certain activities, such as telling stories, arts and crafts, various didactic activities, so on – or they may be given an assignment concerning a particular child, as in Yoni's case.

The teacher's assistants come to our kindergarten without any previous training, even though they are the only staff members to spend hours every day with the children as a group. In addition, they are charged with the formidable challenge of bringing the child closer to his functional tasks, to which he is utterly indifferent. In addition, they must continually regulate and organize a reality that is constantly overwhelming. Therefore, their role is far more intricate and taxing than those of the other staff members. We view the ongoing training and containing of the assistants as being of utmost importance and this meeting is the chief framework for addressing this need. Once a week, for an hour, they are not required to carry out any functional task and are invited to sit down, think and speak their mind. Throughout this meeting, the coordinator tries, in light of the description of the everyday routine given by the teacher and her assistants, to account for the myriad implications, splits, emotional detachments and overloads in the various children, as well as for the interpersonal dynamics between the different staff members, which are a direct result of the children's functional-emotional reality. This is the time and the place for working through raw feelings of aggression, envy, competitiveness and the like, which surface among the staff members, harming their function. This hour is of great importance for the assistants and plays a crucial role in the ongoing operation of the kindergarten.

4 *Staff meeting*: this meeting is also dedicated to a different child every week, in a fixed rotation, and the child's parents are invited to take part in it. This is a multi-professional forum designed for thinking together with the parents

– who themselves partake in a psychodynamic guidance session every two weeks, but have no regular contact with the therapists or the teacher.

5 *Coordinator meeting*: in this meeting, I, as the head therapy-coordinator, meet with the coordinators from the different kindergartens to bring each other up to date and think together. Having already elaborated on the complexities of the role of coordinator, it goes without saying that they, too, need containing, supervision and an opportunity for sharing.

Now is the time to complete this portrayal of the staff's joint thinking circles and depict the inclusive supervision circles: the psychodynamic supervision of the psychotherapist by a supervisor from the senior staff; the psychodynamic guidance offered to parents by the child's psychotherapist; the psychodynamic supervision of each of the allied health professionals and sector-heads[5]; and the psychodynamic supervision of coordinators by the unit coordinator. In addition, each staff member receives professional supervision from a senior supervisor in their respective field. This abundance of supervision, intent on highlighting clinical material and the individual case, is supported by reading groups which meet regularly every week. In these reading groups, all allied health professionals study whatever theoretical material psychoanalytic theory can offer regarding normal development, as well as theories dealing specifically with autism. As we perceive the kindergarten, first and foremost, as a therapeutic space, teachers regularly attend these reading groups as well. In this manner, psychoanalytic theory and the developmental perspective serve as a common ground for the entire staff and as a foundation for ongoing dialogue.

At the therapist meeting, based on everything we have already learned about Yoni's needs, we decided to start the therapeutic plan with psychotherapy: the initial relatedness was already there and this entailed a potential for modifying the overwhelming anxiety characteristic of his admission to our kindergarten. The psychologist felt that a more profound acquaintance with Yoni will help her offer better holding for the parents (though this is not always the case). Due to the lack of sensual regulation and the concomitantly high levels of anxiety, it was decided that the occupational therapist and the speech therapist begin with establishing a relation with Yoni and working with him in the kindergarten environment (the third circle), before engaging in individual therapy in the consultation room (the second circle). The occupational therapist elaborated her initial suggestion to roll Yoni in a mattress in difficult moments, offering a comprehensive sensory program for facilitating his initial regulation and organization. This program was to be carried out several times each day by the occupational therapist or the assistant already related to him, who was to be instructed in this matter by the occupational therapist.

This example shows the unique benefits of the concentric holding circles. The coordinator was able to hold the staff's difficulty, resulting from the fact that the burden, the challenge and the attention are all placed on the shoulders of a single assistant and that the execution of such personal programs decreases the kindergarten's available manpower, which is already taxed by treating young, children who are not toilet trained, even without such special tasks. She offered to structure this sensory program so that, in its initial stage, it will be applied only during joint activities, such as daily gatherings and mealtimes, and its subsequent stages will be applied gradually and later on, in accordance with staff availability. Nevertheless, the staff found it difficult to accept her proposal and this created an unpleasant atmosphere. The occupational therapist insisted that Yoni needs the entire sensory program to be applied immediately. In the ensuing discussion, splitting became more and more dominant, with each professional pulling in her respective direction, as if we must start all of these treatments and right away. Even the speech therapist expressed a sense of urgency: we must begin a program of supportive communication in order to extricate the child, as soon as possible, from his lack of understanding and expression, which in turn contribute to his lack of regulation. The teacher shifted between the desire to apply all these professional plans for Yoni and her identification with the difficulties of the pedagogic team. Finally, the coordinator had resolved this tension among the staff members by helping them see the massive projective identifications Yoni had created between himself and his environment and how his intense anxiety forced his environment to accommodate his needs without delay, obfuscating his own difficulty in tolerating the discrepancies between inside and outside. This understanding allowed the staff to bear their frustration with this compromise a little better and to be more empathic toward the parents, who were often experienced as bothersome and endlessly demanding. The staff no longer saw their desire to find a perfect and instantaneous solution for their child – refusing to accept reality or hold the notion of process – as strange or intolerable.

The individual psychodynamic supervision sessions provided the time and place for each staff member to deal with the difficult emotions that arose in this meeting as well as in their encounter with Yoni's anxiety. In this manner, they were able to experience Yoni's emotional state and it affected their professional interventions. In the pedagogic staff supervision meeting, the teachers and assistants worked through their experiences of non-existence and objectification vis-à-vis Yoni, with the help of the coordinator. This working through helped them see Yoni and make their conduct toward him more empathic and less patterned and perfunctory. Every several weeks, the psychotherapist met with the coordinator, informing her about the therapy and parent guidance sessions. The coordinator's knowledge of what was happening in psychotherapy helped her bring greater depth into her contemplation of Yoni's overall developmental profile, processing such difficult material for the benefit of the staff. Meanwhile, the coordinator had also brought Yoni's psychotherapist up to date regarding his actual kindergarten environment, aiding her in integrating the developmental and clinical information at her disposal.

Throughout the following months, Yoni calmed down a bit. The rhythm and continuity of his fixed daily schedule facilitated his experience of 'going-on-being' as well as his growing ability to predict kindergarten occurrences. The kindergarten's sensory program was adapted to his needs in a good-enough manner and the physical coalescence embedded in his activity on the trampoline and the deep-pressure joint compression,[6] several times each day, had organized him in a way that was more conducive to relatedness, while teaching the staff to handle moments of anxiety. In group gatherings, Yoni became more aware of the presence of other children and in the occupational and speech therapy groups he grew more at ease and more cooperative. While we were tempted to stay in this new comfort-zone, reality brought along the maturation of new potential and we thought it best to help Yoni fulfill it. Yoni's awareness of the presence of other children had beckoned us to commence a process of joint work with another child – in small doses, at first. The speech therapist, in the time frame dedicated to intervention within the kindergarten space, had initiated a structured mediating activity he could share with another child that showed readiness. Without the mediation made possible by the therapist, this kind of interaction would have been impossible for Yoni at this stage.

As the first year drew to a close, some of the children showed initial signs – according to the teacher and the coordinator – of being ready for diaper-weaning. Multi-professional deliberations were dedicated to each and every child and we also wondered whether the time was ripe for Yoni as well. The coordinator consulted with the psychotherapist, who told her that in their psychotherapy sessions, Yoni had begun playing with the water in the sink. At first, he was interested by the rate of the flow and then he put in the stopper, checking to see how high the water can reach before he had to turn off the tap. Then, he took out the stopper and, after the water had drained, began drinking with his mouth right on the nozzle, as if joining together these entrance and exit openings. He poured water-color into the water, watching the pattern it made on the sink's surface as the water drained, and used his hands to smear the color inside the sink. He listened to the noise made by the water as it entered the drain-hole, laughing and rejoicing when the therapist had imitated this sound in a loud voice. He wanted to repeat this again and again. The therapist viewed these actions as a process of becoming acquainted with the function of the container: understanding the notions of entry and exit, filling and emptying, and noticing the residues left in the sink – these were delightful signs of the maturation of the psychic organization required for weaning. In her psychodynamic guidance sessions with the parents, the therapist had shared with them these developments in Yoni's emotional development. With her help, they worked through, to the best of their ability, their anxiety of setting adaptive demands in hopes of accelerating Yoni's development. In the following staff meeting, the last one for that year, the parents unexpectedly began 'pushing' in this direction of their own accord. The staff was already prepared for this kind of demand. The rest of the staff members had also noted the change and the teacher related that Yoni knows when he is wet and asks to be changed. Furthermore, she could already tell by his expression when he was defecating. The staff had decided on a weaning process and discussed its execution: the speech therapist will work on making an image-story with Yoni, providing the weaning process with a communicational context containing the entire range of emotions this process may evoke. Naturally, Yoni would also be able to use this story they create together in a repetitive and patterned manner, while the speech therapist will continue working with him twice weekly – keeping close watch and gently adapting him for further progress, both practically and in terms of his subjective experience of weaning. Meanwhile, the occupational therapist will focus on strengthening the notions of sequence and planning, essential to the weaning process, on the motor skills required for taking off and putting on his pants and the like. The teacher set up this process and asked the parents to provide a good deal of tightly fitting underwear, to make sure that Yoni still feels enveloped and held.

Regular parent guidance sessions enable an uninterrupted working through of the meaning of the internal space that occasionally emerges – but is still very fragile – as well as of the links we must provide Yoni through the accommodating and secure environment. All this may sound like an almost ideal coordination and indeed it is. Reality places many obstacles in the way of such aspirations for coordinated synchronicity that require ongoing adaptation. Differences in opinion occur regarding the timing, the manner of application, the degree of involvement and virtually everything else. As always, attempts to clarify and think through are carried out in the various frameworks I have depicted above, some are successful and some less so.

We now part from Yoni in order to shortly observe the thinking and decision-making process revolving around another child, whose needs are quite different than Yoni's. This will also help clarify my own role, officially defined as 'unit coordinator' and practically serving as the external membrane joining all others. While our encounter with Yoni mostly entailed the convergence of developmental difficulties into a permanent excess of anxiety for both the child and the parents, I now turn to four-year-old *Matan*, for us to encounter the other end of the autistic spectrum, characterized by detachment and faintness.

During the first few weeks of every school-year, I conduct clinical observations of all three kindergartens, in the hopes of minding each individual child, all the children as a group and the three kindergartens as a single unit. While observing, Matan seemed to me to be younger than his actual age; he spoke very little and in a repetitive and patterned manner. He was a quiet child, slightly stooped, with a face void of all affect. At breakfast, Matan would sit with his back to the table, climb down to the floor, go under the table, lie flat on the floor and eat right off it. He would occasionally scan the people around him with limited and superficial emotion. He would rise and head to the corner to play with eating utensils, taking them off the shelf and putting them back on it. He would mutter something in gibberish. He would handle Dora shaped magnets,[7] moving them away and putting them back in place, again and again, saying 'don't . . . don't . . . don't . . . Dora', as a kind of rhyme or chant. While I was rather close to him, he did not seem to notice me. He looked detached. I was having a hard time focusing my attention on him and it drifted away to the other children. The next time I saw him, the children were attending story-time. Matan was lying on his back in one of the corners, away from all the other children, mumbling to himself in gibberish and caressing his leg. He then lay on his side, utterly detached. He didn't seem to be listening to the story. His back was turned on the other children, touching the couch. He then stroked the wall in the corner, peeking at the others from a distance.

In the psychodynamic supervision session the coordinator held with the teacher, they discovered the troubling fact that the teacher does not take Matan 'into account' as one of the kindergarten's children. He simply slips her mind. . . . She is unable to describe him. . . . He's outside her field of vision. . . . The coordinator tried holding for the teacher the psychic functions required for holding Matan within the kindergarten's activities, keeping him present in her memory and her attention, in order to 'bring him back' to the teacher. To their amazement, they discovered that Matan still kept slipping away from them. The coordinator brought the matter up in supervision with me during our weekly meeting. She sought a better understanding of the active forces characteristic of Matan's presence, so that she could perform the task she had taken upon herself for the sake of the teacher – instructing her so that she, in turn, could instruct the assistants.

At the staff meeting, everyone shared the same experience hereby depicted: the child is totally inaccessible. He blends into the surface of the wall or the floor, envelops himself in gibberish rhymes, avoids the presence of both children and adults, escaping our minds. This gave rise to a difficult experience at the meeting, one that was riddled with guilt. We had a hard time taking in the fact that not one staff member had noted Matan in their observations. Each member rolled the guilt onto the next person like it was a hot potato – each time, the accusation was shot in a different direction: there's not enough manpower . . . the parents bring him in late, when everyone else is already engaged in some activity . . . the occupational therapist was meeting with the parents when she was supposed to have been with him . . . maybe he's used to this kind of isolation from home . . . and so on. The coordinator collected all these projections in hopes of cooling this hot potato and viewing Matan as a child suffering from an extremely difficult physical experience, looking for any possible means of existing away from people – who are essentially unpredictable – by clinging to immobile stimuli such as walls and floors. This cleared up the atmosphere and, for a few moments, the teacher and the assistants properly held Matan in their minds. Nevertheless, this holding only lasted a short time before fading away once more.

During my next observation at the kindergarten, I focused on Matan and took the following notes:

> Matan is in the far end of the yard. He's there alone, unseen by the staff. He stands for a full five minutes with his face to the wall. His head is bowed down. I approach him and in response he leaves the area, stepping away from me. I linger in the spot where he just stood and see water dripping from a pipe. This must be what he was looking at. I say, 'there's water'. He looks at me and comes closer. I reach my hand under the water as he watches. I extend my wet hand to him, offering the water for him to touch and feel. He touches it, literally caressing it. I say, 'wet, water'. He touches it again. I place my hand under the water again and then reach it out to him, he touches it again, looking at me. I ask him if he wants to put his hand under the water, but he makes no response. He climbs on a nearby jungle gym and stands over me. I approach him, saying, 'hello, Matan'. He hides and so do I. I say, 'where's Matan? Matan is hiding from me, there's Matan!' For a minute, he is smiling, even laughing. He turns to the slide. I ask if he wants to slide. I feel him drifting back apart. His blank expression is back. He slides an object down the slide and I catch it at the bottom end. He repeats this action with various objects he finds. Something feels less forced now, more mutual. I think to myself that he would have kept on sliding these objects even if I weren't there to catch them. The realization that my presence is meaningless for him at these moments is very powerful.

As a more distanced observer than the rest of the staff, I realized that those constantly interacting with Matan, including the coordinator, accumulated these moments of emptiness and detachment in their experience, but were unable to accrue these fragments of relatedness and communication that I certainly found in him. Regardless of the causes, it seems that Matan's fragmentation mechanisms were so active that even the minds of the staff were under attack, creating an existential state in which it is impossible to continuously feel or think his presence. We had to think of ways to create for the staff a *density* of situations in which Matan could exist in reality and in the mind of those around him.

We prepared a program that entailed, beyond the individual treatments, a thickset array of diverse and fixed activities for the staff to engage in with Matan. We relinquished any spontaneity and prepared a detailed timetable determining in advance each staff member's engagement with Matan as part of the daily schedule. With guidance from the psychotherapist, the occupational therapist and the speech therapist, we formulated work plans that were tailored to each assistant's personality and emphasized working on Matan's impaired physical and psychic foundations. In addition, we decided to hold three weekly psychotherapy sessions, instead of two, each of them thirty minutes long. The goal was to facilitate a denser experience of being, without having his psychotherapist lose her own presence. These three sessions would require the therapist to come to the kindergarten a total of six times: every time she picks Matan up or brings him back, she alerts one of the staff members to his absence or his return.

The reality of working with children exhibiting fragmentary personality structures or functional characteristics, with tremendous fragmentation anxieties, brought to my mind the image of Russian nesting dolls – a system of shells, each placed inside the other, each holding the one inside it – and all of them together, holding the smallest, most internal one. This image approximates our aspiration to create for these children a safe and stable environment in which they can survive. The image of the nesting dolls may evoke thoughts about inside and outside, the kindergarten environment and the therapeutic setting, holding and containing, fragmentation and linking, the intolerable anxiety, which leads to fragmentation and the rigid autistic mechanisms that freeze life into a tree-like rigidity in order to avoid all contact with this anxiety. This image may be apt, but it is far from perfect. It tempts us to solidify our tendency to split experience into static states and it lacks the dynamic nature of the spaces designed to facilitate linking and distinction and the communication between them. We must set aside our tendency to grasp this structure as static and try to imagine it as embedded in a woven fabric, a web that is spread or hung as a hammock: whenever one string is pulled, the entire web is shaken, propelling, through interrelatedness, the processes of change. This dynamic motion is the living aspect of this model and its perpetual agitation requires us to constantly reorganize, reevaluate, adapt and alter it. In the course of our work, we all oscillate between the immediate – the here and now – and moments of distance and observation. The dialogue between these two modalities is always present, whether consciously, as in the therapeutic session or in supervision, or unconsciously, as when the mind wanders to faraway places in the session. This endless dialogue allows us to create a reality which inspires our psychic space and the thought that shapes it, in turn. This ongoing reciprocal inspiration establishes a process of growth and development in each of us as an individual and in all of us together as a team.

Notes

1 The initial model was developed in an ASD kindergarten run by the Association for Children at Risk, in collaboration with the Preschool Department at the Ramat-Hen Mental Health Center.
2 In order to maintain the confidentiality of the parents, the psychologist has chosen not to reveal her name and to serve as a 'general example'.
3 That is, a thought that is divided into two parts, which are experienced as identical despite their eminent difference. See Meltzer, 1975.
4 These meetings are held regularly, once every 2 weeks.
5 Sector heads provide professional supervision for the allied health professionals. They also engage in psychodynamic supervision in order to facilitate more integrative thinking by observing supervision material from their more specific professional perspective.
6 Joint compression is a technique that encourages sensory regulation by stimulating the proprioceptive system through deep pressure. Together with the use of the trampoline, these activities constitute a 'sensory diet' – a comprehensive interven-

tion aimed at improving sensory regulation, a process that is vital for ASD children, which often have no physical regulation. While the notion of 'sensory diet' belongs to occupation therapy, at our kindergartens, we aspire to apply this therapeutic response as well, making it available for the children several times a day – a tremendous change from their perspective.

7 A character from an animated television series for children.

Chapter 3

'I'm not moving, don't you move!'

Treating a child with an organic disorder and autistic defenses – an integrative case study

Orly Shalev

Discussion group:

Orly Shalev – psychotherapist, dance and movement therapist; Tamar Tsabary – kindergarten teacher; Tami Marx – speech therapist; Orit Bar – occupational therapist.

This chapter presents a multi-disciplinary case study which illustrates the dynamic-developmental approach and the structure of everyday practice at the Shaked kindergartens. In terms of presentation, the psychotherapist offers the main voice and provides the binding thread, gathering together the various therapeutic aspects. Quite unusually, in this case she is also the kindergarten's therapy-coordinator. The presentation will include the perspectives of the various other therapists – the speech therapist, the occupational therapist and the kindergarten teacher – in order to offer a broad view of our integrative practice. We have chosen to write about *Elay*, a six-year-old boy now spending his third year at our kindergarten. Elay was chosen because we often encounter the particular developmental characteristics he presents and because his case raises some crucial therapeutic issues. Elay suffers from a developmental deviation which affects every aspect of his function. While resembling children with severe learning disabilities, Elay also suffers from impaired communicational skills and a limited ability to relate to others. Today, Elay's functioning manifests considerable gaps, which may be viewed through several prisms: emotion, cognition, sensory integration, learning abilities, language and communication. This multi-disciplinary presentation will allow the reader to observe the course of Elay's integrative treatment. It will present the contribution of these combined processes to the emergence of his self, as they serve as the ground on which the capacity for relatedness can grow, alongside his development in terms of language, learning, thinking and playing. This case study will explore this process, from the initial stages of acquaintance, in which we felt that Elay exhibited considerable developmental potential, to our acknowledgment of his extensive difficulties and deficiencies, as well as the paths still open for future development.

We begin this case study with the tale of 'The Tailor and the Moon', one of Elay's favorites: the story tells of a tailor charged with sewing a coat for the moon;

despite his relentless efforts, the coat is always either too big or too small to fit the ever-changing moon. In the end, the tailor decides to make thirty coats, one for each day of the month. In a parent guidance session, Elay's mother told me that Elay loves this story and that he asks her to tell it to him every single night. We wondered what it was about this particular story that he found so captivating. We also contemplated this storytelling ritual, which repeated itself with immutable regularity, presenting a predictable sequence which offers a steady sound that enveloped Elay. We also wondered whether the story's content was relevant, whether its meaning could magically touch upon Elay's oscillating sense of self, or perhaps upon his budding interest in the effort to adapt to a changing reality, an effort which resonates that of his therapists and his parents to adapt themselves to him.

Our presentation is organized around three periods in Elay's self-development:

a First period: Stillness and merging relationships
b Second period: Budding separateness and acknowledgment of gaps
c Third period: Structural difficulties versus the desire to develop and live

Background

Weighing 3.7 kilograms, Elay was born on the forty-first week, after a healthy pregnancy and an uneventful delivery. He was described as a nervous baby, who cried often; during the day, he spent much time being carried around by his parents and he frequently woke up during the night. He was breastfed for some six weeks without gaining weight and, after having tried bottle-feeding as a supplement, refused subsequent attempts at breastfeeding. When his parents switched him to puréed food, he found it difficult to sit and eat at the table for extended periods of time and would only eat puréed fruit or cheese from the bottle. His motor development was faster than normal: he barely crawled, was able to stand at seven months and walk at eleven months. In contrast to his exceptional gross motor skills, he did not speak at all until he was two – except for the occasional sound or mutter. After turning two, he began enunciating words – his speech was highly patterned and restricted to the third person and he would simply repeat the sentences spoken to him, answering questions with a question. He occasionally used pointing, exhibiting normal eye contact. He would spend much time looking at rolling objects, throwing objects in the air and rolling them on the floor; he was interested in their formal characteristics rather than their significance. He enjoyed playing with his ball by himself. Elay's mother went back to work two months after giving birth. Following a failed attempt to integrate him into a pre-nursery group, Elay stayed at home with his grandmother until he turned two and was then placed at a daycare center. His adaptation to daycare proved very difficult: he cried a lot, would not communicate with any of the staff members – save for one teacher, with whom he only communicated in whispers – and no matter the activity, he would always stand back and watch, ignoring the other children.

Parenting a child with a deficient organic and mental foundation is a difficult task for any parent and it cannot rely on normal parental intuition alone. Moreover, a child such as Elay may end up disrupting parental function instead of enriching it. Alongside Elay's congenital deficiencies, the external circumstances to which he was born were also very difficult. His family was in the midst of a protracted crisis, involving a transition into a new family setting and a series of illnesses and accidents. The family was led by post-traumatic parents, who exhibited significant organizational difficulties and employed manic defenses. Sincerely seeking help and loving their child very much, Elay's parents invariably came to each and every therapy or guidance session the kindergarten offered. Much like Elay, they too captured the therapists' hearts. Still, while they were very eager to cooperate, it seemed significantly hard for them to internalize instructions. The therapists experienced them as a container wishing to be filled but too perforated to allow the accumulation of any meaning.

At the age of three, when Elay first came to the kindergarten, we met a clearly boyish child – with a heart-winning smile and flirting behavior. This so-called normalcy contrasted with Elay's deficient organic foundation, which hindered his ability to construe processes and integrate any kind of information – sensory, affective, emotional and verbal. Bombarded with stimuli that remained unfathomable for him, he seemed confused and under attack. His verbal development was arrested – his speech was highly patterned and echolalic and mostly expressed in the third person. He found it difficult to learn, would not internalize rules and boundaries and apparently had not mastered the symbolization and abstraction processes required for effective language acquisition. He exhibited an extreme mental and functional dependency on external objects for containment, regulation and information processing. His innate deficiencies made it hard for him to spontaneously learn how to understand and orient himself in his natural environment.

First period: stillness and merging relationships

In the early stages of our relationship, Elay turned out to be a very charismatic child, with heart-warming smiles, who soon won everyone's special attention. Sadly, he utilized this kind of involvement to avoid participating in individual and group activities and to keep clear of having to learn or experience anything new. We realized that the relationships Elay was forming were undifferentiated and entailed a seductive element which, at this point, still evoked phantasies of great potential in his caretakers. In the various therapies, individual relationships with Elay within a containing, regulated and predictable environment enabled optimal adaptation, which was manifest in a merging relationship and a lack of separateness. In these contexts, Elay was experienced as a lively child who longed for relatedness, while requiring absolute dependence. Outside the therapeutic sessions, Elay was frozen and avoidant. When asked to join group activities, he stood apart from the group with eyes wide open, motionless and stiff. We understood this to be a reaction to an organic difficulty, precluding adequate cognitive and perceptual information processing. Elay had trouble establishing an internal rhythm, the steady beat of new links that enables learning. The rhythm of the various therapeutic sessions embedded in the kindergarten's daily routine disrupted his sense of consistency; the potential for adaptation and learning – which he experienced as forced – evoked nothing but anxiety: his drive was impaired and things came to a halt. At kindergarten and therapists meetings, we reached a consensus: at this point, any work with Elay had to be done in small, repetitive units that would be accumulated and processed by the pedagogic and therapeutic staff. In an attempt to attain maximal adaptation to Elay's rhythm and ability to process, we aimed to establish a steady beat throughout the familiar and predictable schedule of the kindergarten routine, the group work and the therapeutic sessions.

As the kindergarten teacher put it:

> In his first few days at the kindergarten, Elay was standing as still as an icicle in his regular corner, while the rest of the kindergarten bustled around him. I try getting him to talk, but he shows no indication of hearing or understanding me and refuses any kind of movement. Sometimes, I take the initiative and hold him in my arms, carrying him from one place to the next. Still, he does not alter his position, only relaxes his muscles, allowing me to move him about. I have no access to his thoughts or feelings, except for his evident anxiety. Strangely, when he is out in the yard, Elay is loose and full of life and engages other children in various primary games. Once he enters the kindergarten, however, he is frozen again.

While the length of these freezing spells gradually grows shorter, Elay freezes again and again throughout the day. He stands frozen and stares whenever we change places or activities, whenever he has to leave for or come back from his therapy sessions, when someone new comes to the kindergarten or when he is challenged with an unfamiliar assignment or cognitive task. I call out to him from across the room and then come closer, leading him – with no resistance on his part – to the current activity. Only then does he relax and join in or sit in sullen resistance, very withdrawn and inaccessible. Eventually, Elay enters the kindergarten on his own. He walks over to his regular corner and waits for me there. I join him for a simple game involving Teletubby dolls, which he repetitively shakes and throws up in the air for me to catch. I am reluctant to alter the rules of this game or initiate any new moves, afraid that any change may interrupt the complete predictability Elay needs to establish relatedness. I am utterly drawn to Elay and he responds by giving in. My role in the kindergarten requires me to divide my attention between all the children, so I must step back from focusing solely on Elay. Whenever this happens, even with ample preparation, the game ends abruptly and Elay resumes his petrified position in his corner.

Let us continue to explore this first period, by looking through two prisms: the autistic mental structure, which seeks to merge with the object; and the specific character of his communication and speech, which manifests Elay's tendency for concrete thinking and his difficulty in creating representations and symbols.

Elay's psychotherapy began a few weeks after he joined the kindergarten. After the initial consultation between the coordinator, the kindergarten staff and the therapists, we decided to begin implementing the therapeutic program, despite the fact that Elay was still not fully oriented. We estimated that he was overwhelmed and could use the regulating setting offered by the consultation rooms, a setting which would facilitate his orientation and adaptation processes. As he was not exhibiting any differentiated relationships, we decided to begin with psychotherapy. Elay refused to enter the consultation room and join me; he stood still and stared, ignoring my invitation. Finally, he agreed to enter the room accompanied by one of the kindergarten staff members, 'just for a peek'. He peered in and went back to the kindergarten. After this first session, his presence was transformed. Elay became very lively and needed me to be present at each and every moment of the session, expecting me to physically follow his every action like a devoted shadow. 'Come, come',[1] he often said with a big, inviting smile. Whenever my thoughts wandered for a moment, he immediately asked, 'are you tired?' indicating his hyper-sensitivity and absolute dependency. Elay was hungry for me to observe him, for my impressed and kind gaze; he called out to me after every action, whether routine or unusual, 'look, Orly, look'. I experienced him as a child who longed for a live and engaged object. As a dance and movement therapist, my sessions were held in a movement-therapy room, which offered a variety of physical interactions. In the initial stages of our relationship, Elay chose the hammock, the trampoline and the tunnel – objects which he used to invite close physical contact. Within the stillness of the quiet room, Elay invited me to join him in the tunnel. Inside it, I felt that we were sitting 'together'. When he asked me (in his words) to 'go in the outside', I realized just how impaired his distinction between inside and outside was, whether because he was developmentally unable to make this primary distinction or because this capacity was under attack. In addition, Elay often asked for the hammock, which was opaque, made of a sturdy and somewhat rough fabric and offered a sense of being held. One could lie in it and be enveloped by darkness or sit up and peek outside. When inside the hammock, Elay would look only at me, detached from all the other stimuli around him, ensconced within himself with a very limited field of vision. I rock him at a steady pace, closer and further away; he wants me to keep rocking him, again and again. Now, the rhythm is up to me and I feel as if everything is just right, as if I don't need to think about anything else – just keep on doing what I am doing (look, rock, smile) and everything will be fine.

The hammock, which feels so much like being held in someone's lap, created a rhythm, a point of departure for Elay's deficient orientation – a point from which he could set out to explore, a subjective springboard, an axis from which he could relate to his surroundings. In this first period, most of my interventions were designed to enliven and create meaning. Mentally, Elay expressed great urgency in his need for our adapted 'togetherness'. He desperately needed my gaze, my role as a vocal admirer and a live and present observer, my actual holding, my mirroring and my validation. On the physical level, I imitated his movement patterns (climbing, sitting, standing) and his motional rhythms.

In time, Elay came to acknowledge the fact that a state of complete adaptation is only an illusion and that, in reality, one must constantly communicate in hopes of attaining it. Elay, who now had emerging awareness of the distance between us, was trying out new ways for finding the proper distance. He would often say, 'it's too far', 'it's too close', and mostly expressed his physical and mental discomfort through statements such as 'it itches'. When he sensed that I was a little tired, when I did not come right away or did not look at him with the admiration he needed, he tried 'switching me on' by asking me to hold various things – all kinds of balls, musical instruments, scarves. . . . This was his way of asking me to perform a containing, organizing and accumulating function for him. These were the first indications that the container function was emerging. While holding Elay's things, I realized from my countertransference that this was a sign that his various parts were gradually coming together.

As time passes, due to the characteristically autistic course of development, which creates something new and then undoes it, the same activity makes me feel as if he is striving to fill – or perhaps plug – my mind in order to leave no room for anything other than him. Physically and mentally, he is burdening me with more and more things, until I can no longer hold them all. I am trying, struggling, to hold everything but Elay keeps piling them on and they start falling over. I am trying to hold and thereby establish myself as a container. I offer no interpretation for this experience of 'impossibility'. Instead, I keep searching, right along with him. I sit down, so that my legs can support the bottom of the container and increase its capacity. I struggle to keep holding this assortment of objects in my cupped hands, trying to provide some kind of structure for things that are still unformed, as if I were saying: 'I am here, trying to hold what is pouring out of you. Things are pouring out of me too, but I am still searching, still trying'. I am trying to create the opportunity for Elay to find a new way of being, a different kind of presence.

My physical inability to hold and join together was a manifestation of Elay's mental experience: random, isolated items, void of any structure or common thread. His container-contained relationship was so vulnerable to attack on linking, that the potential for the emergence of a container stable enough to establish links was precluded (Bion, 1962).

Throughout this period, my thoughts often wandered and I was not keeping Elay in my mind. From a distance, I became more aware of his unanswered difficulties. Denied of any healthy motion between oneness and separateness, Elay immediately reacted with intensified anxiety. Any separateness was experienced as traumatically excessive, petrifying Elay's vitality with sheer terror. I began feeling that Elay's impaired aspects were too exposed, unpredictable and difficult to process. In the session, Elay began cutting adhesive tape and taping the carpet. Sometimes, he was taping in a functional way; at other times, he placed the tape upside down, so that it slid right off, became tangled in itself and would not stick. In the undifferentiated autistic mental structure, one often encounters the kind of ritual activity that negates meaning (Tustin, 1994).

One session after another, Elay scattered marker pens and picked them up again, creating nothing new. I felt deadened. Physically, as well as mentally, I tried finding a place that would be neither too close, impinging or threatening, nor too far – so that I could keep him from slipping away entirely. I wondered why he found this act of scattering and picking up markers more stimulating and interesting than our relationship. Elay's vitality was deficient in a way which put his further development at risk and he needed me to actively seek him out in order to sustain it. In an attempt to enliven him, I sat down next to him, trying to get my own markers, stressing the fact that I was observing and casually describing what I saw – 'scattering and gathering, scattering and gathering' – while also trying to interpret his actions as obscuring his difficult feelings concerning our separateness. Elay gave me a brief interested glance and then resumed his activity. I felt the threat of psychic death: meaninglessness, obscuration and an inability to think were affecting my ability to write down our sessions and discuss them in supervision. I found it very difficult to express the depths of despair and was even uncertain about what actually took place: was Elay hearing my words? Did he feel or understand what I was saying? The task I found most challenging at that time was keeping the flame alive when it was so small and imperceptible that it was nearly extinguished. Technically, I was trying to maintain 'live company' (Alvarez, 1992), to send out the message that I noticed his attempt to share his feeling of falling as well as being dropped by me.

Was he actively dismantling (Meltzer, Bremner, Hoxter, Weddell, and Wittenberg, 1975) thoughts and meaning? Was he using markers as an autistic object (Tustin, 1981) which sealed out all meaning? One could also see the experience underlying Elay's repetitive behavior – endlessly scattering markers and picking them back up – as expressing the phantasy of negating all separateness, a phantasy in which time is infinite. Later on, we will describe this deficiency in the perception of time from a cognitive perspective, in the account offered by the occupational therapist. Maiello argues that 'children in an autistic state cannot recognize the temporal aspect of reality. There can be no beginning, because beginnings imply endings and endings are inconceivable as they involve termination and separation' (2001; the author's translation). Furthermore, an appropriate sense of space-time or causality at the very least requires one to have the notion of two steady points of reference. Meltzer *et al.* (1975) offers a spatial metaphor for the dimensionality of mental space, describing autistic mental space as one or two dimensional. Cyclical time, a temporal modality characteristic of autistic mental space, manifests the omnipotent phantasy of endless repetition and provides a mental shield against intolerable separation anxieties.

The perspective of the *speech therapist* offers insight into the relation between the emergence of the self through the negation of separateness and the capacity for communication and language:

Right from the start, Elay surprisingly has no problem leaving the kindergarten for therapy. He strikes me as a child with a healthy interest in me, as part of the human world, as well as in the world of objects, the toys I pick for our shared activities. Nevertheless, he has a strong need for control. He wants to dictate how things are done – which games we play and how. He goes for the primary games that he already knows – soap bubbles, balloons. After choosing a game and starting to play, he can make room for both of us. Elay can name, protest, command or ask, but I am particularly moved when he blows a big soap bubble and shares his enjoyment with me, cheerfully calling out: 'look!' In fact, he is initiating the kind of communicative intention which is rather rare in ASD children – sharing a subjective experience. It makes me feel that Elay's therapy will be fruitful, that we already have much to work with.

Our point of departure is Elay's highly patterned and repetitive use of language. I realize that he is having significant difficulties in both understanding and articulation. His auditory memory allows him to repeat certain phrases, but he still does not distinguish male from female, confuses tenses and fails to comprehend the use of pronouns. This means that Elay does not yet understand the roles played by these different kinds of words. He perceives language in chunks, as entire phrases, unable to break down or rejoin different semantic units.

My work with Elay begins by establishing a repertoire of shared activities. Our shared experience and attention serve as the foundation for our work – our path to growth. Elay soon settles on a relatively narrow range of activities, which includes a Teletubbies memory game and the book *No, David!* (Shannon, 1998), which features illustrations of a child doing things he is not allowed to, repeatedly earning the reproach – 'no, David!' However, alongside this burdensome repetition, we began to develop a deep sense of intimacy, a tremendous infatuation, which for me is not at all restricted to the consultation room. Elay is the one child in the kindergarten that I am automatically drawn to, the first child I attend to, the one I sit next to at breakfast. In the kindergarten, Elay is frozen and detached but once inside the consultation room, he looks at me with eyes wide open, hungry for any words or demonstration I may offer. He takes my words as is and in the following week I hear him repeating them. He imitates the way I use objects and once more, I see myself through his eyes. It is as if he is trying to fill himself with the ideas, feelings, words and games I provide and instantly practice them as his own. In other words, he is practically incapable of creative and independent elaboration, but gladly seizes what I offer.

In the speech therapy sessions, I notice that Elay never handles actual objects, even though the room has many accessible toys. Rather, he is drawn to picture books. This adherence to visual representations is characteristic of ASD children, who find it hard to understand spoken language. Words are fast, they come and go, ever-changing, always sounding different; but pictures never change. You can revisit them again and again, trying to process and understand.

Therefore, the book *No, David!* is repeatedly used in our sessions. Elay learns it by heart and even memorizes the slight alterations I make to the original text. Reading this book evokes considerable affect. Elay is angry, mad at the mischievous David. We are annoyed together, yelling at David to stop. Despite certain variations in this emphasized affect, however, the activity remains repetitive. After consulting the other staff members, I decided to limit our engagement with pictures and try working with real objects, to try and bring them to life and use them. I bring in all kinds of relevant objects, suggesting that we imitate whatever David does in the picture. Elay goes along with the idea. In one picture, David is making noise by striking a pan with a spoon, the text reads: 'David! Be quiet!' I say, 'let's do what David is doing', and point Elay to the kitchenware drawer. We rummage for utensils that look like the ones in the picture and when we find the right ones, Elay plays along. He lifts the spoon high with one hand, raises the pan with the other and . . . freezes! Just like the motionless picture. There is no movement, the spoon and the pan never meet and so – there is no sound. I ask myself – if there is no sound, why would one need to keep quiet? I am astounded to learn how much Elay fails to understand the story. He did not relate these pictures, that we have been looking at for the past several weeks, to any meaningful event or actual experience in his life. He is not connecting the dots, unable to infer from the picture about the kind of movement and sequence of actions required to make noise with a spoon and a pan. The words are simply hollow. Once I demonstrate, he understands immediately and in the following week offers to do it himself. He runs to the kitchenware drawer, pulls out the spoon and the pan and bangs away joyfully. I join him with my own utensils and we make noise together. Then, I suggest that we try to see what else can make noise. Elay agrees at first, but soon grows tired. It seems that he is only able to concentrate on a limited number of noise-making stimuli.

This experience with the picture-book provided me with a moment of distance and renewed observation of Elay. I was struck by this gaping disparity in a child who knows a story by heart and can employ a suitable affect so convincingly, without understanding its real meaning. This unsettling discovery prompted me to take a step back and reexamine Elay's needs. I realized that in order for Elay to learn and understand, he has to take part in actual, tangible experiences that could bring together sensation, sound, movement and sequence. This way, the words he learns might be related to an actual experience in his world.

Second period: budding separateness and acknowledgment of gaps

Throughout this period, we became more deeply acquainted with the complexity of Elay's difficulties and with the essential confusion between his impaired constitution and his compensatory abilities, which attested to his potential. We came to understand that Elay was employing a mechanism of confusion in order to eliminate premature separateness. For this reason, he was defensively limiting himself to familiar activities, avoiding experiences that required the kind of information processing that was beyond his capacities. After our first year of working with Elay, the nature and severity of his difficulties in processing, learning and establishing differentiated relationships became abundantly clear. Our initial excitement turned into despair. We experienced a child who was full of holes – his language was patterned and limited, his general knowledge was practically nonexistent, his understanding of arithmetic and verbal infrastructure were deficient and his social understanding was nascent. We were confused: can he, or can't he? Does he know, or doesn't he? In our staff meetings, we agreed that the pedagogic-therapeutic environment should aspire for clarity while trying to simultaneously hold Elay's abilities and difficulties in mind. When working with a child like Elay, we must offer a tight and integrative holding framework: a container that would enable us to find the right distance, the kind of relatedness that arises through the adaptability and attunement of a sensitive and accessible object that can oscillate between identification and external observation.

Elay's difficulties, his defensive use of stillness and his disinterest and avoidance throughout this period will be presented through his impaired functioning in his everyday environment. The *kindergarten teacher*'s perspective will help us understand these aspects more clearly:

> As a kindergarten teacher, I do not feel that our relationship is really differentiated. As I described earlier, I feel much warmth, intimacy and tenderness when I do something close and unchallenging with Elay. We are immersed in some shared game that has certain DIR[2] qualities and Elay devotes himself to it. Still, like a pendulum that alternates between extremities, as soon as our playful and joyful merger ends, Elay stays frozen in space as if I had disappeared. Naturally, though quite unfortunately, our assistants react to this stillness by keeping their distance, afraid to approach him. Therefore, any kind of functioning is impossible at these moments – both on Elay's part and on the part of the adults. This anxiety limits the general ability to make his repertoire of coping strategies more flexible. This issue comes up again and again at our kindergarten meetings and requires us to work it through repeatedly, each time from a new perspective.

Elay cannot maintain his potential for relating in his actual functioning; he has trouble understanding and following what is going on in the kindergarten and is unable to see me or use my help in these dynamic situations. I begin to understand that when Elay seems lost, he needs the staff to be endlessly supportive, mediating and adaptable, but also separate in a way that would allow us to confront him with various frustrations. I instruct the assistants to make themselves especially available to Elay, so I will not be his only link to the world, to stick to the daily schedule and to not be alarmed by his paralyzing stillness. Flexibility is important and very intricate here: they must adapt to the various levels of development on which Elay functions, working very gently while presenting clear and consistent demands.

As time goes by, merger gives way to a process of separation which is difficult both for Elay and for me. Being just another figure in the background makes me sad, but I can see that Elay is thawing and slowly adapting to reality. Our relationship seemingly becomes dramatically limited, but it now appears to have greater quality and diversity. He can now face me as a kindergarten teacher who sets boundaries as well as a playmate or a source of comfort. We have created a soothing space. Elay focuses his interest on one matter at a time – such as playing with a ball – immersing himself in a single endeavor until he completely exhausts it. At first, he still seems unripe, clumsy and slow. It is as if he chose a task that is beyond his capacity and therefore needs more and more of the same, without giving any sign of having understood the gap between the task at hand and his skills. Then, all of a sudden, he succeeds and can even own his new skill, applying it in different contexts and using it well.

Given Elay's difficulties in processing several things at once – that is, creating distinctions and links – we see difficulties emerging in all those 'background' areas that lie outside his fields of interest. In group activities, Elay sometimes seems attentive, but when I ask him about the subject at hand, he remains frozen or tries to complete a word I started regardless of its actual context ('we are going to have a birthday pa . . .' – 'pumpkin'). When I am laughing, Elay joins me and tries to get the other children to laugh. They surprisingly become the core of his motivation – he is trying hard to make them laugh and draw their attention. These social interactions are a good sign, but I also notice his distractedness and the limited range of his attention. I make everything especially simple for him, addressing him and reminding him, and he utilizes this to improve his learning. In the staff meeting, I realize that the difficulty lies in understanding and maintaining sequences. Elay finds it difficult to understand complex sequences, so he avoids them altogether. I make sure someone is there to help him and, with the proper support, Elay enjoys sitting, raising his hand and participating throughout longer periods of time. Elay is acquiring his primary concepts. He remembers songs and knows the symbols of the different holidays very well. But when I ask him more complicated questions about how or why, I encounter profound ignorance. Elay is mastering the explicit layer of knowledge, but not the subterranean layers of meaning that involve knowledge and its experience; he never asks why or how things work.

As it is hard for him to take in information sequentially, I devote the morning group activity to playing a version of hide and seek that entails several activities that require the children to think. I believe this playful method offers the children a link between actual experience and various concepts (under, above, behind, before, inside, and such). I lay out several objects on the floor; one of the children volunteers to hide an object, while another child leaves the room and waits for us to call him back in. When the child returns, he has to guess which object was taken and then look for it. Elay is immensely excited and very eager to go out, come back and discover the object. But once he comes back in, he is unable to remember which of the four objects is missing, even though he already saw it and recognized it. I try using fewer objects, but to no avail. We play the game for days on end and whenever one of the objects is hidden, Elay has trouble remembering it. In supervision and in the therapists meeting, we wonder whether this is a cognitive difficulty or a mental inability to tolerate absence. We remind each other that there is no point in engaging in splitting and we must be aware of how these two aspects interact. We try helping Elay by calling out instructions – 'hot-cold' or 'near-far' – but he does not understand these hints. Elay will only look in places where he likes to hide objects, or places previously used as hiding spots. Once he realizes that the object is not where he thought it was, he finds it hard to keep moving – both physically and mentally, to consider another person's thinking and subjectivity. None of our hints helps him keep going, except for physical guidance – literally 'pushing' him in the right direction. When it is his turn to hide an object, he always goes to the same predictable spots. I find myself surprised by the contrast between his eagerness to leave the room and wait – so full of anticipation, vitality and true childish joy – and his heavy, lost and anxious reentry.

Throughout this period, the organic aspect of Elay's emotional and communicational difficulties stands out and this issue is constantly reexamined in staff discussions. The perspective of the *occupational therapist* offers a more in-depth exploration of its manifestation, even in individual therapy in an attuned and regulated environment.

As part of the therapy, I try to examine Elay's difficulties in playing 'object hide and seek', as described above, under different conditions. I am trying to see what kind of mediation Elay needs in order to be able to play the game. Elay picks up a car and tries to hide it. He places it, with me watching, in the ball pit and asks me to find it. I pretend to look in different places around the room and finally 'find' it in the pit. Again and again, he places it in the pit and asks me to find it, ignoring the fact that I am watching him and unable to come up with additional hiding places. We change roles. I ask him to close his eyes, explaining that while his eyes are shut I will be hiding the car for him to find. He opens his eyes, looks at me, but will not budge. He has no idea about what to do and where to start looking. I mediate the search process for him by raising possibilities, as I am looking over various hiding places around the room – 'could it be . . . in the barrel? Could it be . . . under the bean bag?' – until he is able to find the car.

One perspective that might prove useful for understanding Elay's difficulties is the cognitive one. Elay finds it difficult to relate to two sources of information at once and has limited mental flexibility. He has difficulties filtering and organizing the information stored in his memory in categories or patterns or in light of existing knowledge, so that he could adapt to it and use it more efficiently. Such impaired information-processing disrupts his ability to respond in a way that is expressed, among other things, in his freezing and his poor recall. Deficient information processing is characteristic of children with learning disabilities as well as ASD; when this deficiency is compounded with difficulties in relating and communicating, it has considerable impact on their ability to adapt to the world. The occupational therapist continues:

> Throughout his first year at the kindergarten, I joined Elay at breakfast. Elay, who only recently started naming colors, is wearing a red shirt with a Spiderman print. I ask him what he would like to eat, even though I already know the answer – a slice of bread with jam – the same thing he has every morning. I tell Elay that the Jam and his shirt are the same color. 'No', he says, 'my shirt is Spiderman'.

During his second year, as we made our way back to the kindergarten after his therapy session, Elay would stop at the entrance and refuse to move. My explanation is that his sense of time was disrupted: he left the kindergarten during play-time and is now coming back to a different situation. Elay cannot maintain the experience of a sequence which lasts throughout change. This results in anxiety, which he expresses by freezing.

Elay also suffers from a cognitive deficiency in problem-solving. In one of our sessions, hoping to help him link together the different elements of his experience, I suggest that we turn the light off and use candles and a flashlight to light the room. Elay declares that he will turn off the light. He looks at the switch, realizes that it is too high up for him to reach, takes a chair and places it under the switch. Then, he notices that right next to the switch there is a stool that is even taller than the chair. He sets the chair aside, climbs up on the stool and turns off the light. When presented with a relatively simple, or perhaps familiar, problem, Elay seems able to identify the goal, come up with a plan for reaching it, change his mind and come up with an alternative, more effective plan and make decisions. I am curious to see how he will deal with a more complicated problem: the room is not completely dark, because light is coming in through the window. I ask Elay what we should do about the light from the window. He seems to have an idea. He climbs back on the stool and turns the switch on and off again. At first, I am not sure what he is trying to do. Finally, I have to face the fact that Elay is trying to turn off the sun by pressing the light switch. Elay confirms my assumption: I ask him if he succeeded in turning off the sunlight that way and he says that he did not. He has another idea. He goes over to the air conditioner, which is right under the window, and tries pressing its button – a response which suggests a false over-generalization. But still, why won't Elay turn to me for help? I am there for him throughout this entire process. Elay stands there staring, all out of ideas. I decide to lend him a hand, explaining that we need to draw the curtains. We do so together and the room is finally dark. Elay turns on the flashlight, I light the candles and we sing 'happy birthday'. I ask who we should sing to and Elay looks around, examining the objects in the room. He then suggests that we should sing 'happy birthday' to the tunnel. The tunnel, I wonder, how can you sing 'happy birthday' to a tunnel? But that is Elay's suggestion and that is what we do. To my relief, when the song is over, he suggests that we sing to me. Then, for our third go, he suggests singing it to the flashlight. This transition between me, as a significant figure, and random objects is quite deceptive.

In terms of graphomotor skills, Elay is avoidant and has little interest or motivation. Even though he is five years old, Elay neither colors nor draws. He seldom takes part in the kindergarten's creative activities. In terms of his motor skills, his difficulties are minor at best and cannot account for his adamant avoidance. For Elay, coloring a work sheet is a practically impossible feat, as he complains: 'doing this again? We already did it'. 'I'm tired' and 'I can't' are two more frequently-heard phrases. Otherwise, he would color a little bit, then stop and look at me, as if he was waiting for me to tell him to go on. I break up this task for him into little units and cheer him on: 'now do the body; let's see if you can do the arms; come on, Elay, you're almost done . . .' Elay only uses a single color – red, his favorite, and will not use any other color. This task, which he finds so pointless and meaningless, takes a long time. Elay seems surprised that he was able to finish coloring. He says several times that he colored everything, as if he did not believe he would be able to do so. He is apparently satisfied with the final result – asking to take the coloring sheet home to show his parents. Still, this does not make him any more eager about coloring the next time. It feels as if there is no process: Elay is frustrated by the coloring sheets and his mechanisms are not getting any less rigid. I take comfort in the fact that the kindergarten teacher is reporting a certain improvement, saying that Elay is a little more cooperative. However, this too, as is often the case with Elay, is inconsistent.

When I try drawing with Elay, I find out once again just how unbelievably limited his knowledge of the world is. I ask Elay what color the sky is. He looks at me in amazement and eventually says that he doesn't know. We go outside; I repeat the question while pointing at the sky. This time, he says 'blue'. When I ask him what is in the sky, Elay hesitates and finally says: 'moon'. On a completely different occasion, we draw a road. Unsurprisingly, Elay has no idea what color the road should be. We go outside again and look at the road. Elay says that it is blue. I have no idea why – was he even looking? Is he mixing up the road with the sky? In one of our sessions, Elay talks about a traffic light and I suggest that he should draw one. Drawing, much like coloring, remains a task that only I initiate and which he takes part in occasionally at best.

But then, just as I am convinced that all is lost, that no progress is being made, that there is no motivation to speak of, Elay manages to surprise me, big time. In one of our sessions, I hesitantly ask Elay to draw over the letters of his first name, which are presented to him in dotted form, instead of me writing his name for him on the sheet he just colored. Elay succeeds and is very excited: 'hey, I wrote me'. From now on, he displays a capacity for learning which leaves me dumbfounded. He starts internalizing the meaning of letters and numbers – not in the autistic fashion, which only relates to their forms – but in a way that is appropriate for a child his age, who is beginning to develop literacy skills. He can recognize the letters of his name and soon goes on to recognize letters from the names of the other children. A few days before Independence Day, he comes in the room and informs me that he knows how to draw a flag and a Star of David. A Star of David? Elay? That shape is a little tricky for a boy just over five. But Elay draws one and keeps drawing more and more. He might also have a hard time believing his success. It feels as if writing is empowering him – and he writes and writes and writes. I ask myself where these academic skills could have sprung from, given his fundamental cognitive difficulties.

Writing is power and it serves Elay emotionally as well. During last year's summer camp, the children were in the 'pool', a large tub that we placed in the yard. One day, Elay's father came to pick him up for a doctor's appointment. Elay asked us to wait for him to come back before going in the pool, but that was not possible. When he came back and saw the other children bathing, he was angry: 'they didn't wait for me', he kept repeating, 'they didn't wait for me'. Something went wrong in Elay's plan and it seems as if he just couldn't get over this hitch. But rigid as it may be, this response shows how far Elay has already come: he is not simply freezing anymore. Sitting in his bathing suit on the bench next to the pool, Elay refuses to go in the water and keeps complaining. One of the other children splashes water at him and Elay starts crying. Pool time is over. All the children go back into the kindergarten, but Elay is still sitting on the bench. I try talking to him and explaining the situation, but he wouldn't budge. I carry him back inside and now he starts crying again. He says that he will tell his father that 'they' did not wait for him. I suggest that he should write his father a letter and Elay agrees. Elay says: 'they didn't wait for me and I'm angry at them'. I dictate the individual letters for him and he writes the letter. Then we take an envelope and put the letter inside. Throughout the rest of the day, I see Elay walking around the kindergarten not at all distressed, with the precious envelope in his hand. The clear and fixed form that writing gave to his complex and meaningful experience was movingly significant to him.

Elay's development is felt in the kindergarten as well. The *kindergarten teacher* describes how Elay stubbornly refuses to sit at the arts table:

> He is frozen and looks out of reach. I help him understand that while he is not required to participate, he has to sit at the table along with everyone else. I lead him to the table and he grumpily sits down. He never really took to creative activities. Elay has significant difficulties in integrating, establishing sequences and being creative. He can create a whole by copying various parts, but he doesn't seem to fully comprehend what he created. Still, Elay is very eager about learning to draw complicated forms. This way, he learned how to draw a Star of David and a bow and arrow. Elay can feel shallow, absent or empty but also momentarily full and present. It is very difficult to tell deficiency from avoidance or anxiety about his ability or lack thereof. While his ability to draw freely remained undeveloped, Elay suddenly discovered writing. He shows a great interest in and enthusiasm about letters and words. He learns how to write his name, asking how to spell the names of all the

other children. He masters the alphabet very quickly and, to everyone's surprise and astonishment, starts using letters to form words. He does this all day long, deeply enjoying the sense of control it affords him. Elay's use of letters and words is different than that of other ASD children – he appears to be using words in a meaningful way, as part of his attempts to understand the world. He only writes names that are meaningful to him – family members, the other children, the staff members – and his preoccupation is far from detached. He puts together new names by breaking up words he already knows, instead of monotonously learning more and more meaningless words. Nevertheless, he still has no phonological awareness and does not make the connection between a given letter and a particular sound. His reference to letters is strictly visual at this stage and it takes Elay some time to grasp their more profound meaning.

The material presented by the occupational therapist and the kindergarten teacher shows Elay beginning to develop sequences in his self-experience and his object-relations. His recovery and his subjective involvement with the significant figures around him are apparent.

In psychotherapy, Elay starts playing with dolls. He sometimes creates domestic scenarios, but his core activity represents the kindergarten, with each doll named after one of the children. Every doll has a single characteristic, by which Elay decides its identity. The most significant doll is that of Maya, a child who tends to stand out in the kindergarten, with her broad smile and her pink hairpins and hair bands. Elay's play is almost entirely concrete and very confused. When Elay presents a beating episode, it is hard to tell who the offender is – Maya or himself. Elay does not understand when I relate to this confusion as meaningful. After repeated attempts at finding a plot or a story in Elay's playing, I realize that I have to speak in a simple, positive manner, without question marks. I refer to the excitement and the difficulty manifest in this encounter. Elay represents himself with two dolls. One was molded as a stiff immutable unit; the other has joints that allow movement and a potent, 'live and flowing' feel (Shahar-Levi, 2004). Elay picks a different one each time but sadly, he eventually leaves out the movable doll, which represents the ability to physically and mentally distinguish between the different parts of the body, a prerequisite for any manner of live engagement. Elay abandons it, adhering to the immobile one. Was he erasing or freezing the distinct feelings that were beginning to emerge and the nascent potential for mental motion? Alongside this defensive rigidity, the sprouts of development continue to flourish, insisting on their right to exist. In one of the sessions, Elay chooses a little girl doll, whose movement resembles that of the jointed boy-doll. He says: 'Maya dreamed about my mother. Why is she dreaming? It's not her mother. It's my mother'. This play gives rise to surprising feelings of envy, potency, anxiety and intimacy as well as a clear distinction regarding whose mother it is. I am excited to realize that this also exhibits a dimension of depth, dreaming and phantasy. Out of repetitive, rigid, formal and age-inappropriate play, so characteristic of the autistic mental structure, an emotional experience has emerged.

In another session, Elay sets the dolls aside and asks me to swing an empty hammock. Session after session, I keep swinging the empty hammock. At first, I feel that we are sharing a phantasy in which Elay is cradled to an attuned and adapted rhythm. I feel that, by now, rhythm and the notion of time are somewhat more established in Elay's mind. The hammock has a holding and containing quality and the swinging allows one to use rhythm to create an internal beat. In time, despite Elay's developing abilities for conceptualization and play, feelings of emptiness and meaninglessness began to surface in the countertransference. If I waited long enough, will a baby be born in this hammock? I am irritated – sometimes I experience the hammock as a potential space, awaiting realization, waiting for Elay to find it and fill it – like Bion's 'empty thoughts', thoughts looking for a thinker, a potential which meets a realization. Sometimes, I am horrified that the hammock might remain forever empty, meaningless and somber as a symbolic emptiness (Alvarez, 1992). I bring this up again and again in my supervision, where this dilemma meets other deliberations concerning Elay's needs. Should I initiate, opposing Elay's wish to dictate an infinite time, and 'plant a seed', or wait for Elay's initiative to ripen, for his realization of some idea or wish?

In one of our sessions, I intuitively place a baby-doll in the hammock. While it took a long time for this intervention to mature, I am still wondering what kind of interpretation it offers. Is it a functional or a pedagogic intervention? Is this an expression of my difficulty in tolerating emptiness? Elay looks at the doll curiously yet unsurprised. He puts it in his lap and examines its face, eyes, ears and mouth. Was this Elay as a newborn baby? Our newborn baby? My countertransference guides me to tell Elay, 'the baby has eyes and ears too and a mouth'. In the following sessions, Elay changes the baby's diaper and puts it to sleep, he even adds a bedtime story. ASD children repeatedly confront us with the question of how meaning can grow from such vast emptiness. Perhaps Elay needs more active participation – mine as well as his mother's – in order to realize an internal potential that is an 'unthought known' (Bollas, 1987, 17) and transform it into a 'thought known'. I have faith in the enormous significance of the time it took this idea to mature within me. The ability to contain emptiness and nothingness enabled the notion of 'a baby' as a creation of life. Alongside the 'birth' of this baby, Elay also acquired writing – a skill which is much more than strictly formal, drawing on much deeper layers. Elay is developing his capacity for symbolization, abstraction and representation, allowing his sensory experiences to become imbued with subjective meaning.

Third period: structural difficulties versus the desire to develop and live

We kept trying to broaden and deepen the process by which Elay was endowing meaning, by emphasizing the sequences and the connections between action and emotional experience; the therapy and the kindergarten; the kindergarten and his home environment; and between learning and actual experiences. Seeing that the other children have much of the same difficulties as Elay, each in his own unique way, during Elay's third year at the kindergarten, the kindergarten teacher, her assistants and the speech therapist established a new communication work-group that focused on everyday experiences. The *speech therapist* tells about Elay's participation in this group:

> Elay is already using different kinds of compound sentences and has acquired the use of various grammatical rules, such as gender and numeric agreement and the accurate use of pronouns. I notice the funny mistakes he makes when trying to use language creatively. However, his difficulties in understanding and his poor knowledge of the world still stand out. While he can describe things and tell stories, there are many underlying gaps. As a result, he has trouble understanding the more intricate levels of language. He is unable to make the necessary connections and thus has trouble understanding sequence and causality and drawing conclusions. In addition, he is familiar with very few fields of knowledge and therefore has a hard time finding more diverse subjects of conversation and elaborating on them.

Mere observation or talking 'about' did not make Elay or the other children in the group more familiar with their world. At an early age, Elay could not master the learning principles which allow children to employ a set of rules instead of learning each word or event separately. It feels as if one still needs to make the world accessible for Elay, by creating tangible experiences – of sight, touch, movement, taste, smell – in order to give meaning to all the words he is already using in a shallow and detached manner. It feels as if one has to fill one gap after another and start rebuilding meaning from the very beginning. Elay's knowledge of the world is so limited that it often seems like an impossible task. Our basic assumption is that with children like Elay, nothing can be taken for granted and even the most familiar actions, which we find utterly trivial, may not be entirely clear to him. Therefore, beyond the satisfaction drawn from a given experience, we also try to present every experience to the children in a variety of contexts. Maybe by delineating experiences, noting causality, sequence and the way the different parts make up the whole, these children could begin experiencing in a new way. Instead of only dealing with specific situations, we provide them with tools, which they can then internalize and develop for dealing with new situations.

We call this group the 'home group' and we base it on sharing the children's everyday experiences at home. We also decide to make the parents as actively involved as possible. As we go from one subject to the next, the parents are notified and receive a 'sharing sheet', so that they could continue the activity at home and discuss it with their child.

As soon as the group is on its way, the gap between Elay's ability to take part in the preparatory conversation and his ability to participate in the actual experience becomes very noticeable. Elay insists on being very actively involved in the conversation, picking on his friends, trying to take control of the situation, trying to make us laugh, moving around – and when all these attempts fail, he claims he is too tired to go on. He finds it very difficult to keep up with a multi-sided conversation, which requires him to process information from several different sources, and he simply gives up in advance. We begin to wonder whether Elay is suffering from an attention deficit disorder, but as soon as we begin the experiential activity, he springs back to life, takes an active part and participates in every task.

Take, for example, a 'laundry' activity: Elay could not answer basic questions such as – 'what makes clothes dirty? What do you do with dirty clothes? Does this shirt need washing?' But when we brought out the water-filled tubs, he joined the process from beginning to end – washing, wringing out and hanging. After a while, he even went out to the yard to see if his clothes were already dry. While the group allows children to learn different fields of knowledge, it also stresses social interaction. At this point, the presence of other children begins to increase his motivation. Elay has a good friend, whom he often follows around – Elay sees him as an example, mimicking his actions. As part of an activity about getting ready for bed, the children were asked to bring their pajamas from home. After putting on their pajamas and making their bed, Elay and his good friend are happily lying side by side, listening to a story. Then, they make loud snoring sounds and 'refuse to get up' once the 'morning' has come, laughing together under the blanket. It appears that Elay really registered this experience, for in the next group session he is already able to describe the sequence of actions one has to perform at bedtime.

At some point, we began leaving the kindergarten and taking walks around the neighborhood, getting the children to 'learn through their feet'. We walked over to a cactus garden, to the grocery store and to a nearby playground. The children are encouraged to notice the things we see along the way. Elay and his good friend are holding hands and Elay, who usually does not even look up at the sky to see what color it is, was starting to mind his surroundings. 'There's a car!' he calls out excitedly. 'There's a date-tree!' he rejoices (shortly after the children learned about trees). His friend shouts, 'look, dog poop!' and they enjoy a good laugh. Sadly, the cactus garden, the destination of our first walk, is closed. Standing outside it, I use this opportunity to talk to the children about feeling disappointed. But this feeling does not last long, as the world is full of tempting offers. On our way back, we see a crane lifting furniture into an apartment. Elay is very curious about it. He shouts out, 'look! Crane!' We spend minutes on end looking at the crane taking furniture up and down. Back at the kindergarten, each child is asked to tell the group about something that happened during our walk and Elay, with much excitement, talks about seeing the crane. On our next walks, he looks for the crane, but we never see it again.

When we come back and the children are asked to share an experience, Elay enjoys unfolding his story and is able to clearly depict what he had just experienced. It seems that connecting to a meaningful and pleasurable experience from the recent past helps him organize his description of his personal experience. When Elay shares his perspective on an experience, it is surprising to see how creative his description is. I enjoy watching him in the group. Socially, he seizes every opportunity for interacting with his contemporaries; emotionally, he enjoys himself, flourishes and is moved; in terms of language and communication, he is learning new concepts, engaging in conversation as we walk and coherently describing his personal experiences to others. At the grocery store, we look at different categories of food – fruit, vegetables, meat, pastries, canned food. Every child has some small change and is asked to pick out a product. Elay knows exactly what he wants. He goes for a Kinder cake and even walks up to the clerk, asks how much it costs and buys it. At the kindergarten, Elay relishes eating the cake he bought and asks, as one might have expected, to go back and buy more things.

Throughout the group's activities, the kindergarten teacher made a point of documenting the special experiences they shared. She uploaded the pictures to the kindergarten computer for the children to watch and enjoy. Elay spent a long time looking at the pictures. Now, these were no longer a frozen message, but an invitation to converse with the staff or the other children, an opportunity to share his experience or exchange information. The group focused on learning by connecting the whole-body experience and the attending affects, which endow it with meaning. I feel that this way of learning is right for Elay. The ability to make connections, practiced under ideal conditions as mentioned above, was now part of a multi-sided discussion in the children's everyday lives. As the *kindergarten teacher* recounts:

> Not too long ago, Elay had trouble recalling experiences and could barely describe what he did the day before. He had a very hard time taking into account what his listeners knew or did not know and when he formulated an idea it was very difficult for us to understand its context. The more he developed, the deeper these gaps became. We felt that if he could succeed only once, the dam would break open and the big bang would finally arrive. As always, this phantasy was only partially realized. Throughout his last year, Elay was sometimes able to share his experiences at home as part of a joint effort by the entire staff to help him organize and reconstruct sequences. I noticed that his ability to hold sequences had to do with the intensity of the experience and the degree to which its stimuli were overwhelming. After the Passover break, each child told the group about the Seder (Passover dinner) he attended. However, Elay, having attended a very crowded Seder that was too busy for his abilities, could not even recall where it was held. Only after repeated attempts to enliven the moment was he able to tell us that they went to his grandmother's. Today, when the conversation is clearer and draws on knowledge he already acquired, Elay is better organized and his recall is quite moving. During a morning session, we are engrossed in a conversation about summer. The children recall joyful moments from their summer

vacation. The sea takes up a significant portion of the conversation. What it looks like – what color it is, how big it is and what's inside it. Elay actively participates: 'the sea is big and blue, not like a pool'. The children share their experiences of going to the beach. Elay keeps silent and then says, 'I want to go to the beach too'. Elay already knows a thing or two about the sea. He knows that it is big and blue and also that he has never seen it. I suggest that he asks his parents to take him and he does. The next week, I ask, 'have you been to the beach?' 'No!' He is holding this idea, 'you can't go because of the jellyfish!' (does he know what these are?). Elay's mother sees me and confirms his report. The end of the school year is almost here and Elay still hasn't been to the beach. When the year is over, I say goodbye to the children and, about a month later, I stop by the kindergarten when the children are in summer camp with the substitute staff. I come across Elay surrounded by his friends and holding a shoe-lace that has virtually become part of him. He stands next to me, a little stiff, and says, 'I went with mom to the beach'. What a good boy. . . . He was able to remember how important this was. So much effort to hold his will, his thoughts and his desires in the context of his relationship with me. All this was rolled up into this short sentence. I had been waiting a long long time for this to happen, right along with him.

Here we are, sending a little boy off to school, one who knows all about letters and numbers, writing and cutting with scissors, who is well organized with his school bag and his pencil case, who can follow instructions (more or less), handle a work-sheet and join meaning to his experience. A little boy is off to first grade.

According to the *occupational therapist*, after Elay's years at the kindergarten, one sees a child who is significantly more whole:

> Elay has clear fields of interest, he takes part in the various kindergarten activities (all of them, though not consistently), he is capable of learning, thinking, adapting and coping. It seems that he has developed a sense of his own abilities, alongside the capacity to deal with tasks that are difficult for him. It appears that his information processing and memory capacities have expanded, enabling him to better preserve his experiences in the world. His thinking process has developed; information is now more available to him and he has a bigger pool of strategies to choose from. He can internalize new knowledge faster and maintain his attention for longer periods of time. His knowledge of the world has increased and the world seems less frightening and intimidating for him than it used to be. The kindergarten teacher and I have been facilitating a first grade preparation group and it is far from easy for Elay. He has trouble listening to our explanations, understanding our instructions and carrying them out diligently. Still, despite his difficulties, we are amazed at his participation: he is there with us, constantly learning and pushing forward. He used to give up right away, but now he is not giving himself any breaks.

In his last year at the kindergarten, Elay and four other children are integrated into a kindergarten for children with normal development. On the days when I join him in the integration process, I observe the soccer game that emerges spontaneously. The game is not exactly soccer, more like playing 'catch' with their feet. The hidden goal of this game seems to be kicking the ball as hard and as high as possible. Elay manages to kick it harder and higher than anyone else. While it is difficult to maintain mutuality in this kind of game, it appears that the other children appreciate Elay for the strength of his kicking. In the therapy room, I try to take Elay's playing up a notch, realizing that soccer is an important preoccupation for him and thus a fertile ground for learning. I mark two points, explaining to Elay that these mark the goalposts. Elay is not taking this in. I try to practice counting the number of goals scored, but he is unable to remember or understand that I scored one goal and he scored two. I am tempted to imagine Elay, later in life, playing soccer in a team, but maybe I am being too optimistic. How will he learn all the rules? How will he deal with losing? What about the need to react quickly and be creative, to plan, think ahead, try and understand what the other players have in mind? Elay keeps moving forward, growing and developing, but it feels as if he will always have these gaps, barring his way to higher functioning.

And back to the *psychotherapy*: one day, Elay throws up at the kindergarten and his father comes to take him home. After staying at home for a few days, he tells his psychotherapist about being sick in great detail: 'I threw up at the kindergarten. Dad came to take me home. Mom wasn't home. We called her. She came. I was in bed. I threw up again. I went to sleep for a long time and then I watched television. That's the story! I told you so many things today'. Elay is excited by his growing sense of ability and I choose to confirm and reinforce his joy, 'I like it when you tell me. It was a story about you'. 'Yes', he says, 'an interesting story'. Elay is telling me his story and I can imagine it and contemplate it. A story about the internal objects which are kept and digested or expelled when they are toxic; about his father's ability to be attentive and serve as a container for his undigested feelings; about the ability to keep his mother in his mind, even though she was not present; and about his ability to use the therapy in order to allow what he says to become endowed with further meaning.

This is a significant step forward in terms of his capacity to think and communicate. This newly developed ability can be conceptualized as overcoming what Alvarez called a 'wondering disability' (2012, 16), by developing the ability to 'wonder' and wander around in one's thoughts. When this ability begins to develop and contents start being more important than form, it is both crucial and exciting. A child who has never used his imagination can now say, 'I have an idea'. The possibility of looking for an idea is now an actuality and ideas sometimes appear even when one has not gone looking for them. According to Alvarez, realistic thinking does not depend on attaining the depressive position; it begins to emerge along with the first thought that is related to a present object, rather than an absent one, as Freud conjectured. Nevertheless, knowing the present object requires a correspondence between the infant's processing capacity and the nature of the stimulus in terms of rhythm, intensity, predictability and complexity. If attention is rushed, thoughts may acquire a patchwork character.

Throughout Elay's years at the kindergarten, the intense and densely woven fabric of the various therapies facilitated the development of his capacity to self-regulate, organize his thoughts and create sequences. The therapies made Elay's processing mechanism more adaptable to the potential of sharing everyday stimuli, thus enabling a new and essential level of thinking and communication. Stern (1985) indicates that the development of a sense of a 'verbal self' goes hand in hand with the development of a 'narrative self'. The ability to tell stories arrives much later than language itself and when it is mature it paves the way for new aspects of the self. In childhood, most of one's autobiographical plots are constructed through the help of others. In therapy, one may witness the very act of putting a story together under laboratory conditions: the story is woven by endowing an experience with meaning – not when it happens, but when it is reconstructed. Elay is growing more capable and when I respond by saying 'I like it when you tell me', I am referring to his joy and pride at having grown and realizing that we can converse and imagine together.

For Elay, a damaged organic foundation and an overly complex mother-environment met in a way that shaped his development as full of islands of misunderstanding. These immense developmental gaps evoked profound anxiety that made him choose to maintain shallow structures of understanding wherever depth was inaccessible to him. When Elay began to develop the ability for emotional thinking, subjectivity and the formation of narrative, his capacity for symbolization began to emerge.

In the therapy room, Elay starts writing. In normal development, the functions which begin to appear at the age of two, fully mature at the age of five: fine motor skills and symbolization reach a level that allows for the transition to writing. For Elay, the use of symbols has only partially matured and this development is surprisingly intense. Elay is excited about his emerging abilities and he rushes into the room with great eagerness to practice again and again. 'I'm practicing', he says and then adds, 'I didn't practice skating on my skateboard in a while'. Reflective processes are now in motion and Elay, affected by them, is wondering at the miracle of his development, asking 'how am I doing this?' As if he was asking, all surprised: 'how am I growing?'

At first, when writing letters, Elay mostly relates to their formal aspect rather than their meaning. On the page, the letters are placed as if suspended in midair, scattered and in disarray, lacking any order or direction; but in Elay's mind, they come together to form words, to spell his name. I admire his ability and trace his letters with my finger: 'E, and there's an L and here we have an A and last in line, the Y'. Still, for a long time, the letters will not come together. I talk about his difficulty in joining them and allowing them to belong together. Elay has a hard time figuring things out by himself, so after a while I tell him that the letters should be next to each other in order for them to know that they are together. I connect them as I did the different parts of his body. The E next to the L, which is right by the A and finally, the Y: 'each letter has its own place'. Elay is writing and his letters are starting to belong to each other. 'Just like a family', I think. Elay already knows all about his family unit, he is also writing the names of the other children that he sees posted on the kindergarten's drawers and on the board that says 'who came to the kindergarten'. Then, he writes 'dad', 'mom' and the names of his brothers and sisters. Suddenly, he stops. Drawing a blank? 'Who else?' he asks. 'You wrote and wrote and all of a sudden you ran out of names'. 'Yes', he says, still unable to think of any more names. 'Who else do you know?' I ask. Elay gives me a glazed, puzzled stare. 'Sometimes we're just out of ideas', I say. Silence. 'Maybe grandpa and grandma?' 'Yes!' he rejoices. His eyes light up, 'I have two grandmas and one grandpa', he tells me. From there, he moves on to his cousins and even remembers to write my name – 'Orly'. He realizes that he is actually capable of writing any word that comes to his mind, which has grown so very much.

This experience of moving and growing is not easy for Elay. In the therapy room, he is acting all grumpy, resisting and breaking boundaries, hoping to derive a sense of power and ability. In his playing, he associates himself with evil and aggressive characters, while perceiving 'good' characters as weak. He is exhibiting the first inklings of splitting, which indicates the emergence of a mental structure. Elay turns to areas of experience in which he is more knowledgeable and capable. He can kick the ball very hard around the room, enjoying this quite a bit. His movements grow more and more precise and he can aim the ball, trying to kick it to various spots, such as the tire in the corner of the room. At first, I allow this, thinking that experiencing powerful movement helps him develop another layer of his self,[3] a positive and non-destructive vital urge that will help him attain separateness. But this force is unregulated and Elay is looking around the room, savoring the sight of things falling down and crashing to the floor by the force of his kicking.

In the countertransference, I feel helpless, physically and mentally bombarded. Gradually, I begin to feel anger and alarm. I try regulating his activity, interpreting the importance of force, the impact of falling objects, but my words fall on deaf ears. In one of the sessions, Elay kicks the ball and breaks the clock. As we pick up the pieces, I interpret his desire to kick as a wish to either stop time or rush it forward, in the context of his coming separation from me and the kindergarten. His attack was severe and I was looking for a way to maintain a live presence in relation to his panicked reaction, which created the feeling that the room was filling up with bad objects. The danger presented itself through extensive use of projective identification (Bion, 1962), so that we were both struck by uncontainable dread. I offered Elay a softer ball to replace the hard one, as if I were telling him: 'I think that you got really scared and I got scared along with you, but now I am finally able to help you survive this panic and acknowledge a softness that will facilitate, rather than limit, your movement'. Elay made use of this understanding. As termination drew closer and we recalled the shattered clock, he asked, 'Orly, you brought the clock to the room, right? Why did you want it?' While I am wondering whether I should explain about the clock being a representation of time, Elay went on to ask, 'so why did you get a clock that breaks? Why didn't you get a plastic clock?' For a minute, I was surprised, why did I buy that particular clock without thinking that it could break? With much grief, which was also the grief of the actual separation at hand, I said, 'would you like me to find a special clock, one that never breaks, even if you kick it? One that would be perfect for you? Maybe you would like a clock that would be just right for our time, a clock that would make it so we didn't have to say goodbye?' Reality sneaks in. In therapy as well as in the kindergarten, reality is usually adapted and modified to suit the child's developmental needs, but I need to help Elay bear the fact that his mental mechanism must adapt itself to the vast real world and that no imaginary clock could ever stop time.

In one of the sessions, Elay finds a pair of soft mice-shaped toys. He names them 'Blue' and 'Red' after their colors. He holds them tightly in his lap, keeping them safe and asks me to be the mice – who are facing a great many dangers – while he will be the hero who protects them from all these unpredictable perils, which he imagined as vicious monsters. Elay is establishing a good and bad split (Klein, 1952). We are trying to protect the good from the bad and the plot becomes quite complicated – we are making traps for the bad guys and a home, a tent full of pillows, for the good mice. Suddenly, whether it is after a few minutes or after several sessions, potential space collapses. Elay stands up, looks at me with glazed eyes, void of any ideas, as if he saw me as alien and empty. All meaning is drained from the game and our train of thought is lost. Maybe this anxiety was evoked by the threat of evil trying to destroy good.

Toward the end of the year, something moving and unexpected happens once again. Elay is taking his first steps in rope-tying. The kindergarten teacher says that Elay has been spending time with a 'strong' boy, the kind of boy who rekindles in Elay the familiar notion that strong is destructive. Elay spends weeks wooing this boy: making significant concessions, making sure he never goes last, always asking to sit next to him and so on. Unfortunately, Elay is always last in line for this boy, who keeps inviting other children over to his house and never lets Elay have his favorite plate. This makes Elay very sad, but in time, this motion between impotence and omnipotence is peppered with more and more moments in which Elay feels potent. One day, a parcel of toys arrives at the kindergarten. In it, Elay finds a butterfly with a string attached to it. He tries repeatedly to tie the string and gets in a bind, but he already knows how to ask for help. The admired boy and another friend take an interest in Elay's attempts at tying. When all three of them work together, the string ties together Elay's mind and also serves to tie all three boys into a single bundle. This astounding tying ability is applied throughout an ever growing range so that magically, the entire kindergarten is suddenly tied up. Their joint activity is full of playfulness and creativity – toy-trucks are tied together, various objects are tied in a chain and dragged all over the kindergarten, pieces of furniture are tied to one another and so forth. Elay is experimenting with deepening and honing his tying skill in *occupational therapy* as well:

> He brings a string into the room and shows me how he ties the bicycle to the trapeze-swing. But his knot comes undone. I show Elay how to tie a double knot and he learns quickly, comparing one kind of knot to the other. As a goodbye gift, I decide to make Elay a book that is bound with a string and tied just like shoelaces. When I show Elay the book, he shows no interest in its contents, but is deeply impressed by the string binding. At the staff meeting, we wonder whether he is deliberately ignoring the meaning of the book by focusing on the knots, so as not to feel the significance of our goodbye. Maybe he can only relate to the concrete, rather than the emotional 'tie'. In the occupational therapy room, Elay asks me, 'how did you make this knot?' and I demonstrate. He tries but is unable to tie it. Throughout the two weeks left before the end of the year, whenever Elay comes into the room he immediately asks to try the knot. He says that he wants to do it all by himself and when he fails, he asks me to help him in a very adapted manner. I am impressed by his motivation for learning and the urge to keep trying until he succeeds as well as by his ability to use my help. I am less excited about the act of tying itself, which I find esoteric and inefficient. Sadly, the year is almost up and Elay has not learned to tie the knot. In my concluding meeting with his parents, I tell them about his interest in tying knots. I still have one more session left with Elay.

On the last day of the school year, Elay sees me coming into the kindergarten and says, 'now I know to tie the knot, just like you'. I suppose that his parents taught him how. He holds a piece of string I once gave him and shows me how he ties a knot around the leg of the table. Then, he wants to tie my hand. He is trying to tie everything around the kindergarten: a chair, a table, a cup, a game board. He keeps tying and untying, tying, and untying.

On that same day, one of the assistants, who used to work at the kindergarten and went on maternity leave, comes for a visit. She used to be very important to Elay – he would rely on his relationship with her and had a hard time giving up her presence. When she walks up to him to say hello, he completely ignores her. She asks him if he wants to come and see her baby. No response. I tell Elay that I am going to go and see her baby and I ask him if he would like to come along and tie the baby's stroller. He agrees to come, confidently steps up to the stroller and ties it. One of the other children is trying to talk to the baby, tickling it. I tell the boy that he is very good with babies. Elay, after not so much as glancing at the baby, says, 'me too', perhaps as a result of some healthy envy. Then, he asks me to come outside and says, 'pretty baby, huh?' On the surface, it seemed that he avoided any active communication with the assistant and her baby and was strictly preoccupied with tying the concrete knot. But it was evident that implicitly he was intently preoccupied with the very possibility of making connections in his thoughts and imagination. It is still crucial that we build a bridge to reality for him, again and again, due to the immense gaps between his intentions and his difficulties in initiating connections in terms of meaning and communication.

Elay brings this potential for tying knots to *psychotherapy* as well: he picks one of the ropes that are lying about the room and ties it to a hula-hoop, he pulls and unties, then ties and unties again. I try to link his rhythm of tying and untying to our relationship – stating that it seems to symbolize our separation. Elay looks up with glazed eyes. 'What? What did you say?' He does not understand, or maybe his understanding is far away, lost at the bottom of some deep well. Elay tries to tie the rope to other objects but fails. He seeks but does not find. One spot is too small or cramped; another is too challenging for his present skills. He keeps tying the rope to the same object. I look around and notice a tumbler toy that has a large wide strap. After thinking it over, I decide to offer it to him. Elay's eyes light up. He ties the rope to the tumbler toy and pulls it toward him. The tumbler toy reacts and leans his way. Elay lets go and the tumbler toy swings back. He ties a hula-hoop and asks me to hold it, to keep the rope tight and walk backward. 'Pull it', he says, 'pull it more, let go. No, not now, in a little bit'. Precision is very important. He tells me where to stand and we try again and again. Elay is pleased, the timing was perfect. I let go at just the right time and the tumbler toy swung back to its original position. Today, when I think about the tumbler toy, it occurs to me that it is soft, flexible and very moveable and that its shape is even reminiscent of a breast. Could it have served as a transitional object? (Winnicott, 1971b) Naturally, I was the one who suggested using it, so that it is not his exclusive creation. Still, he rediscovered it in a way that made it seem as if it was never my idea to begin with. He used it to negotiate moving closer and further apart throughout our separation. I hold on and let go; the toy is under his control, but not completely.

Elay is moving toward a post-autistic organization (Meltzer *et al.*, 1975). We are tied together in a mental hoop. He pulls and lets go and I adapt myself to his movements with a deep relational resonance. Elay already knows how to write words and think thoughts, but still cannot grasp the significance of tying and untying the rope to the hoop as a symbol of our coming separation, perhaps because of the pain it involves. Nevertheless, the emotional impact of relating and being detached is already fathomed through myriad unseen threads.

A moment before our final goodbye, Elay experiences yet another developmental step. He finds the soft mice, the ones named 'Blue' and 'Red' that he kicked around as if they were a soccer-ball. He smiles and asks, 'don't look now'. I say, 'I can close my eyes'. Elay is surprised by this absurd idea. 'No', he says, 'don't look now'. I say, 'you know, when I close my eyes, I can't see you'. His eyes light up in understanding, 'okay, close. But don't open them until I say'. I calmly close my eyes, but I am also excited and full of anticipation; I can feel the thread that is tying us together just like the rope and the hula-hoop. 'Now open', he says. I open my eyes. Elay has joined the two mice together. These mice that were once kicked about are now joined to one another in an embrace. Elay, who once could not bear to see my eyes wandering away from him, has developed the capacity for depth and for meaningful relatedness. This three-dimensional experience is so different from his early desire to tape different surfaces together, joining nothing to nothing, like the adhesive tape to the carpet. With these mice, Elay is capable of so much more. He prepared a surprise for me and I am excited and moved. For a moment, with my eyes closed, I am imagining what it would be like after we say goodbye and stop seeing each other. When I open my eyes, the mice are joined together; joined, rather than glued together.

This has been Elay's story. I have chosen the above clinical material to serve as a prism, one of many no doubt, that would allow us to discuss both the autistic aspects and the developmental aspects – the mental elements which make time stand still and refuse to acknowledge a process of growth and change – the part that says 'you won't move and I won't move', alongside the mental functions that compel us, as therapists, to move developmentally: 'move, so that I could move too'.

Notes

1 Grammatical gender is very prominent in Hebrew. There is a difference between male and female nouns and here, as in other occasions, Elay addresses the female therapist with a male form.

2 DIR (Developmental, Individual, Relationship-based) is a method for treating ASD children, based on S. Greenspan's developmental model for expanding circles of spontaneous communication.

3 Shahar-Levi calls this positive aggressive movement 'selforce'; see Shahar-Levi, 2004.

Translation: crying over mom

Chapter 4

In the beginning was the Word?

Some theoretical and technical considerations in working with ASD children – a case discussion

Joshua Durban

For the past several years, as part of a joint discussion group, I had the privilege of getting to know and deeply appreciate the profound work that is carried out daily at the Shaked kindergartens. To the best of my knowledge this kind of integrative inter-disciplinary psychotherapeutic work with ASD children is unprecedented, in Israel and abroad. When thinking about applying certain clinical practices to the child and its developmental environment, one should take into account a comprehensive theoretical model that spans the width and length of six different dimensions: the structural, the dynamic, the genetic, the geographic, the economic, and the epistemological. More simply, we need to constantly bear in mind the child's psycho-physiological make up; his use of internal and external spaces; the nature, content and quality of the object relations in his internal world; his emergence process as a person within his family and society and his way of constructing his capacity for thinking. I believe that the case of Elay, and the manner in which it is reported and conceptualized, endows these theoretical notions with both immediacy and vitality and is therefore immensely relevant to our clinical practice. As the case study suggests, the integration of these different dimensions throughout the therapeutic work eventually led to three very potent expressions of the transformative journey this child had made at the kindergarten. The first was Elay's use of the *hammock*. This served as a matrix for a psychological re-birth. The second expression was the appearance of the *string*: the string that oscillated between clinching/gripping – much like Elay who was gripped inside a deadly numbness – and binding/linking. The final, third expression was *Elay's use of the string to tie the two mice together:* an astounding manifestation of object relatedness. The cruel and persecutory mice were bound together, linked. At this moment, we encounter an object relations' dynamic that can finally move from the earliest anxieties-of-being, through the paranoid-schizoid spectrum and toward an almost-depressive phase. I think that the hammock and the string were not simply new structures that had emerged in Elay but also his way of acknowledging the beneficial presence of kindergarten and the entire therapeutic staff. They were actively binding, delineating, linking, and relating all that was frozen, empty, and perforated in him, giving it life and form. These are prime instances of transferential relatedness.

Elay's case and the therapeutic staff's mode of work highlight the need for renewed consideration of both theory and technique. It is quite obvious that when working with ASD children we often make extensive use of gestures, actions and a total body-mind presence, which differ from classic psychoanalytic interpretative techniques. Nevertheless, they are based on a deep psychoanalytic understanding of early mental processes and traumas. They therefore contribute to a better understanding of adults and of the appropriate modes of encountering damaged early mental states within therapy.

The changing shape and use of interpretations in the psychotherapies of ASD and psychotic children

I wish to share some thoughts regarding my experience in the treatment of ASD and psychotic children when, often intuitively and unawares, we momentarily resort to different modes of being and interpretation, in order to establish some immediate contact with the unconscious of the withdrawn, unreachable, fragmented and non-verbal child. These *pre-symbolic realizations*[1] assume the form of concrete acts. Thus, they do not qualify as symbolic play. They might therefore be regarded as acting in and out of the sessions and as a deviation from traditional technique. However, I believe they constitute an inevitable part of the therapy of such children, through which certain aspects of the child's mind might be reassembled, repaired and sometimes even virtually created. There are two points which for me seem to be at the heart of the matter: the first is the link between the level of representation and the level of anxiety evident within the session, and the second – the necessary technique which is then called for in order to establish contact with the child, mobilize anxieties and promote representation, integration, and reparation.

I Detecting the deepest levels of anxiety

Let me start by reminding ourselves of John Steiner's observation regarding difficult-to-reach patients. In his book *Psychic Retreats* (1993), he writes:

> *I want to make a distinction between understanding and being understood, and point out that the patient who is not interested in acquiring understanding – that is, understanding about himself – may yet have a pressing need to be understood by the analyst.* Sometimes this is consciously experienced as a wish to be understood, and sometimes it is unconsciously communicated. A few patients appear to hate the whole idea of being understood and try to disavow it and get rid of all meaningful contact. Even this kind of patient, however, needs the analyst to register what is happening and to have his situation and his predicament recognized (132, italics added).

How this 'being understood' is to be accomplished and registered as a means for psychic contact and transformation when dealing with difficult-to-reach or encapsulated patients, often fragmented and aggressive, remains one of the most urgent questions in therapy. Steiner himself advocates the use of therapist-centered interpretations, although he mainly uses it to verbally interpret paranoid-schizoid anxieties, defensive pathological organizations and their accompanying unconscious phantasies.

A related approach lays more stress on the role of primitive anxieties in preventing or destroying symbol-formation and representation and, as a consequence, hindering the possibility of understanding and relating. It is therefore crucial to detect them at their maximal level of operation and interpret them. Our work with ASD children and with children suffering from severe psychosis has shown that, alongside early paranoid-schizoid and depressive anxieties – that is, besides the drama of relationship – there is a deeper layer of anxieties, which might be called 'anxieties of being'. These 'unthinkable anxieties' (Winnicott, 1962) involve our threatened sense of existing as bounded, psycho-biological units. They include the experiences of having no body, existing solely through the senses, which are often mixed and dislocated, having no inside or outside, leaking out and emptying, liquefying, freezing, burning, falling, dissolving, having no sensation of time and space. These 'anxieties of being' are characterized by a deep sense of confusion and non-differentiation between self and object and by futile attempts to attain some level of cohesion while fending off the threatening environment with the help of adhesive identification (Meltzer, 1975), annexation (Rhode, 2012) and autistic objects and sensation shapes (Tustin, 1981). The child gripped by these anxieties lives in a nightmarish world where the backdrop of safety is replaced by an uncanny landscape where no good internal object can develop. From my experience with these children, it is not so much that unconscious phantasies do not exist but rather that they disintegrate into their components. That is, there is a slow dismantling (Meltzer, 1975) of the psyche's connective tissue, severing links between body, mind and object, with each of these disintegrating and splintering in turn. These anxieties can be alleviated in two ways. The first is by finding a 'real' development-promoting object to be gradually implanted within the mind; this object will supply the patient with its total body-mind presence or 'mantling' (by the therapist). The second is by resorting to an internally deadening pathological autistic organization, dominated by the tyranny of the non-differentiated senses, which holds the seductive but false promise to save the patient from nameless dread and catastrophic change.

While the patient is in the grips of these 'anxieties of being', we find him often in pre-verbal, pre- or non-symbolic states of mindlessness: frozen, shattered, and terrified of anything human. It is often very tempting to interpret these anxieties on the paranoid-schizoid level, but the therapist soon discovers that this is at best unhelpful and at worst deepens the gap between him and the child's unconscious. It is then that we realize that alongside these more 'organized' anxieties and object relations there is the deeper layer of 'anxieties of being'. In other words, bad objects only fill an internal void where there is a no-object, an un-object, or a disintegrated one. In the case of multi-determined developmental pathologies such as ASD or children suffering from psychosis or schizophrenia, there is usually a combination of a hyper-sensitive constitution (which in itself is traumatic since the 'body as a mother'[2] or as a good object becomes persecutory and traumatizing) and a tragic, harmful course of development where there is a difficulty in establishing a good, containing object consisting of a parental couple joined with love.

All of this can only be achieved through special kinds of therapist-based interpretations, which utilize the therapist's own memories, experiences, bodily sensations, and his capacity to think, feel, relate, and integrate. But above all, it is the therapist's unconscious willingness to let the patient use his own good internal objects and bodily container that promotes integration and makes some reparation possible. Houzel (2004) sees this phase of the treatment when these 'anxieties of being' begin to leak, to 'hemorrhage' into the session permeating the therapist's mind, as a 'transference onto the container' (228). Melanie Klein called it 'absorption'. It is characterized by a flooding of beta-elements and by frequent states of hallucinosis in both patient and therapist. Before a movement to what Bion called a transformation in K is possible, the therapist must contain and suffer this situation, this transformation in hallucinosis as long as it is needed by the patient (Bion, 1965), in order to start incorporating and subsequently internalizing the therapist as a good, continuous, 'real' and live object, as 'live company' (Alvarez, 1992).

To sum up: the lower we descend on the representational developmental ladder (from representation, to misrepresentations, to un-representations, pre-representations, or miss-representations), the more we encounter 'anxieties of being', which are closely linked to early infantile trauma (constitutional, internal, or environmental) which needs to be addressed and handled. This is achieved mainly through therapist-based interpretations, relying heavily on his total body-mind presence. This total presence, reflected in our state of mind and in our interpretations, brings about an 'object implant' by which the primary good object becomes the therapist and his link with his own internal objects (Durban, 2014).

2 The need for an expansion of analytic technique

I would like to briefly describe eight principles that I find useful when working in these areas. I wish to emphasize that all these additional modes of interpretation co-exist with and are later elaborated by and worked through verbal ones. Within each session there is an interplay between the following modes of interpretation:

Corporation – the construction of a *bodily container* (Pollak, 2009) for patients with a disintegrated or confusional bodily representation. We often need to help the patient differentiate between body parts, inside and outside, self and object.

Present-ness – this means making the child present for himself as a person, rather than an object or a random assortment of behaviors and sensory organs. Naturally, this is made possible due to the incessant efforts on the part of the therapist and the environment to present themselves in a way which the child finds bearable, while still outside his usual boundaries. This does not mean adaptation or optimal adaptability, which often only serve the child's malignant unconscious merger phantasies; rather, it means creating a live presence which allows for separateness and frustration as well.

Personification – presenting the therapist as a *live companion* who utilizes his total body-mind presence within the session. This entails the reversal of objectification: making the inhuman human, especially within the transference. We translate any attempt of the child at objectification and dehumanization as a meaningful and namable action performed on/with a person and by a person and thus – inevitably human. Personification includes the therapist's willingness to be projected into and invaded, to experience somatic hallucinations, as well as making his internal world of object relating available for the patient. Personification necessitates a close monitoring of the therapist's psycho-somatic countertransference and *somatic hallucinations as a means of autistic communication.* The combination of corporation, present-ness, and personification promotes the development of *multi-dimensionality* and *orientability*, which are impaired in the ASD child.

Reparation in action – using varied techniques such as *imitation*, affect enhancement and *amplification* (Alvarez, 2012). In this sense, we often need to initiate an act, a gesture, which signifies in a near-concrete way the possibility of integration and reparation.

Reassembling the linking function – actively and concretely re-connecting the disintegrated elements of unconscious phantasy. Linking is one of the most complicated principles in the sense that the therapist needs to constantly and actively link together senses, feelings, actions, intentions, and thoughts – even when all these are primary or fragmented – into a single sequence or string, much like the one Elay walked around with in the final months of his treatment. I think that this string also reflected his appreciation and deep understanding of the therapeutic process he underwent.

Reclaiming (Alvarez, 1992) – pulling the patient back from his withdrawn state into the relationship within the session. Reclaiming is the insistence on bringing the child back to us from his frozen state, fighting for whatever healthy parts are inside him, even if these are hidden and out of sight. In terms of the countertransference, this capacity relies on the existence of hope within us, on the belief that a self-less object can become a self that has an object. Our reliance on this 'developmental reverie', often severely impaired in the child and in his parents and resulting in deep despair (Durban, 2014), is dependent on our ability to hold on to theory, to the staff, to our own intra-psychic sources of hope and nourishment or, in short – to our good objects.

Allowing 'virtual patient' phantasies – images representing the therapist's hope for the patient's successful future psychological development. I have chosen the term 'virtual' following Freud's description in *The Interpretation of Dreams* (1900): 'everything that can be an object of our internal perception is *virtual*, like the image produced in a telescope by the passage of light-rays' (p. 611). This is a memoir of the future child.

Trauma and the death-object in ASD children

I will now elaborate on trauma as an omnipresent element in the treatment of ASD children and the relation between this trauma and nothingness, emptiness, perforation, and stillness – or what I term the 'Death Object' (Durban, 2012).

All children who suffer from considerable developmental deficiencies are traumatic or post-traumatic in several respects. First, the very fact of constantly existing in a state of confusional void, which is the main experience manifest in Elay's case, is traumatic for the child. In fact, the child is always on the verge of annihilation and non-existence as his mechanisms for feeling, experiencing and thinking – on which he relies for survival in the world – are deficient. We need only recall the chilling description of Elay's various structural deficiencies: a congenital structural disorder manifest in the disruption of his capacity to relate, learn, and develop; a deficient organic foundation in terms of his ability to decipher, process, and piece together any kind of information – be it sensory, affective, emotional, or verbal. This makes Elay extremely vulnerable and dependent on external objects, not only in order to carry out his practical functions, but also in order to be able to develop his psychic functions. Elay has cognitive deficiencies, which hinder his spontaneous learning in his natural environment. In terms of learning, Elay needs a great deal of repetition and precision and for others to find the exact locus of his difficulty as well as the thread that could bind him to the material at hand. Constantly bombarded by stimuli, Elay cannot understand its meaning and experiences it as confusing and impinging.

The developmentally deficient child is also in serious danger of having a shattered psyche, as a result of *multi-traumatization*: stemming from actual developmental or structural disasters and from his internal catastrophe – that is, living under the constant threat of annihilation. Following Freud's insights in 'Beyond the Pleasure Principle' (1920), Tustin depicts trauma as 'an overwhelming experience of helplessness in the face of an accumulation of excitation, whether external or internal' (1990). This helplessness could be caused by the organism's structural-functional inability or its immaturity, or by real situations that are simply 'too much', or a combination of both. For example, Tustin describes the autistic shell as a kind of defense against trauma, for which one pays the dear price of annihilating one's capacity to feel, think and create phantasies. According to Tustin, the most crucial component of the therapist's approach to the child's trauma – and to her own personal trauma that arises throughout the therapy – is 'the therapist's state of mind'. Tustin argues that the cases in which she was able to help the child were those in which she could, through whatever means, feel at home with herself and her surroundings. She indicates higher success rates among children whom she saw at her home, in contrast to those treated at her clinic. In my view, unlike the uncanny feeling that this kind of mind-body deficiency evokes in both the child and the therapist, this feeling of being 'at home' requires the utilization of all the techniques I previously described. Throughout the case presentation, I was deeply impressed by the cozy and home-like feeling expressed by the participants as well as by lively flow of the clinical material in each account and between the different accounts, even when discussing very difficult moments. I have no doubt that this home-like feeling, generated first and foremost within the staff's collective unconscious space, contributed much to Elay's progress.

In Greek (as well as in various medical and surgical contexts) trauma means wound or 'puncture'. It refers to the damage caused by the tearing of the skin or cell membrane or by an external force which affects the entire organism. Sometimes, it refers to the kind of damage caused by internal injuries, without any tearing or breaching of the skin, as in cases of internal brain trauma or degeneration (Laplanche and Pontalis, 1967, 465). We should add, given everything we know today, trauma caused by considerable developmental difficulties. Freud's greatness lay in the fact that he understood the destructive implications of events that could not be processed (whether by the sensory-motor system or by the cognitive-representational one) in the psychic system. He claimed that trauma temporarily shut down the pleasure principle, which is the principle of life and growth, and that the psyche becomes preoccupied with various attempts at controlling and binding these traumatic events, so that they could be processed at a later date. This brings to mind Elay's string which appeared after his initial habit of flinging things in the air. Moreover, this 'shutting down' of the pleasure principle or life force strengthens the anti-life forces, first and foremost aggression and destructiveness. We can only imagine how much aggression and despair, and the ensuing destructivity, arise in a child who is constantly attacked by a confusing annihilating structure-cum-world.

In traumatic situations, we witness the emergence of the death drive, whose hallmarks are fragmentation, delay, suspension and endless repetition and whose aim is to return to a state of unfeeling, to avoid all stimuli and to resume a cessation of existence. Freud's portrayal of the death drive is a very apt depiction of Elay, when he is in his frozen-repetitive states. The prominent indicators of trauma in the psychic system are anxiety and splitting, that is, the attempt to reposition the trauma outside the frame of one's consciousness, which endows it with its own world and its own rules (Freud, 1926). It is interesting to note that one of the related phenomena mentioned by Freud is the disjoining of symbol and symbolized, meaning that one encounters an unnamed stimulus or a name without a stimulus. It is fascinating to see how Freud is already outlining the various future developments in the psychoanalytic study of trauma, mainly the relation between container and contained and un-mentalized states.

The impact of trauma, especially the kind of trauma that involves the dread of annihilation and extinction, on the emerging infantile self is immense. Trauma disrupts the self's sense of continuity, effectiveness and existence. It disrupts thought and language-related processes, as being overwhelmed with stimuli precludes any distinctions between symbol, icon and index (Peirce, 1992, 1998).

One of the most well-known effects described in analytic literature is the absence of representation. Cohen (1985) describes how an experience that is too powerful and overwhelming to be symbolically attached to a wish needs to be worked through or modulated by means of what he calls 'need-mediating objects'. Cohen describes how, in these situations, experience becomes a psychic hole, void of structure or representations of need-fulfilling interactions and one is left without any foundation for symbolic interaction with the world or for goal-oriented behavior. Similarly, in Elay's case, we find a developmental progress in terms of finding such mediating objects, whose pinnacle is the invention of writing and numbers. Green (1998) argues that when the maternal container is unable to assimilate projective identifications, one is hemorrhaging representations, suffering a pain that entails no representation of the wound but only a state of emptiness, a hole. In contrast, Salomonsson (2006, 2007a, 2007b, 2007c) suggests, in light of his analytic work with young infants who have suffered various traumas, both physical and otherwise, that the hole itself is a sign or a representation. In other words, the hole can serve as a kind of need-mediating object, as Cohen put it, or, if we take into account the workings of the death drive on the phantasmatic level, as the abode of a dark and alluring object which narrates some trauma. Bion has taught us that nothing and no-thing are interchangeable in the psychic system. This means that nothing is represented as something, as a bad thing: no-breast equals a bad breast. In other words, the hole does not merely stay a hole – it is filled up with bad things replacing nameless grief and catastrophic threats. There is a defensive attempt to turn nameless dread into something with a form. When the thing that has no name can be turned into a person, then one can do something about it.

Bohleber (2002) discusses the collapse of the dimensions of time, space and sequence in those suffering from trauma as well as the difficulty in creating a meaningful personal history. Rhode (2012) demonstrates how the autistic child is unable to form an identity based on memories because instead of internalization he just adds-up, or 'annexes', external elements taken from his surroundings. In therapy, progress indicates that 'life as a trauma' begins to make room for a re-enactment of the trauma and for painful mourning of its losses. For instance, the ability to create a narrative of loss as a precursor of the ability to mourn is evident in Elay's story about his father and his throwing up. Words and feelings such as love, longing, and care are then present in the therapy room in an interpersonal context. In order to carry out the arduous task of making progress and of mourning, we must first deal with the massive internal presence of death anxiety and turn it into an object.

Elay's being is in itself a trauma. He is constantly experiencing near-death which in itself is a repetition of his developmental catastrophic experiences. He is living in the grips of what I call his 'death-equivalents', that is, the experience of being closest to death while still being alive. In addition, traumatization is exacerbated through the encounter with reality and the deficiencies it involves, starting with the encounter with the traumatized-traumatizing parents and recurring at each new level of development. We witness the emergence of a vicious cycle, in which external and internal traumas reinforce each other, creating an environment in which existence is not safe. In Elay's case, his gaps and holes echo a family that is already in the middle of a protracted crisis involving the choice to have children, illness and accidents. The parents are post-traumatic, exhibiting significant difficulties in functioning as well as manic defenses. As the case study suggests, every new spurt of growth and development gives rise to a new encounter with deficiency and nothingness. Dangerous death, which Elay initially manifested as paralysis, hole-ness, repetition and passivity, becomes an increasingly angry and persecutory element.

Thus, the developmentally vulnerable child feels in constant danger of being annihilated and destroyed. The fear of death inhabits all of us, as a fundamental element in our development and our personality; we engage it in a kind of internal dialogue that is based on various pacts and agreements designed to appease it or to learn how to live with it. Throughout development we create a kind of well-demarcated, inner death that is made up of developmental experiences that are registered as near-death in our psychic system and are thus death-equivalent. To mention just a few of these 'death-equivalent' experiences: the experience of birth and being torn or separated from the mother's interior, losing continuity, falling apart, falling into bits, liquefying, burning, freezing, suffocating, extreme hunger or pain, loss of orientation, moments of emptiness and non-thinking, emotional numbness or emotionless-ness, losing a love object or a parent, being exposed to the death of others, and so on. Such death-equivalent experiences are accumulated and eventually make up the portrait of a personified death object, which oscillates between a partial-sensory object and a whole object, with which one can form a relationship. These experiences can happen to anyone at some point in development. In the context of a more or less normal development, the person has recourse to various psychic manipulations that could help them cope with the danger of death or annihilation – it can be voided, fragmented, mitigated by vitality, love, creativity and goodness or manifested as a clearly defined object (a 'bad-object' which can be fought). As far as the disabled child is concerned, however, we are not talking about mere glimpses or moments of these experiences but about an ongoing state of being. The child is bombarded not only by non-digestible stimuli, but also by real dangers and the threat of psychological extinction, which are experienced in a most concrete and physical manner. Inside this autistic entrapment, the developmentally impaired child cannot apply any efficient psychic maneuvers, like those I mentioned earlier, simply because his capacity for object relations is minimal, if not altogether absent. Therefore, the fear of death is manifest as a constant physical-behavioral presence rather than as a distinct object, confronting us with a frozen, repetitive, perforated and fragmented child. All of these are indicators of physical as well as psychic deadness. That is, instead of creating a death object that one can enter into dialogue with – as pathological as this dialogue may be – the child is caught in death's clutches, unable to move. It is no coincidence that the most frequent words we hear are 'no' ('No, David!'), 'gone' etc. The rigor-mortis-like rigidity with wide open eyes, is often replaced by a soft passivity, a tendency to liquefy and dissolve which equally belongs to death's deconstructive actions. Many of the children we encounter have indeed suffered a near-death experience: actual death of a significant other, intrauterine dangers[3] and parents inhabited by dead or deadening objects. This is a significant pathogenic element, especially when it meets a child who lacks the basic structural equipment required for dealing with these experiences. The developmentally impaired child cannot endure this and thus 'plays dead', as if he were identifying or merging with his attacker. It is an attempt to 'kill death with death'.

Many ASD children walk about like zombies after having lost all internal vitality. Masked by constant activity and over-stimulation there lay an impoverished, lifeless world. The child often resembles an object rather than a human subject. As therapists, we are faced with the difficult and arduous task of acquainting ourselves with the specific death object of each and every child as well as with the 'death-equivalent' experiences comprising it. We need to engage in a direct and unflinching dialogue with it while offering our therapeutic live-presence as a substitute for death-relations. It is no coincidence that Ann Alvarez chose to name her book 'live company' (1992). In the psychic domain, death is not simply a description; it is a presence with its own set of rules, behaviors and goals. It aims at crushing, fragmenting, making things shallow and one-dimensional, numbing and non-thinking. Its clinical signs are repetition and obfuscation. That is why it is so important to confront all these with internal vitality. We must maintain our capacity to think, feel, relate and integrate (everything Orly referred to as 'positive answers and responses') – all of which are abundantly present in the material at hand, in every therapeutic excerpt as well as in the structure and an overarching world-view practiced by the kindergarten staff.

Grounded as it is in providing meaning through interpretation within a given relationship and by means of continuity, regularity, consistency and the gradual piecing together of the split-off, denied and fragmented parts of the psyche, psychoanalytic therapy serves as a 'life-object'. It is thus capable of mitigating the presence of the 'death object' in one's internal world.

Elay is a fascinating and intriguing child and the entire staff responds accordingly. On the one hand, Elay is frozen, empty, fragmented and, on the other hand, he is charming, alluring and loveable. His stillness, as well as his quasi-masculine, semi-erotic charm, have several meanings. As I already elaborated, his stillness is the psycho-physiological manifestation of extinction resulting in a defensive merging with its representative: the death object. This merging is characterized by repetition, negation, mindlessness and detachment. At the same time, however, this stillness is also an attempt to create a continuous unity that would replace the gaps, the lack of sequence and the incoherencies. That which was melted and frozen shall now be unified and hard. Tustin describes a paralysis which is caused by the attempt to fend off persecutory and deadening internal objects. But stillness is always also a frozen traumatic moment which waits for the right opportunity for unfreezing, with the right person. The movement between sleep and wakefulness seems to narrate some developmental failure in a child who slipped away or failed internally, who is looking for reparative understanding, for the right gaze which will awaken him and put him back on his developmental track. Throughout the therapy, we find a fascinating dynamics involving gazes – Elay looking at his therapists, as they look at him looking at them, and trying to learn how and what to look at. This therapeutic hall of mirrors brings something back to life, perhaps echoing or even restoring the function of the brain's 'mirror-neurons'. It seems to me that Elay's stillness is present as a message to the entire staff, reminding them that he needs to be rebuilt from scratch. In order to do so, he utilizes a psychic maneuver that he learned from his parents: charming and being charmed, or what is often described as a premature and inappropriate eroticism. Still, this use of charm serves as a guarantee that the staff will not abandon or leave him or freeze in response to him freezing (which indeed happens at first). Elay's use of seduction and his immersion, which invites one-on-one intimacy, are also a kind of Siren's song, as if he were saying: 'come, merge with me, and let me in so that I can liquefy and dissolve and thus finally obtain the pre-separation oneness I crave so much'. Indeed, this 'charming' approach attains its goal in terms of internally motivating his therapists. Nevertheless, right behind it one can see the death object rearing its menacing head. In Elay's case, this object is mainly incipient, formless and exists merely in terms of sense-perception, stimuli and movement: it is flinging things in the air; it is the soap bubble, the 'no', the colorless sky, the fear and the repetitiveness. As therapy runs its course, the split between the stillness and the charm, that is, between Thanatos and Eros, lessens. The death that had Elay in its clutches now becomes the string with which one can bind, restrain and relate.

Reality steps in. We must remember that the journey into post-autism is arduous and sometimes even dangerous. Change for the ASD child is often quite traumatic (Durban, 2014). Elay wakes up into the world and, with the help of the entire staff, he starts living in this world, with all the good and bad that are in it – confronting these, essentially, is what makes us alive.

Notes

1 Pre-symbolic realization is a developmental precursor of Sechaye's 'symbolic realization' and interpretive reparation of a broken link between pre-conception and its realization (Bion, 1963). Without its establishment in the mind of the autistic child any object presenting is meaningless.

2 The primary body is first equated with the mother's body. Then, with the growing sense of separateness, it is projected into her as an object. The safe establishment of a sense of body-mind relies on two simultaneous developmental capacities. The first is the attainment of covers or containers throughout development (the womb, the skin, the breast, the mother's insides and her mind and then the whole object in union with another object). The second is the establishment of links – neurological, emotional and cultural. In ASD children, these two capacities are impaired, resulting in feelings of 'nowhere-ness'.

3 There is some fascinating research concerning misrecognition during pregnancy between the maternal immunological system and the fetus's, resulting in a failure to transform killer cells. Although these situations are often resolved and do not result in miscarriage, there is some evidence which links these states with the later appearance of autistic states (Ben Bassat, 2017).

Translation: hands; belly; feet; fingers

Chapter 5

The body-schema and the development of the self

Tamar Meidan and Karen Peleg

Discussion group:

Tamar Meidan – dance and movement therapist; Karen Peleg – clinical psychologist; Hilla Matodi – speech and language therapist; Orit Bar – occupational therapist; Nilly Kedem – educational kindergarten manager and DIR therapist[1]

Introduction

In the course of our clinical work with ASD children at the Shaked kindergartens, we encountered many children who were preoccupied, during psychotherapy, with their body and its basic functions. Presumably, these children were seeking to stabilize a schema that could distinguish between and connect physical and mental experiences in a way that facilitates development. Although developmental interventions focusing on the 'body-schema' traditionally belong to the domains of physical and occupational therapy, the clinical reality in many cases is that children, especially ASD children, bring these issues with them into psychotherapy as well. In such cases, the therapist is required to address the child's physical concreteness as a basis for mental representations and mental structure.

The handling of the body in psychotherapy raises many technical and theoretical questions. In some cases, it seems that this preoccupation with the body is related to the working through of infantile sexuality; in others, it fulfills the function of auto-sensuousness – a common autistic defense (Tustin, 1981). However, our focus will be on those many other cases in which the body becomes a dominant therapeutic tool, as part of an effort to establish a 'body-schema' as a central developmental aspect. In autism, this aspect is always disrupted and the children exhibit a wide range of bodily manifestations indicating various body-schema disorders. We find this phenomenon – its intensity, magnitude and extensive variety – far from surprising, since familiarity with autism leads to the understanding that a preoccupation with the fragile body-schema is inevitable and deeply embedded in the roots, consequences, and disruptions of the developmental path. In order to examine the connection between the body-schema in normal development and the results of its constitutional distortions in autism, let us turn first to its definition.

The body-schema

The physical body is an object with a given structure and the body-schema is a subjective and abstract representation of that functioning object. Establishing a body-schema requires, therefore, a transition from concrete somatic sensations to representations. Ayres (1970) defines the body-schema as the conceptualization of the body's anatomic structure and the manner in which the various body parts work together in motion. It is the image of the body as a three-dimensional unit, a general sense of the body as one whole unit, an inner feeling of the positions of the body parts and an awareness of their existence, which is independent of sight. The body-schema is a unique, dynamic, and flexible kind of self-knowledge, which develops gradually and changes throughout life. It is a sort of map, created by combining sensory information with the body's neurological memory, its parts, their interrelations, weight and size. The body-schema integrates information originating outside the body with that originating from within.

The body-schema is created and developed out of one's innate bodily potential. The mother's care and the infant's active investigation and involvement with her and with objects in the world promote the creation of the schema through feedback from the sensory systems that process perception and bodily motion. Various sensory systems are involved in the creation of the body-schema:

1 *The proprioceptive system (the deep sensory system)* is a central component in the formation of the body-schema. The system's receptors are located in the muscles and joints and it supplies information about the positions of the various body parts and their interrelations without the need for visual input (i.e., even with one's eyes closed). In addition, the system reacts to the movements of the body as a whole and to the motion of body parts in relation to the surrounding space, thereby enabling a sense of body unity. The proprioceptive system contributes to the understanding that the subject, rather than the environment, is in motion, and thus enhances the 'me' and 'not-me' distinction. Neisser (1991) introduced the notion of the 'proprioceptive self', that is, a basic self-awareness that is based on sensations of motion and action and which also includes the motion of the eyes in the process of visual input. The respiratory and digestive systems also contain proprioceptive receptors and the information they provide facilitates the establishment of a sense of inner space that is based on the experience of fullness and emptiness.
2 *The vestibular system*, located in the middle ear, is responsible for the maintenance of spatial balance, but also for identifying changes in posture while the body is in motion. Whereas the proprioceptive system provides information pertaining to the relations between various body parts, the vestibular system involves the body's spatial relationship with gravity, that is, with the external world.

3 The receptors of the *tactile system* are spread throughout the surface of the skin, that is, around the entire body, thus giving rise to a cumulative sense of envelopment. This system demarcates and defines the boundary between inside and outside. Developmentally, it plays a central and primary role in intersubjective non-verbal communication between mother and baby.
4 *The Sensory System* includes the sense organs. It regulates perceptions from the outside world, allowing movement in three-dimensional space and plays an important role in the formation of the body-schema. It plays a central part in object relating and in exploring the outside world. It is also highly significant to sensory-emotional regulation. Stimulation, sound and movement are already experienced in the womb. Intrauterine studies have shown that all the senses (except vision) are already active at the beginning of the second trimester and, therefore, from that point on, the fetus responds to touch, pressure, motion, heat, sound, taste, and pain. In addition, it is possible to identify individual fetal movement patterns. Thus, it is reasonable to infer that there exists a primal body-schema – a primal orientation within the uterine space – a pre-organized stage, yet not entirely random. It involves psycho-physical and behavioral characteristics which persist into early childhood and beyond.

The body-schema needs to be clear and stable enough to allow orientation in physical space and in the experience of the self, but must also be able to develop and change throughout life. It must be flexible enough to accommodate changes such as growth, weight gain, or an increase in muscle mass. A rigid or an over-conscious body-schema might interfere with functioning and development. Let us now proceed from reviewing the development of the body-schema from a somatic-functional perspective to understanding the space in which this development takes place.

The subject develops and lives in a space where two kinds of 'gravity' are at work: the physical force of gravity and the mental 'gravitational pull' of object relations. The body-schema, then, is created and develops through the feedback embedded in experiences of involvement with the physical world and object-related interactions. Gravity is an external force that is constant, absolute, and has a fixed directionality: downwards. The direction of motion is negotiated between the force of gravity, pulling downwards, and the force of motivation, which pulls upwards. Interpersonal 'gravitation', the innate tendency toward object-relating, constitutes emotional 'gravity'. Maternal holding and handling, by providing an adequate response to embodied and mental needs, promotes the formation of the body-schema through caressing, cradling, making sounds, hugging, holding, regulating, and the like. In addition, the body-schema is formed and develops through the baby's active investigation of the world's objects, by means of activities such as inserting, removing, throwing, opening, closing, and so on. (Shahar-Levi, 2004). Many children's songs include references to body parts, movement and touch as channels, which intuitively address the development of the body-schema, for example: 'If You're Happy and You Know It', 'The Hokey Pokey', 'This Little Piggy', and so on.

The body-schema from a psychoanalytic-developmental perspective

Many psychoanalytic theories have addressed the relationship between physical functions and the development of the self. Freud was the first to discuss the relationship between the body and the ego, arguing that the ego is first and foremost a bodily ego (Freud, 1923). Klein (1952) focused mainly on the digestive system as the foundation of psychic functions. The psychic mechanisms described by Klein, such as introjection, projection, and splitting, are all based on the bodily activities of incorporation and excretion, while emotions such as love or hate are based on sensations of hunger and fullness. Using the same analogy, Bion (1962) emphasized its transformative character – since only a transformation of the materials entering the body makes them useful to us. Alongside the central importance of the internal digestive system, psychoanalytic theory has often referred to the skin as the physical envelope, which serves as a definitive boundary for the subject and maintains a complex relationship between inside and outside.

Bick (1968), Anzieu (1989), and Ogden (1989) have suggested various forms of psychic organizations, which precede Klein's schizo-paranoid position – a primal organization based on the somatic experience of the skin. Bick depicts a passive baby that experiences its body and psyche indiscriminately as a clutter of unintegrated part objects, collected by the skin, having no internal binding force. The skin, imbued with the experience of maternal holding and physical handling – which ideally includes the nipple in the mouth, alongside the contact provided by the mother's holding, voice and smell – facilitates the baby's identification with the primal experience of being enveloped as the potential for the psychic container. It gives rise to a boundary between inside and outside as a precondition for introjection and projection processes.

Anzieu (1989) coined the term 'Skin-Ego' – a primary formal signifier of mental space, present through the experience of the skin as the body's surface. The skin enables the baby to represent its inner space as a container for psychic representations. In Ogden's description (1989), the roots of the primary mental organization lie in sensory experiences stemming from tactile imprints experienced as bounded surfaces. He refers to the initial organization of these experiences as the 'autistic-contiguous position', a primal, pre-symbolic position preceding Klein's splitting (schizo-paranoid) organization. This position stems from tactile sensory imprints experienced as bounded surfaces. According to Ogden, the rhythmic sensory contact at the surface of the skin is the basis of infantile object relations.

Body-schema and the development of the self in autism

ASD children are born with various organic impairments. Those affecting the formation of a body-schema are difficulties in regulating and organizing external sensory input, as well as impairments in the proprioceptive system and motor function, including motor planning. These mechanisms are directly interrelated and, as a whole, have a crucial influence on the development of the body-schema detailed above. As for the body-schema itself, it has a crucial influence on these mechanisms, since the organization of sensory input is vital to regulation, just as the autonomous capacity for regulation is vital to the successful organization of sensory input, as well as to the maturation of motor planning and coordination abilities (praxis). Various studies conducted in the last decade have examined the prevalence of motor deficiencies among children on the autistic spectrum. One study (Ming, Brimacombe, and Wagner, 2007) found that the main motor symptom was hypotonia, found in 51 per cent of ASD children; motor apraxia was found in 34 per cent; and the tendency to tiptoe was reportedly found in 19 per cent of children. Another study conducted that same year (Provost, Lopez, and Heimerl, 2007) found that 100 per cent of the children diagnosed with ASD were late in developing either gross or fine motor skills or both. A study by Green *et al.* (2009) found that 79 per cent of ASD children had motor impairments and a further 10 per cent were borderline impaired.

In autism, organic-neurologic activity is disrupted to various extents but, according to the psychoanalytic view, difficulties in the physical foundation are not the only factor disrupting the development of a proper body-schema. The nature of autistic mental space also proves a significant obstacle to the normal formation of the body-schema and its relation to the self: it is widely accepted that the recognition of physical separateness is a cornerstone to the development of the body-schema. An impaired capacity for psychic separateness, a central and fundamental part of autism according to currently accepted psychoanalytic theories, may lead to a substantial impairment of the body-schema as well. Tustin (1981) sees autism as a post-traumatic response to the infantile recognition of physical separateness, given the baby's innate disposition for extreme merger. According to Tustin, the baby experiences its separateness from the mother's body as a loss of part of its own body, and thus the foundation for its body-schema is disrupted from the outset. The massive defensive array of auto-sensuousness described by Tustin is also closely related to the fundamental disruption of the body-schema. Ogden's 'sensory floor' (1980) and Anzieu's 'psychic envelope' (1990) are distorted through the utilization of autistic sensory forms and objects. Therefore, the impairment of the psychic 'floor' and 'envelope', the experience of separateness as bodily rupture and fluidity, the perception of orifices as holes and the experience of physical growth as a gluing together of parts that are unrelated to the bodily self, can all be explained and conceptualized more generally as essential and critical expressions of a basic disruption of the body-schema. The resistance to separateness, as one of the central characteristics of autism, inevitably leads to impaired object relations and to an avoidance or distortion of the process of investigating and experiencing the external world. This process is, in fact, the space in which the schema develops: through the given body and its experiences in relation to the maternal object and the physical world. In this state of affairs, the sensory and motor experiences of those two aspects are substantially and comprehensively impaired and it becomes significantly difficult to use the maternal function for regulation, feedback, communication, holding, and containing. The capacity for representation also depends on the capacity for separateness – since nothing is identical to its representation. Autism involves difficulties with separateness and difficulties with leaving sensory concreteness behind in favor of representations, as well as an active assault on these abilities. All of the above also undermine the ability to create links and connections, so that the development of a stable body-schema that could accommodate developmental needs is impaired. Autism can be seen as an inverse realization of phantom pain: in both cases, the brain does not send the correct signals corresponding to the actual physical experience, rendering the body representation unusable.

Observation, inquiry, and clinical experience with such disorders, which are so apparent in the children we work with, are very helpful in attaining a deeper understanding of the formation of a healthy body-schema.

The 'body-container' as a primal psycho-physical schema

Thinking about the relationship between the physical and mental disruptions she encountered while working with autistic children, Pollak (2009) suggested the body-container as a primal schema. This body-container is just as physical as it is mental, since it precedes the differentiation between physical and psychic experiences and forms the basis of pre-reflective contact between the subject and the world. The schema refers to anatomy and its concrete functioning in a way that links the physiological given with the subjective meaning in the context of object relating, like two roots nourishing the same developmental process.

According to Pollak, since its inception, psychoanalytic theory has been looking for a way to describe the self's need for cohesion, differentiation, and autonomy, while also describing and conceptualizing the absolute human need for openness and dependence. The role of the body in relation to these complementary needs has already been addressed: the skin envelope (Bick, Anzieu) and the digestive system (Klein, Bion) were presented as the physical-functional actualities underlying the mental functions. Pollak believes that in order to describe primal psycho-physical space, it is necessary to outline a schema which views these two systems as interrelated and, furthermore, to describe a more complex network of differentiations and connections that enables an unmediated realization of the subject's psycho-somatic exchanges (incorporation-transformation-excretion) with its environment. At the body-container level, the potential for survival, development, and meaning is realized as a result of the convergence of three elements: an envelope, a vertical axis, and a horizontal axis.

The sense of envelopment emerges from the skin, as the vast and multi-directional sensory organ constituting the body's boundaries. The vertical axis is what Pollak calls the 'frontal spine', since, anatomically, the body orifices are located at the front of the body (Pollak, 2009). The orifices, each an organ as well as a function, are interconnected in a structure that suggests a spine: distinct elements that are interconnected as to establish a functional sequence. The 'frontal spine' includes four vertebrae: (1) the outward-facing sensory organs/orifices, located in the face (eyes, ears, nose, and mouth); (2) the respiratory and cardio-vascular systems (trachea and thorax); (3) the digestive system (esophagus and navel), joining the second vertebra to form a felt inner space; (4) the lower sphincters, which allow control and closure, thus keeping the inner body from being experienced as a breached tube. The interrelations between these vertebrae contribute greatly to the organization of three-dimensional experiences and to the establishment of depth in psycho-physical space. The movement of the tongue inside the mouth, the movement of the expanding ribs and chest and the ability to hold in air, feces, and urine, provide a sensed experience of a flexible interior space whose characteristics can be discerned using the deep sensory system. The disappearance of food into the mouth and the transition – so accessible through swallowing – of things visible and tangible into an unseen place, only vaguely and implicitly felt, creates in our body the continuity between the visible and invisible, absent and present, conscious and unconscious. It is gravity that dictates viewing the frontal spine as a vertical axis, rather than a multi-directional network of functions. Verticality connects us to the fact that the body is by nature both a material object and the root of subjectivity. This middle axis is not only vertical, but also frontal, which involves the openness of the horizontal axis, where face-to-face contact, as the most powerful expression of object relations, forms the basis for all other encounters. The horizontal axis attains its full meaning when it echoes the functions of the frontal spine and, at the same time, the frontal spine attains depth when it meets the horizontal axis. The full significance of the body-container is felt when the intersections of these two axes resonate within the envelope in the creation of organized, regulated, open, and distinct vitality. In practice, we often encounter the permutations that arise from the interplay between their mutual influences. This schema is given to us as an innate potential but, because it is a manifestation of the interdependence of a considerable number of psycho-physical functions and because of its dependence on their proper functioning, it may also bring us closer to the frailty of the child's primal constitution. The full force of this frailty is revealed in ASD, where we encounter a very diverse array of disruptions to the many connections depicted through the schema.

This schema is not available to autistic children as a present, intuitive, and applicable basis. Since it is the subject's psycho-physical origins, it is not surprising to learn that difficulties in its formation are manifested as disorders in the entire range of physical and mental functions.

Clinical accounts of body-schema deficiencies in ASD children

Doron joined the Shaked kindergarten at the age of four, after being diagnosed with ASD. Doron suffered from an acute developmental delay: as a baby, he was diagnosed with hypotonia and joint hypermobility (especially of the hip joints).

He suffered from difficulties in emotional regulation, his motor development was lagging, his existing motor skills were cumbersome, and his gait was characterized by a slight inward twist of one leg. As a result, Doron often fell and hurt himself. In addition, his language skills developed late and with much difficulty. He did not establish any relationships with the other children, only with adults and his relationships were characterized by a lack of distinction between self and other. His emotional structure was confusional (Tustin, 1981) and lacked proper differentiation between inside and outside.

During the first year of psychotherapy, Doron seemed mainly preoccupied with his body and its functioning, a preoccupation which in retrospect can be understood as an attempt to establish a body-schema. In every session, Doron repeatedly asked the therapist to read and reread the book *Let's Go – From Head to Toe* (Frankel, 1979). The book is about a mother who, on a rainy day, goes with her son Naftaly on a journey across the body. The mother points out Naftaly's different body parts and explains their function: the head and its movement, the eyes that can open and close, the mouth and its myriad functions, the arms, the legs, the back, the stomach, and others. Doron listened to the story again and again, apparently requiring many 'different go's' in order to map and internalize his physical organization. While listening, Doron would alternate between looking at the therapist and looking at the pictures in the book; the therapist would point at the relevant body parts, her own as well as Doron's. While he was read to, Doron would alternate between two postures: he sometimes lay in a rounded fetal position, wrapped in a blanket with one foot outstretched toward the therapist, who would hold it and apply pressure to create proprioceptive stimuli. At other times, he would sit upright, actively exploring his various body parts. It seems that these two body positions are related to different developmental phases and to several central characteristics of the body-schema. In the first position, in which Doron is lying down wrapped in a blanket and held in a primal manner by the therapist's body and psyche, he globally experiences the envelope and the proprioceptive stimuli, which precede the possibility of separateness, a prerequisite for differentiating the various body parts. The therapist would hold this differentiation for him, by telling and elaborating the story of the various body parts. In the second, more separate position, Doron behaved as a curious and eager infant, who actively explored his body and experienced the use of its various parts. Additionally, the two positions in which Doron explored his body enabled the development of two cornerstones of the body-schema: a sense of a distinct self that is separated from the world by an envelope, as well as a deep body sense and intra-body differentiation between the various body parts. Doron did not undertake this important psycho-physical investigation in a void, but within the framework of transference relations, that is, within the therapeutic relationship, which is reminiscent of the development of the body-schema in the context of a mother-infant relationship.

Since he was a baby, Doron suffered from severe stomach aches, which were later diagnosed as symptoms of a chronic hereditary condition. Thus, his hypotonia, his joint hypermobility and his difficulties in sensory regulation were not the only factors affecting Doron's difficulties in establishing a body-schema. His frequent and acute stomach aches led to an over-stimulation of this specific part of his body and may have even been experienced as an internal or external assault, since the differentiation between inside and outside were not sufficiently established. Moreover, Pollak (2009) describes how disruption in one element of the frontal spine necessarily affects the other elements, eventually disrupting the ability to establish a body container.

In the course of the therapy, Doron's body-schema gradually stabilized, thereby enabling a different processing of the body-mind organization. Doron began drawing human figures, although those figures reflected a pronounced distortion in body conception (apparently, this was not the result of any graphomotor difficulties, but a true expression of his experience). Doron would draw several figures on one sheet of paper, each having a complete body except for the legs, which he replaced with a floating mermaid's tail. Moreover, the figures were all entangled with each other by their hair and limbs.

Presumably, the substitution of the tail for the legs and the lack of separateness between the various figures was a true expression of Doron's body experience: the expression of a deficient sense of physical stability stemming from his hypotonia and his clumsiness, of the immature separation between the two sides of the body (the two legs) or of his disrupted sense of envelope and proprioception. It is also possible that drawing a fish-tail instead of legs, as well as entangling the various figures together, expressed confusional (psychotic) mechanisms or an assault on the adaptive processes initiated by the recognition of the body's reality and separateness. It appears that all these factors, whether physical-sensuous or emotional, joined to form this chaotic experience. In such a cyclical dynamic, all of these factors influence one another, feed one another and eventually lead to an impaired body-schema.

In one session, Doron drew a legless torso on one sheet and enormous dinosaur legs on another. He asked the therapist to glue the two sheets together – to connect the dinosaur legs to the torso he had drawn. When the two sheets were connected, he began striding about the room, taking long, heavy and thunderous steps, saying: 'look, I have huge legs, like a dinosaur'. It seems that the heavy and cumbersome dinosaur legs, clearly incongruous with Doron's slight build, reflected his sense of being overburdened and his crude perception of his own legs at that stage.

Later on, Doron began to address the back side of the figures he drew: he drew their heads, back, and legs from behind. It seems that his psycho-physical experience already involved directionality: front/back, up/down, and left/right. The figures gradually became more human and more complex. Pollak (2009), in her conceptualization of the frontal spine, emphasizes the differences between the rear – the back – and the front side of the body, each of which meets different and complementary needs: the rear is opaque and hard, in contrast to the soft front, which contains most of the orifices. In the infantile state, when the baby is held by the mother, the rear side provides a sense of stability and support, whereas the front side maintains the relation to the object and the world through the orifices. In later developmental phases, both sides are integrated and we then experience them as the middle-axis of the self, which is surrounded by objects.

Alongside the establishment of directionality and the emergence of a 'mental spine', Doron started asking the therapist to cut the figures out and separate them from the sheet of paper. Each figure became separate from the next and obtained a clear boundary. He would occasionally ask that the figures be re-attached to their background or to other drawn figures. Presumably, he wished to represent an experience of envelopment and external boundary, while navigating the axes of differentiated versus undifferentiated, merged versus separate.

In time, Doron began to move around more stably on his feet, falling less often. He frequently jumped off stairs and, with the therapist's help and organization, managed to land on both feet. At that time, Doron began to use the words 'myself' and 'me' more clearly and distinctly. He would stand in front of the mirror and say: 'this is me, myself'. This important turning point attests to the stabilization of Doron's more mature and well-defined sense of self, which was also apparent at home. Doron was now more stable, both physically and mentally. He moved more freely in space, recognized and expressed desires and frustrations, sought contact with the other children and formed more distinct relationships with the adults.

In our view, Doron's increasingly integrated sense of self was a direct result of a more mature body-schema and it would not have been possible without the hard work done in psychotherapy. In earlier stages, Doron used the therapy to clarify, organize, and consolidate his perception of his body parts, their positions, and their functions. He used storytelling, drawing, paper cutouts, and his relationship with the therapist to do so. He also needed to repeatedly test and check not only the various body parts, but also their motion in relation to the object and the surrounding space. In addition, he needed to experience envelopment and proprioceptive touch in order to establish his body-schema.

Doron is not alone in this and it sometimes seems that we are witnessing a universal phenomenon. In fact, most of the children we have encountered in the course of our work at the kindergarten, even those diagnosed as relatively high-functioning, are preoccupied with the difficulties and disruptions of their bodies, motivated by the need to further develop. Occasionally, we encounter children whose preoccupation with the body-schema is all-consuming, whereas at other times this preoccupation is merely implicit or only apparent in states of extreme anxiety; but it is there in almost every single case. Moreover, throughout the years, we have witnessed in children such a wide range of manifestations indicative of different body-schema disorders, that these seem infinitely varied. Again, we find this phenomenon – and its intensity, magnitude, and variety – far from surprising. On the contrary: in our opinion, it is inevitable and deeply embedded at the foundation of the multifaceted disorder called autism.

We will now present several more examples of children who suffered from body-schema impairments and who grappled with the various forms of these impairments in psychotherapy.

Noam entered the Shaked kindergarten at the age of four. He suffered from hypo-sensitivity of the proprioceptive system; hypotonia, especially around the mouth; and severe oral motor dyspraxia. His body-schema may have been damaged due to the hypotonic and hypo-sensitive proprioceptive system, leading to impaired motion planning. In the first year of psychotherapy, Noam would run around the room, often falling and bumping up against the walls. It seemed that Noam's body experience was fluid, that he was being 'spilled' around the room, in a painful and non-functional search for body boundaries and a sense of deep touch. Noam was frequently drooling, so that his shirt stuck to his body like a second skin (Bick, 1968).

In time, Noam began seeking the deep body sense and the envelope in a more adapted manner: he would sit in the therapist's lap with his back to her, asking her to hold him and wrap them both in a blanket. The therapist understood that, due to his physical impairments, Noam's body-schema could not spontaneously develop as a basis for the development of his self and therefore allowed him to experience the deep body sense and the envelope in the therapeutic relationship.

Mika, aged six, was an extremely detached and disabled child. Mika made little contact with her environment, expressed herself in very few words and her physical organization was severely impaired. In the kindergarten and in occupational therapy, distinct difficulties concerning her body-schema came to light, manifest in significant motor encumberment and an inability to assemble even a basic human-figure puzzle.

Mika's parents reported that, as a baby, she suffered from extreme sensory sensitivity and would become highly distraught by the touch of even a gentle breeze on her skin. Because of this, her parents were afraid to touch her and rarely did so. In psychotherapy, Mika would pile layers of Plasticine on a sheet of paper, forming a sort of geographical structure or a thick armor. On this structure, she would ask the therapist to carve different shapes or objects, sometimes human, some of which she would partially erase with her finger. She would ask the therapist to carve more and more objects, until a cluttered jumble of engravings, objects and object-parts emerged on the lumpy surface. The preoccupation with Plasticine can be understood not only as a representation of an autistic armor, but also as an expression of a psycho-physical experience, in which the Plasticine represented the skin/body and the engraving of objects on its surface represented Mika's fragmentary experience of the world and of herself. The extreme sensory sensitivity, combined with the lack of concrete parental contact – essential to the development of the body-schema – may have created an experience of intense and isolated impressions that did not allow for a sense of unity, sequence and continuity. The damage to the body-schema, as it was manifest at that stage of therapy, was expressed in terms of the envelope and the holistic body experience, which was inchoate and had not yet matured into a human-shaped unit.

Later in the therapy, alongside her preoccupation with the Plasticine, Mika initiated singing body-related children's songs together with the therapist. It seemed that she was trying to make contact with and feel the various body organs.

In subsequent sessions, she abandoned the construction of the Plasticine armor and asked the therapist to draw various garments such as a hat, shirt, gloves, pants, and shoes, while she moved her hand to the appropriate places for depicting a 'human figure'. It is conceivable that this request expressed an autistic experience, in which Mika erased human attributes and perceived disparate objects instead of a human body. But from the body-schema perspective, it can be seen as an attempt to maintain a complete and unified physical experience that has the form of a human body, but which is not derived from a sense of the body itself, but from piecing together relevant external elements (articles of clothing).

Some months later, Mika made drawings of human figures that began to correspond to the initial developmental stages for such drawings. From the body-schema perspective, this can be seen as development from a lumpy structure, represented by the Plasticine in a primary and concrete fashion, to the more abstract representation (drawing) which reflects a more mature body-schema structure.

Merav entered the Shaked kindergartens when she was three and a half years old. In addition to impaired relational and communication skills, Merav suffered from severe hypotonia, delayed motor development, hypo-sensitivity of the proprioceptive system, hyper-sensitivity of the auditory system and significant difficulty in motor planning. In the course of addressing her difficulties in occupational therapy, massive body-schema disorders became apparent. Emotionally, Merav was very anxious and confused, exhibiting considerable confusion between inside and outside, as well as between her home and the kindergarten. Merav rarely spoke during her first year of kindergarten, but was very verbal in therapy. However, her verbosity was usually not directed at another person, but served as a kind of sensory envelope, probably designed to create an experience of self-holding and a sense of continuity.

When she first began psychotherapy, Merav would enter the consultation room dragging her feet, her body limp, muttering phrases that had a constant rhythm, which seemed to envelope her, and which the therapist could not decipher. During the sessions, Merav would stare into empty space and ask: 'where is Merav? No Merav . . .' (at this point, Merav was already familiar with the therapist and consultation room). In those situations, the therapist became very anxious and confused and, in response, gripped her shoulders in order to provide deep touch and said: 'Merav is right here, we are right here in the room', while pointing at Merav, at herself and at the room. Consequently, Merav turned to the mirror in the consultation room, observing her reflection at length. It appeared that she was looking for visual validation of her existence. Following this, Merav lay on the inflated rubber wheel, her body limp and her legs dangling out. Again she stared around the room and muttered to herself, 'no Merav . . . no Merav . . .' The therapist again became anxious and felt the need to hold her so she would not be lost in space. She held both her feet and said: 'Merav's feet . . .' Merav smiled, a mischievous sparkle glistened in her eyes, and she said aloud, 'here's Merav!' Later, she went back to looking in the mirror, studied her movements, jumped and made faces, as if she was making her sense of existence more present.

Merav's case illustrates a serious impairment of the experience of psycho-physical presence, which is apparently intensified by anxiety. Merav's impaired physical constitution (mainly her hypotonia and low registration of information from her proprioceptive system) created difficulties in forming the body-schema. In turn, the impairment of the body-schema, especially of the sense of presence, influenced the development of a stable and continuous sense of self. Merav's psychic structure is confused, which may have also hindered her capacity for representation, which is essential to the development of the body-schema. For Merav, contact and intimacy are an overwhelming and intimidating experience, which evokes the anxiety of being engulfed by the relationship. Perhaps that is why she wants to disappear, or make the therapist and the room disappear. It appears that her anxiety and defense took on the features of Merav's body-schema, that is, the experience of a lack of physical presence joined hands with the possibility of psychic disappearance. In the therapy, the containment of anxiety, along with the concrete physical intervention, addressed both physical and mental aspects.

Michael was a low-functioning child who was completely non-verbal. In psychotherapy, he began to develop the ability to hold 'twoness'. During that time, he first began using his hands in therapy. Until then, his arms would dangle lifeless at his sides as he moved about the room, as if he did not have them at all. He then began reaching out toward the therapist, pulling her toward him, pushing her away, indicating through gestures where he wanted her to stand and examining things around the room. In addition, he appeared less rounded – his back straightened somewhat and he began to look directly at the world.

The therapeutic response

In the course of our work at the kindergarten, we have encountered many different variations of possible body-schema disorders. We have found that an integrative practice, which addresses physical, mental, and functional impairments and involves a speech therapist, occupational therapist, psychotherapist, and an adapted environment, could prove helpful. This engagement with the body and the contact with such primal areas of experience confront us, on a daily basis, with fundamental questions concerning therapeutic technique, with issues of therapeutic responsibility and with the need for concrete physical contact in psychotherapy. These weighty questions are present in situations – whenever we encounter the body-schema, for example – in which therapeutic practice must be adapted to meet the primary needs that arise when treating ASD children, whose experience is often concrete and demands an appropriately concrete response. Moreover, since it appears that damage to the body-schema is dominant in autistic disorders and since the body-schema is an integral part of the development of the self, the split between these domains does not serve this development and thus, holding the psycho-physical foundation in psychotherapy is of the utmost importance.

Therefore, it appears that an investigation of these primary components, which requires a variety of concrete physical experiences, is also essential as part of

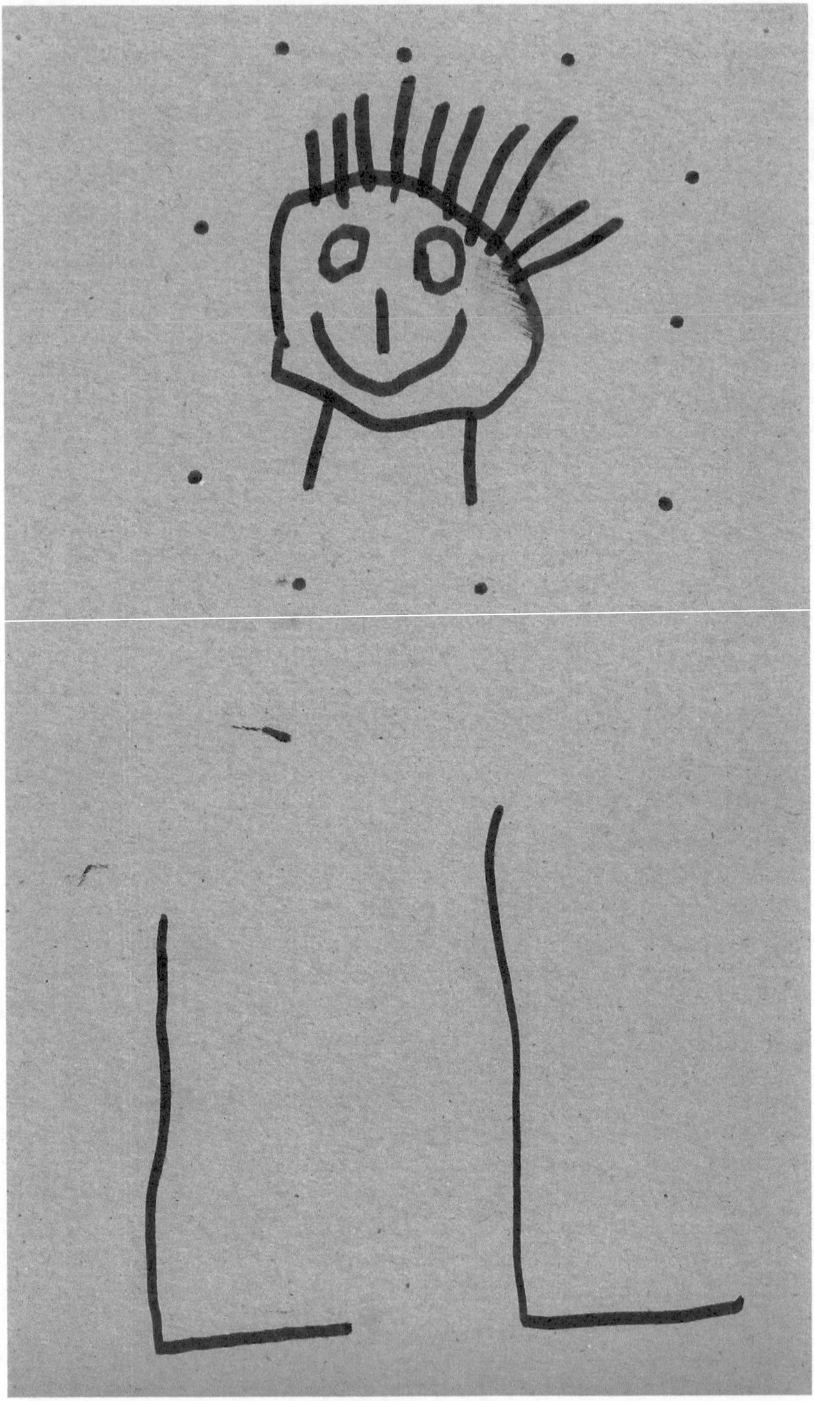

psychotherapy. Words are often insufficient and there is a need for proprioceptive touch, jumping, quick or slow movement, for examining the body parts in front of a mirror, for wrapping, cradling, and actual holding and touching. However, in other cases, when touch stimulates infantile sexuality or auto-sensuousness or when a child suffers from sensory hypersensitivity, it is better to avoid touch and look for other ways to assist in forming the body-schema and providing a low-stimulus environment. Physical contact in psychotherapy is a complicated practice and it requires careful consideration of the question of boundaries that arises in relation to offering actual parental response, as well as of questions regarding the sexual confusion that such contact can potentially evoke. It is usually possible to identify changes to the body-schema through the increasing capacity for separateness and for holding 'twoness': 'me' and 'not-me', two eyes, ears, hands, and feet.

Note

1 DIR (Developmental, Individual, Relationship-based) is a method for treating ASD children, based on S. Greenspan's developmental model for expanding circles of spontaneous communication.

Chapter 6

Thoughts on diaper weaning and its contribution to the development of the self in ASD children

Limor Montal and Yael Eitan

Discussion group:

Limor Montal – clinical psychologist; Yael Eitan – clinical psychologist; Netanela Sheihi – kindergarten teacher; Merav Haim – occupational therapist; Irit Pollak – speech and language therapist

Diaper weaning and psychic development

Diaper weaning is a gradual process, which concludes when the child is able to control the bowel and bladder and relieve himself at the appropriate time and place, day and night. Various terms are used to describe the process, such as 'toilet training', 'hygiene training', 'diaper weaning', and so on. Each term highlights a different aspect of the process and the rich vocabulary indicates its complexity. For example, 'hygiene training' emphasizes curbing the satisfaction gained from soiling and wetting, as part of the child's adaptation to external cultural constraints; 'toilet training' emphasizes the functional aspect and is aimed at habit formation; 'diaper weaning' echoes the primary weaning from breastfeeding. This last term sheds light on the process of relinquishment and loss, both in the concrete sense of the loss of excrements, and in the phantasmatic sense – the gradual relinquishment of the delusion of omnipotence that serves the wish to merge.

The wide age range for starting the weaning process in different cultures, as well as among different children within the same culture, implies a fundamental dilemma regarding the appropriate time to do so. There are cultural differences in the consideration of the infant's physical maturity, which includes continence, as well as in the consideration of psychic maturity, which includes the infant's voluntary acceptance of the external cultural demand, despite the loss it entails. According to the psychoanalytic view, timing is of crucial importance and the manner in which diaper weaning is achieved impacts psychic structure and the development of the mature personality.

In normal development, the child makes intensive conscious and unconscious efforts in preparation for and during the weaning process. Infants often exhibit curiosity, interest, inquisitiveness and motivation to be 'like grown-ups'.

The parents' attitudes toward the child and the process, the timing and method are all important in the weaning process (Menninger, 1943). It seems that the weaning process is enabled by the synergy between the child's desire for growth, the desire to emulate significant others, the understanding that 'poo and pee' belong in the toilet; the comprehension of the concepts of 'clean' and 'dirty', and the parents' readiness and willingness to mediate the process. The decision of when to begin the weaning process depends on the parents' assessment of their child's maturity and competence, their personal cultural conception and their own perceived competence to lead and maintain this process. When the child's surroundings are sensitive to his needs and can identify with them, the external demands for cleanliness and his opposing anal and urethral tendencies can be successfully reconciled. However, when external control is too rigid or when the weaning process begins too early, the child is robbed of the opportunity to experience gradual bowel control voluntarily and freely. Upon encountering his parents' demands, the child may experience feelings of helplessness regarding his own body. He may then cope by resorting to illusory control measures, such as pretensions for autonomy, which preclude the ability to rely on others for help. Alternatively, he might regress into a primal mode of oral control through thumb-sucking, whining, and demanding, or become hostile and intrusive, using feces as ammunition (Erikson, 1950).

The development of continence has four stages: (a) control of nighttime defecation, (b) control of daytime defecation, (c) control of daytime urination, and (d) control of nighttime urination. The psychoanalytic view holds that there is a parallel between the development of control and regulation on the physical and emotional levels. Freud was the first to assign a crucial role in psychic development to the anal phase, which begins with the emerging ability to control the sphincter and during which the focus of the infant's attention moves from the oral to the anal zone. Freud (1908) linked some adult character-traits – orderliness, parsimony, and obstinacy – to infantile anal eroticism. The emergence of physical continence is expressed in the infant's new and improving capacity for muscle control, namely retention and elimination. At this stage, two conflicting functions develop: holding on and letting go. Freud describes how, when the child holds the feces in, the anal erogenous zone is strongly stimulated, arguing that alongside the sensation of pain, there must also be intense pleasure. The infant, feeling the stimulation in his bowel and bladder, senses his capacity to prevent excretion or at least to decide when to evacuate.

The maturation of anal and urethral sphincter-control joins the development of the muscular system in endowing the child with more power to influence his environment: he can reach out and hold on, throw and push his way toward external objects or keep them at a distance. Therefore, this becomes the stage in which the struggle for autonomy takes place (Erikson, 1950). It is also referred to as the anal-sadistic stage, since the pleasure of control is accompanied by a desire to control and exert power over the environment. At this stage, the child relates to the object in terms of possession: any object of desire is something to claim as his own and every object resembles the child's most primitive possession, the feces. Freud emphasized that when body products are cathected with libido, the child cherishes them and considers them as gifts given to the mother as a sign of love. Anna Freud (1965) added that when body products are cathected with aggression, they become weapons, used to discharge rage, anger, and disappointment within the object-relationship. These contrasts between eroticism and sadism, between excretion and retention and between the anal functions and the anal product, serve as a paradigm for conflicts involving ambivalence: active-passive, male-female, separation-individuation.

Diaper weaning also requires relinquishing the pleasure derived from the spontaneous act of excretion and from dirtiness and adapting to the external demand that represents social order. Abraham (1923) claims that these two demands put narcissism to its first serious test. This primal narcissistic injury can then be compensated for and self-satisfaction can be replaced by satisfaction derived from being considered 'good' and 'praiseworthy' by the parents. Another loss that the infant must contend with is the loss of control over its own excretions. The child feels as if a part of his own body has spilled or fallen and disappeared into the toilet. He feels the evacuation as absolute and that his physical integrity is thereby damaged. Experiencing a diaper-less body and the fact that evacuation into the toilet deprives him of giving his parents his excretions as a means of controlling them, fills him with anxiety (Solan, 2007).

Despite these difficulties, toilet training reduces the infant's anxieties regarding his introjected bad objects (Klein, 1952). Sphincter-control allows the infant to believe he can also control his internal objects and the destructive nature of his phantasized fears. When control over evacuation and the mother's demands are in accord, the baby may feel that the damage caused by his excretions to the internal and external objects in his destructive phantasy can be repaired. Therefore, acquiring hygiene habits reduces guilt and provides the impulse for reparation.

Diaper weaning and the various developmental areas

The ability to control one's bowl and bladder and to undertake the social conventions surrounding it spans a broad functional continuum: notifying an adult when feeling the need for relief; the spatial and temporal planning involved in going to the bathroom, undressing, sitting on the toilet; coordinating the cleaning of feces and urine, flushing, putting one's underwear and trousers back on, washing and wiping one's hands. Finally, the child is expected to return to the same place and activity he had left before visiting the bathroom. It is an integrative process, which relies on the maturation of sensory-motor, cognitive, communicative and linguistic, social and emotional development. ASD children exhibit various difficulties in all developmental areas, resulting in functional gaps, which make the processes of growth and integration much more difficult.

Sensory-motor development includes the gross and fine motor control skills required to perform any given sequence of actions. ASD children often suffer from hypotonia, motor clumsiness, and sensory regulation and differentiation, which affect physical development. They may manifest irritable movement, self-stimulation, distraction, avoidance of contact with water, auditory inundation and recoil in response to the sound of water coming out of the toilet or tap, difficulty enduring the sensation of excretions left on the body due to hyper-reactivity or, on the contrary, inability to sense these due to hypo-reactivity and difficulty identifying the exact location of physical sensations. These children also exhibit difficulties in *motor planning* and execution, including posture, movement, balance, body-schema, bilateral coordination, and fine manipulation.

Cognitive development, in this context, includes understanding the situation, the perception of sequence and causal organization (e.g., associating physiological bladder pressure with urination), a capacity for problem solving ('what do I do if the tap is too high?'), transposition and generalization (the child must use different bathrooms in different places), categorization (one eats in the dining room, sleeps in bed and defecates in the bathroom), memory, and imitation. Cognitive maturity also involves the (partial) understanding that excreted material is waste and not part of the body.

Linguistic and communicative development includes the child's ability to notify an adult when he wants to go to the bathroom, to ask for assistance and to respond to the adult's suggestion to use the bathroom. Children at diaper weaning age possess a basic vocabulary that allows them to understand concepts such as 'dry', 'wet', 'bathroom', and others. ASD children often manifest a linguistic delay and significant difficulties in communication, which make the task of approaching adults or responding to their initiative more complicated.

Socio-emotional development: the child begins to show interest in imitating other children. He wants to be independent and grown-up, to get rid of the diaper and use the toilet. The child shows curiosity about the body; investigation of inside and outside and of the experience of filling-up and emptying-out and the pleasure derived from physical control. The child at that age has developed a certain capacity to endure psychic separateness and separation from the excrements as well as frustration and disappointment at being unable to 'deliver the goods'. These areas of development are usually disrupted in ASD children, leaving the psycho-physical infrastructure required for the process of weaning equally impaired. The child often has little inner motivation to grow and develop and might even actively attack this need.

Given such developmental gaps, the child's chronological age cannot safely indicate when to start the weaning process. At our kindergartens, we have seen many children through this process, which is often lengthy, intermittent, erratic, distorted, and generally characterized by stubborn refusal. However, clinical experience shows that despite these enormous difficulties, weaning also involves a significant growth of the self, which is manifest in all areas of development. Moreover, we have found that postponing the process may jeopardize, disrupt, and actively distort the child's development and growth.

The 'container' as psycho-physical infrastructure for openings and envelopment – as opposed to holes and autistic mechanisms

Bion proposed the notion of the 'container' as a metaphor for a psychic space in which raw experiences are transformed into experiences with psychically digestible meaning. Pollak further proposed to break down the container metaphor into constituents, which endow psycho-physical space with the potential for opening and closing.[1] According to Pollak, the (dermal and parental) envelope preserves, protects, and distinguishes between interior and exterior, whereas body orifices are locations where inside-outside relationships are realized. The weaning process entails the child's subjective introduction to the objective fact that his body has controllable openings, through which internal material may leave in a voluntary manner. During development, the baby is unconsciously introduced to the container's various characteristics by investigating his body, the object and the external material environment. Infants can be seen exploring the notion of interiority by pushing their fingers into their mother's mouth or following objects as they disappear and reappear. The internal investigation of 'having an opening' begins during the oral stage and its prototype is the mouth, which can be opened and closed. The diverse dialogue between the good-enough mother, who is attentive to signals from her baby, and a baby with a normal congenital constitution, produces a wealth of experience, encourages development and enables the baby to experience openness and closed-ness. A baby who, for structural reasons, experiences moments of separateness as traumatic, will experience his mouth as a hole or a rupture, through which psychic or body materials may leak out or be pushed in (Tustin, 1994). According to Tustin, in attempting to prevent this horrific experience, the baby uses autistic shapes and objects, which delusionally plug these holes. He is then enveloped in a protective sensory shell, which inhibits development. In ASD children, the psycho-physical experience often lacks the dimension of depth and the subjective meaning of the opening, as well as control over what goes in and comes out, cannot be established.

Diaper weaning as an opportunity for psychic development in ASD children

Hygiene training in ASD children is complex, due to the disrupted establishment of the psycho-physical container. We encounter children who, having chronologically reached weaning-age, still manifest discrepancies between different developmental areas: disrupted function of the psycho-physical container, inconsistent differentiation between inside and outside and experiencing body orifices as holes that can be blocked completely (by prolonged retention and constipation) or leak uncontrollably. In such situations, there is no stable experience of internal space in which bodily excretions can exist. Feces and urine are experienced as part of the self, rather than its products. Thus, apart from the anxieties that normally arise throughout hygiene training, there are also more primary anxieties related to disintegration, leakage, dissolution, and annihilation.

The external demand that accompanies diaper weaning forces the child to identify and create associations between distinctions he had been mindless of until that point. This experience evokes acute anxieties. The autistic child, who had hitherto used sensory mechanisms in order not to see, not to feel, not to pay attention, to ignore, to block and to push away, begins – often against his will – to engage and to feel: pee is wet, poo is dirty, the environment demands change, things come out from inside, what was inside disappears. Conforming to social demands is a crucial decision for these children and it is accompanied by massive anxieties, for the child and his family alike. This anxiety is often felt by the staff as well. For an ASD child to begin the weaning process, he needs at least an inkling of physical and psychic differentiation between inside and outside and some capacity to be contained and aided by others in mitigating anxiety. At the same time, surrounding adults need to recognize the intensity and nature of the child's anxieties, so that they can endure and work through the child's powerful projections. Thus, the child may become familiar with the discrepancy between his catastrophic inner experience and the actual worked through experience, which mitigates anxiety. The accumulation of anxiety-mitigation experiences is very significant for the child's transition to a three-dimensional experience of physical and psychic space.

In our view, the potential contribution of diaper weaning is that physical experiences are subject to additional working through and psychic organization. The combination of a significant physical process, which evokes massive primal anxieties, and the environment's willingness to support this developmental cause, may facilitate the emergence of an ability to contain massive psycho-physical anxieties. Thus, physical experiences undergo a process of mentalization, which allows the emergence of a new level of self-perception and self-organization. For example, during the weaning process, the concept of periodicity and continuity (loss and re-creation: here, gone, here again) develops, strengthening the sense of self-continuity, reinforcing intuitive temporal perception, providing a sense of potency in creating new things, providing control and a capacity for planning and choosing as well as for differentiating and connecting inside and outside. For parents, who represent society, the process is equally significant, symbolizing growth and acceptance by the social order.

Case study: a multi-professional dialogue – between external-functional reality and internal reality

We will demonstrate diaper weaning in ASD children through an extreme clinical example: a child who underwent a very difficult weaning process, a process fraught with primal anxieties that affected the staff and the parents as well. We will emphasize the importance of creating a space for different voices, which can be considered and used as part of a multi-professional discussion.

Itay joined the Shaked kindergartens around the age of three. Our initial impression was of a very anxious child, who rarely made eye contact or communicated verbally and whose behavior was extremely patterned and constrained. Itay's birth was ordinary, in the thirty-fifth week of a complication-free pregnancy. He was described as a calm and quiet baby. Itay had much difficulty with breastfeeding, which may have stemmed from a congenital difficulty in oral planning, which requires sequence, timing, mouth-and-throat coordination and the coordination of suckling, swallowing, and breathing. Since birth, due to a sensitive gag reflex, Itay would often reflux and, at a later age, vomit. Itay's eating habits were problematic and he became very picky about his food. At a very early age, the oral aperture, the first body orifice of admission and investigation, became an opening through which things are uncontrollably ejected. This experience may have led, among other things, to a tendency for excessive control, expressed as extreme pickiness about what is allowed inside. Itay also suffered from auditory and visual hypersensitivity. He had difficulty controlling and regulating the quantity, intensity, speed, and timing of sensory input coming from the outside world, to which he seemed to respond with defensive patterns and a need for control.

Motor development was reportedly adequate, but there were difficulties in language development. When he was one year old, Itay started uttering some words, but those were soon gone and he mostly used pointing until the age of two. When he joined the kindergarten, his speech was limited and poor. His play was also repetitive and poor and he would usually play the same game over and over.

Itay was at home until he joined a mainstream preschool when he was two. It soon became clear that the environment was unsuitable for him and several months later he was diagnosed with an ASD and moved to our kindergarten. At first, he was extremely anxious, crying intensely and screaming ceaselessly at every change or transition. The intensity of his anxiety dominated, disrupted, and paralyzed his life and that of his family. A few months before he joined the kindergarten, his parents tried doing without diapers for a short time, but he exhibited such great anxiety that his parents quickly went back to using them. Halfway through his first year at the kindergarten, Itay's parents wanted to recommence the diaper weaning process, insistently clinging to his chronological age: 'if we wait for Itay, the right moment will never come'. For us this was a fundamental dilemma: when should we start the weaning process? On what grounds should this decision be made? Who decides – the child, his parents, the staff, the therapeutic team?

Limor, the kindergarten coordinator, observed Itay on several occasions in the kindergarten environment and spoke with the pedagogical staff, the allied health professionals and with Yael, the psychotherapist, who came in most contact with Itay's inner world and with his parents. The kindergarten staff felt that it was too soon, because Itay was still adapting to the new environment: he would often stay by himself, ignoring what was happening around him and throwing a tantrum at any attempt to approach him. He exhibited rigid defensiveness, expressed as fanatic adherence to the daily schedule and extreme pickiness regarding food. Itay's limited diet consisted of a single brand of dairy pudding and soft white cheese. When the company changed the logo on the cheese's packaging, Itay reacted with intense anxiety and could not eat. He had 'home food' and 'kindergarten food' and mixing the two was strictly forbidden. We focus on Itay's eating habits, following the assumption that eating represents the primal experience of a body orifice. There is a direct link between eating habits and diaper weaning, which includes experimenting with a novel orifice. In addition, both the staff and the parents reported that Itay was not signaling before relieving himself and was seemingly mindless of it.

The allied health staff was divided. Following her observation of Itay, the coordinator reported that when arriving in the morning with his father, Itay was crying and screaming, consumed by extreme anxiety. He would continue to scream and would not be consoled by the staff. Finding a whiteboard, he would pick up marker pens and begin to repetitively draw closed shapes, filling them again and again, instantly calming down. His conduct in speech therapy was also markedly repetitive during this period. Interestingly, occupational therapy struck a different chord with him: the therapist felt that the relationship Itay was establishing with her was significant and he would let himself experiment with various activities. She was hopeful: 'maybe the weaning process will offer some surprises'. The therapist felt that, based on the relationship and the experiences he created with her, she might be able to withstand the anxiety that was likely to appear. During therapy, which included taking baths in order to familiarize Itay with his body parts and reduce the anxiety involving his body, she suggested that he go to the bathroom. The explicit mention of the bathroom immediately resulted in Itay's refusal to 'go' for many hours. Itay shut off this opportunity. The parents and the staff responded with anxiety: 'maybe it's too soon'.

Yael, Itay's psychotherapist, recounts: 'when I first invited Itay into the consultation room, he immediately gave me his hand, coldly, like a robot, and went along with me. He joined me without trying to find out who I was or where I was taking him. Itay entered the room, looked around, sat down and after a long time said: 'draw, paper'. His voice and initiatives were frail and his pace was very slow. He took a long time before whispering a word out of his mouth and I was attuned and eager to hear what he had to say. He drew a sun and a cloud and said: 'sun, cloud'. Then he moved over to the doll house and placed a table and a chair, saying: 'table, chair'. Then he came back, drew another sun and another cloud and said: 'cloud . . . yellow . . . sun'. Later he saw the box of cookware, took out a pot, a fork and a knife, saying: 'fork, knife', and put them back. There were many beginnings in the room. Every beginning stirred anticipation in me. I said to myself – there, now he will finally start playing. But he just moved on to the next thing. He would go from object to object, naming them, session after session, without any development. When I tried to linger with him on one choice, he became nervous and shouted: 'no, stop!' I felt that my space was very limited and that I had to carefully choose my words and my next steps. I would frequently find myself glancing at my watch in boredom, emptiness, and despair. In many sessions, he pushed the pencil down hard when drawing, making a hole in the sheet of paper. Then he would panic and want to end the session. When I would refuse his request, he would cry and scream. I was infected by his intense anxiety, feeling helpless and unable to calm him. The sessions would end with me looking for regulation, relaxation, and contemplation as channels for transforming our shared anxiety'.

The discussion among the kindergarten staff demonstrates Itay's tendency for abrupt shifts from extreme anxiety to complete relaxation. He was trying to void his anxiety, pain, and loss, as if to eliminate emotional meaningfulness and to avoid facing painful emotions. He was not making use of the human functions available to him, resorting instead to formal elements through adhesive identification. Itay's dominant self-experience is that of a breached container, lacking the quality of a continuous three-dimensional experience. At that point, we felt that diaper weaning would place too much strain on Itay, confronting him with catastrophic anxieties, before he had the capacity to contain them or seek assistance from his human environment. At that stage, it was felt that the process could not commence except on a solely behavioral basis, without the realization of its inherent potential for psychic development – something we were not very keen on.[2] This discussion was ongoing and the parents were fully engaged in it. It was agreed that we did not want to rush things with Itay, because he was beginning to show signs of calming down and the beginning of a three-dimensional psychic space.

Toward the end of the first year, it was felt that the staff were postponing the start of the process and waiting for an 'ideal time' out of anxiety. The mother reacted with anger at the delay. Alongside the staff's acknowledgment of this anxiety, Itay was beginning to show signs of development in every aspect of his functioning. A reduction in the intensity of anxiety was apparent, as was the new ability to negotiate the delusion of omnipotence. The teacher described how he was now exploring his body: checking, naming, comparing his body parts to those of the boy Joshua from the children's book *Once upon a Potty* (Frankel, 1980). The mother excitedly reported that he was painting figures with facial features and a full body. During meals, he began to eat two different foods together, such as French fries with ketchup, which had been unthinkable until then. When saying goodbye to his parents in the morning, he was more willing to accept help from the teacher's assistant. He also agreed to talk about separation after it took place. When his father would go out of the house, instead of screaming continuously, Itay began to say: 'daddy went to take out the garbage', assuring himself of his father's return. Even in transitions from one activity to another, it was clear that he was willing to rely on the staff and not just the schedule. He also began expressing his moods verbally: 'not now', 'stop, I don't like it!' There were numerous signs of a psychic space capable of holding content and emotion. He played for the first time with another boy in the kindergarten: they climbed the slide, went down the ladder and shouted 'help!' together.

The change was also apparent in therapy. Yael reported: 'there was now considerably more engagement and Itay's ideas were starting to emerge and become more whole. More primal notions arose, such as womb, warmth, and nurturing, which brought more relaxation. For example, in one session, Itay took a plate, a knife and a fork, added 'ingredients', cooked chicken, blew air on the food and asked me to cool it. In another session, he asked me to draw a house and a sun – the inside sheltered and the outside energetic, potentially burning. He asked that I add windows and a door to the house – openings for letting things in and out. Itay ventured to open the windows, then the door, but the act of opening frightened him. He lacked regulatory mechanisms: blinds, curtains, measures of control over the entrances to the room, his subjective space. At the beginning of therapy, he made it clear that the notion of an inside was threatening to him. In one session, Itay went to his box and said: 'Itay'. I explained to him that this was his box and he then put a drawing of his inside it. I had the impression that there were moments when he would begin to experience me and himself as containers that can keep things inside of them. Itay was playing with kitchenware and wanted a cake. I suggested that I make one, but he did not want it. I suggested that he did not want it *yet*, thus adding progression and the dimension of time to the discussion. After some time, he began asking me to draw him a cake. I was excited about that request, interpreting it as an indication that Itay was starting to experience the therapeutic relationship as nurturing. He seemed to begin to fill up inside, but was still not really 'taking in' my offers.[3] For several sessions, Itay asked me to draw something, then cut the drawings off the page. He put them in the closet and took them out again, trying to hide and then find them. He would say, 'who is hiding in the closet?' and then find them and say, 'wonderful!' He also began hiding himself during sessions, asking me to look for him. He began feeling that things can exist even if they are hidden from view. A sense of connection between inside and outside was beginning to form'.

Yael regulated and respected Itay's pace, so that he would feel sufficiently in control to open up and let in, creating a space for things like 'still don't want to', 'want a little' and 'want in a little bit'. Itay was moving forward, developing the required sense of space: he began to stand alone in the corner when relieving himself and was no longer mindless about it. However, the act still involved intense anxiety and a stubborn refusal to adapt to external demands. When his mother would read him from *Once upon a Potty*, he refused to even utter the words 'pee' and 'poo'. Still, there was also a sense that Itay, as well as the staff and the parents, now had a repertoire of experiences to rely on in order to endure the coming anxiety. Furthermore, we had the impression that a harmful gap was growing between development in other areas and the lack of development in terms of weaning. A clearer distinction was beginning to take shape between the immature parts of Itay's psyche, his congenital problems and inability to contain anxiety and his active mechanisms of omnipotent desire to control.

We realized that anxiety should not be allowed to trump everything else and that we needed to find 'containers' for the staff, the parents and Itay, so that everyone could endure and contain the anxiety. We set a future date for taking off the diaper, so that everyone could start preparing for the process. We agreed to start with the indirect preparations and discuss the weaning process directly only when the moment arrived. The decision brought great relief: the parents were happy to have a set date and the staff was reassured that there was enough time to prepare.

Preparation – exposure through play

Due to Itay's resistance, we began approaching the issue indirectly, through play with water and receptacles during 'yard time', to enable familiarity and internalization of the cyclical process of filling, emptying, and refilling. Itay would handle syringes, cups and funnels, while we emphasized concepts and actions such as to fill, to empty, to splash, to press, inside, outside, here, gone, and others. Later, this experimentation was carried out near the toilet. Itay began entering the bathroom, tossing toilet paper in the toilet and flushing. Then, he began to squirt water from the syringe into the toilet and flush. These activities were designed to work through the anxiety of losing his excrements, while not directly involving diaper weaning.

After a few weeks, we started reading Itay a story written by the speech therapist. The story featured Itay as the protagonist and was based on the book *Once upon a Potty*, which he loved and was intimately familiar with. At first, he refused to look at the book, but still seemed attentive. In time, he became an active participant and recited the story, although he omitted the words 'pee' and 'poo'. Later, we put more emphasis on changing his diaper inside the bathroom stall and tossing it in the trash can. Four days before the set date, we hung pictures depicting the sequence of actions on the bathroom door. The staff wrote a short story describing how Itay was going to take off the diaper in four days, relieve himself in the bathroom and put on a new pair of underwear. At the end of the booklet, there was a table where Itay would put a sticker every day until the diaper was to be taken off. At home, his parents tried to draw his attention to the bathroom. Until then, his mother said, every time someone had entered the bathroom at home, Itay would hide behind a chair. Gradually, his mother invited him to press the lever that flushes the toilet. Itay now had no problem darting out of his hiding place and flushing the toilet. When the parents put the feces from his diaper into the toilet, Itay initially refused to take part, but finally agreed after a few days.

Separation from the diaper

The moment of truth had arrived – it was time to take off the diaper. Itay made no objections. He tossed it in the trash and put on a pair of underwear. He urinated in his underwear a few times and his response was harsh. He refused to be changed, cried and would not let anyone get too close to him. We tried to let him have 'some time with the wetness', to talk about how it felt pleasant or unpleasant, or 'dirty and needing to be changed'. But it seemed that Itay was flatly rejecting any adaptation to the change. Soon he was refusing to 'go' for hours on end. This caused him physical pain and intensified his anxiety. He suffered from abdominal pain and would writhe on the floor in an effort to keep excrements in, shouting and crying. He was shrouded in helplessness and extreme anxiety. When he could not stand it any longer, reaching the limit of his omnipotent control, he would sit motionless, clutching his penis, letting the urine fill his pants. After such an evacuation and the ensuing physical relaxation, he would be seized by anxiety again and burst into tears. He wanted to keep wearing the wet clothes but he was offered to put them in a plastic bag inside his knapsack, which seemed to provide him with some degree of control and security. After urinating, with his wet clothes changed, he seemed relieved, but would then be tired for the rest of the day, from the efforts invested in control and retention. At that stage, Itay would not defecate at all at the kindergarten, only at home with a diaper on. The kindergarten staff, which was prone to contracting Itay's anxiety when it erupted, was fully involved in these routines and in the daily deliberations about how to help and comfort him.

While Itay was desperately trying to maintain control over external reality, the psychotherapy sessions were becoming more playful, especially through play with gouache. Yael recounts: 'we came up with many ideas. He became more communicative, independent and active in the room and had new initiatives, such as climbing a chair to get the paint or to grab a water receptacle'. Yael felt that she was witnessing Itay's weaning dilemma: whether to go along with development, growth, and external demand or to remain stuck by halting the rhythm of his body. 'During one session, Itay drew a large cake with five candles. He colored the first candle with gouache, using his finger, then wanted to wash his hands. I replied: 'You're struggling. Sometimes you enjoy finger painting with gouache and sometimes not. Sometimes you want to get dirty and sometimes you want to be clean'. In another session, he wanted to hide outside the room and for me to go looking for him. I found him hiding not far from the bathroom. I offered to show him the bathroom and he agreed. That session, he wet his underwear. I suggested that he was debating within himself, whether to pee and poo in the toilet or in his underwear: 'today, you chose to pee in your underwear'.

Despite our decision to absolutely avoid direct discussion of the weaning process in other contexts, in the psychotherapy room I sometimes tried associating it with the gouache. In one session, Itay painted the sink drain, pushing the brush into the hole, as if investigating what was in there. In another session, he washed the brush and wanted to wipe it with toilet paper. I responded: 'you want to wipe the paint off the brush with toilet paper. Like after pooing, when we use toilet paper'. Later in the session, he came to sit in my lap and wanted to mix colors. We prepared various colors. I said: 'orange like an orange, blue like the sky, brown like poo'. On another occasion, Itay mixed purple, 'like eggplant', then brown, 'like . . .' He looked at me and said: 'like poo'. I was so excited! It was the first time he agreed to utter the word 'poo'.

Retention as an omnipotent control phantasy

In external reality, Itay's retention persisted and reached its peak. There came a point when he had not peed in twenty hours and was constantly crying in pain. He 'held it in like a maniac', as his mother put it. He gripped his penis tightly so that urine would not drip out and held his bottom, so that 'tush doesn't run away'. He seemed to fear not remaining intact and fought with all his might against internal and external reality alike. His parents were concerned for his health and asked to meet the psychologist in charge of the kindergarten unit.[4] One afternoon, the mother sent for her to show her Itay screaming and writhing, holding his penis and refusing to pee. It was a frightening spectacle indeed, even for seasoned professionals. In their guidance sessions, the parents reported that when they saw Itay in such distress, they would drag him to the bathroom by force. They began to hold him tightly by his hands and feet, to prevent him from holding in the urine, until he would finally pee in the toilet. They were gentle, sensitive, and responsive parents, who were constantly examining their actions. They were going through a very difficult period and they needed containment and reassurance.

Retention began affecting the psychotherapy sessions as well. Yael recounts: 'throughout the session, Itay was preoccupied with retention, holding in the pee. He cried and would not go to the bathroom. I tried reassuring him, saying: 'it's just the pee that comes out. Your body doesn't need the pee. The pee goes out but you stay intact'. I tried to keep things calm and not let anxiety take over. The 'retentive' Itay was incapable of doing anything during sessions. He would sit on the wheel, crying and holding in the pee. In one session, I suggested that I draw him like that and he agreed. Then he came and sat in my lap and I sang to him. He calmed down, went back to the wheel and fell asleep. Retention was clearly wearing him out. He peed a little in his pants while he was asleep. I was very happy about this relief, even if it came at the cost of wakefulness.

In another session, Itay asked me to draw a toilet. I asked him if he wanted me to draw poo and pee in it and he said yes. Then I asked what else to draw and he said: 'Itay sitting'. In another session, he again asked me to draw a toilet, and then he drew 'a weewee-prize'.[5] But he was still very much holding in. During one of the following sessions, he took gouache and began to apply the colors with his hands. His hands were covered with gouache and so when he needed to pee very badly, he could not hold his penis. He rocked to and fro, shouting and crying: 'wipe with a napkin!' He began wiping his hands with paper and then threw himself to the floor. It was clear that the weaning process was holding back his development. The feeling was that he could not do anything because of the fear of weaning'.

During that period there was an ongoing dialogue between Yael, the psychotherapist, and Limor, the kindergarten coordinator. Limor said that, facing this prolonged retention, the therapeutic staff described experiences of aggression, even abuse. The kindergarten was suffused with an atmosphere of panic and helplessness in the face of Itay's intense anxiety and began wishing for some ideal savior who would 'know what to do'. It was difficult to hold on to the remarkable progress that was still being made in the psychotherapy sessions. Following a team discussion and after seeking medical consultation to assess the risks of such prolonged retention, we began to make some helpful distinctions: gradually, it became possible for us to distinguish between Itay's internal phantasies and anxieties and external reality; between the use of force and a parental position that recognizes Itay's well-being; between his annihilation anxiety and experiences of death and a reality in which it is possible to part ways with excrements.

Other hypotheses arose out of the staff's experiences. They suggested that Itay was equating urination with aggressive, destructive acts towards objects. Itay's difficulty with emotional regulation came up, particularly the regulation of anxiety. An idea took shape – to give Itay one month during which the staff will maintain a very levelheaded attitude toward the weaning process and follow a regular routine with no exceptions: if we see Itay holding in, we take him to the bathroom, stay with him and not let him off the hook.

In psychotherapy, Itay began to squirt the gouache out of its bottles, emptying many in the process. He seemed to be investigating what came out of them: 'during one session we ran out of one color or another. Itay began to panic. I suggested that we fill a bottle with water and he liked the idea very much. A few sessions later, I began to refer to this circular process, saying: 'it's just like when you drink, then there's pee, and then you drink again and then there's more pee'. During one session, Itay sprayed water out of the bottle in all directions. I mentioned urine, which splashes out if you hold it too long. Itay became preoccupied with filling and emptying. I would ask him at the end of each session whether he wanted to keep things or throw them away and he began to experiment with tossing things in the trash'.

At that point, the staff made Itay another book, which told the story of how he said goodbye to the diaper, was feeling confused and afraid of the change and held in until his tummy was hurting. The book also explained that it was okay to release the pee in the toilet, because the pee went away, but Itay stayed and the adults were keeping him safe.

A moment of inner resolution: the hole as an opening – 'alone, open alone'

One December afternoon, Itay was taken to the bathroom to urinate. He went wild, spraying urine everywhere. When the staff tried to clean him up and dress him, he became even wilder, fell and injured his ear. He was so frightened that he would not let them treat his ear. Apparently, this shared traumatic experience was needed for a change to take place: at breakfast the next day, Itay drank a glass of water and again showed signs of retention. At the end of the meal, he stood up and went to the bathroom. He seemed hesitant. He went back into the main room, cried a little and went back to the bathroom. The teacher followed him and they entered the stall together. With her help, he pulled down his pants and underwear and the teacher told him that she was watching over him, that only the pee will go away, but Itay will stay. Still unable to urinate, he asked to sit in the bath and his request was granted. There, too, he continued to hold in the pee and cry. The teacher kept reassuring him, saying that he may be afraid, but she was watching over him. Itay replied: 'not afraid, confused' and asked: 'say again, "watching over you" '. He returned to the bathroom and when the teacher asked him to pee again, he said: 'alone, open alone'. It seems that the containment reduced the anxiety that time, enabling him to become acquainted with the notion of openness in a voluntary and deliberate way. They both waited together until the urine stopped flowing. After peeing, Itay asked to get out of the stall, dressed without crying and went back to playing. That same day, he peed in the toilet at home as well, then stopped and said, 'pee-pee went in the toilet. That's it'. In the evening, he asked to pee six times. Each time he peed a little and finally also defecated in the toilet and said: 'poo went in the toilet, bye-bye poo'. From that moment on, he began defecating in the toilet.

His ear, which remained injured for some time, seemed to have been extremely significant, as if it were a scar, a sign of the psychic and physical pain that he was experiencing around the weaning process. In psychotherapy, Itay asked Yael to draw a toilet and then drew many 'weewee-prizes' around it. Alongside the sense of accomplishment, Itay became interested in the wounds on his body. First concretely, by pointing at a wound on his leg, for example, and then a little more playfully, by pouring red paint on his hand and saying: 'I have a wound'. Through play, Itay transformed the experience that was beyond his control into an experience that he initiated and therefore one he could also investigate from a distance and from another perspective. At that stage, Itay seemed to begin to grasp the idea of recovery from pain, of continuity despite loss.

Diaper weaning as a process of growth

The staff meeting that was held a few months later was very emotional. It was clear that Itay had achieved a very significant and valuable developmental leap, on many different levels – emotional, communicative-linguistic, social and cognitive. The teacher described important progress in consolidating a separate and stable self, enabling development and functioning as well as the emergence of desire, initiative and the joy of independence and growth. For the first time, Itay began to use the first person. He was preoccupied with 'I want/don't want', wanted to do things by himself, but also learned to ask for help when he failed. His parents added that Itay's understanding of the distinction between self and other has also improved and that he was better able to keep some of his feelings to himself.

His developing ability to endure anxiety and work it through was also becoming more pronounced and he was making less use of autistic calming mechanisms. It seemed that the physiological holes Itay was plugging were becoming openings for experience and that he was now alternating more freely between being open and closed to the world. He began to enjoy speaking and singing, trying new foods and eating whatever was on the rotating daily menu in the kindergarten. He continued to explore weaning-related openings with more curiosity and less anxiety. The parents reported feeling that Itay was also more willing to allow greater room for difficult experiences and emotions and to talk about them by saying things such as: 'I got scared', 'I am angry', 'Itay is not feeling so good'.

The teacher also reported Itay's cognitive progress through the development of a three-dimensional conception of time, as well as of gradation, sequence and continuity, which were reflected in utterances such as: 'I want now', 'after', 'later' or 'tomorrow', which were effective in helping him calm down. He also understood the meaning of a cycle better, which helped him, for example, to maintain the understanding that an article of clothing that was taken to the laundry was not gone for good, but was going to be washed and returned.

The speech therapist reported progress in Itay's ability to look for solutions. When she wrote his name on a picture he had painted, but he did not want his name on it, he found his own solution: he asked the teacher to photocopy the drawing without the name. In group speech therapy sessions, Itay became more attentive to children around him, addressing them directly with 'hello friends', 'hello Tom', etc. A year before, the presence of other children bothered him and he wanted them to stay away. He was still having difficulties with changes, but began to seek more help from adults, using them as a calming agent, rather than shutting down and eliminating emotional meaningfulness through autistic mechanisms. He was now insisting on being understood and helped and took less time to recover from distress and frustration.

In psychotherapy sessions, a significant development occurred in Itay's ability to take time to organize his thoughts and actions. He took to sitting in the wheel and describing his experiences for much of the session. He recounted experiences from the kindergarten and from home. It was clear that he now had an inner space, a container where things could be stored and from which it was possible to retrieve memories and thoughts. He also managed to think about the future and prepare for it. For example, he recounted that he and his family were going to move to a new apartment: 'my room will be purple and my sister's will be green and mom and dad's will be purple . . .'. His existential experience was no longer exclusively in the here and now, but the past and the future were also accessible, alongside a sense of continuity. His activities in the room became diverse, creative and more passionate. He began to recite from various stories, such as Aladdin and the Magic Lamp, The Jungle Book and The Giant Turnip. In some sessions, he would draw pictures of a family. Itay's absorption, internalization, and thinking abilities also showed significant development. It appeared that he was observing the outside world and sometimes managing to let things in without feeling attacked.

Itay's parents continue to update us about his progress, which is still accompanied by anxieties and difficulties, but also by touching development and growth. When Itay entered first grade, his mother sent the staff letters with updates: 'since the first day at school, Itay has felt good, liked the environment, leaving home happy in the morning and coming back happy in the afternoon. During the first few days, he wanted to tell the entire family about the teachers' names, about the activities at school, he really wanted to tell us everything. . . . The teacher says that he is very charming and hard-working'. We later received another letter: 'Itay finished first grade with significant academic and developmental achievements. He made a lot of progress with emotional regulation and anxiety management, he wants to experience new things and to explore the world more. . . .'

Conclusion

In this chapter, we discussed diaper weaning: the dilemmas and difficulties that this issue raises and its contributions to the development of the self, in the context of multi-professional care in a kindergarten for ASD children. During the developmental process, the dilemma arises of choosing the right time to begin the process of diaper weaning and assuring its success. We took a long time to reach a decision, trying to determine whether Itay's psycho-physical maturity was adequate. Itay's progress was the result of very complex internal negotiations and was accompanied by grappling with massive anxieties. At the end of the process, significant development was made in terms of self-perception, organization of the psycho-physical container and the capacity to absorb, internalize, and understand.

Itay's case may be extreme, but it reflects a process that we see in many children in our kindergartens. The psycho-physical infrastructure required for the process of diaper weaning is impaired, the psycho-physical container is disrupted, body orifices are experienced as holes and the very motivation to grow and develop is frail or actively attacked. The weaning process is very often lengthy, bogged down, distorted and accompanied by stubborn refusal. Adaptation to social demands represents a significant psychic turning point for these children and is accompanied by grappling with massive primal anxieties, for the child as well as the family and the staff. However, it is important to distinguish between congenital problems, sites of under-development and difficulties in containing anxiety, on the one hand, and on the other, the active mechanisms of omnipotent desire to control reality, to deny the fact that both the body and the world cannot always be under one's absolute control. Postponing the diaper weaning process might actively jeopardize, disrupt and distort the child's growth and development. In order for the ASD child to become mature enough to start the weaning process, it is necessary to have a primary infrastructure of physical and psychic distinction between inside and outside and some capacity to be contained and use others to mitigate anxiety. On their part, adults must recognize the intensity and nature of the child's anxieties, so that they may endure and work through the child's powerful projections and help him differentiate between external reality and the intense anxieties and phantasies of his internal reality.

When the process is undergone with proper guidance, holding and containment, it has the potential to bring about a fundamental shift in psychic organization. The accumulation of experiences of transformed anxiety serves as a significant step in the transition to three-dimensional physical and psychic space. Mentalized physical experiences join together in a new layer of conceptualization and organization of the self. The conclusion of the diaper weaning process usually leads to significant growth that is expressed in all areas of development. The physiological holes once plugged by ASD children become openings for experience and the alternation between being open and closed to the world can finally begin.

Notes

1 See Chapter 1.
2 However, in some ASD children with a more serious cognitive disruption, the behavioral approach to diaper weaning is usually preferred.
3 At home too, his conduct around food and in general was described as 'robotic': his mother was forced to decide when he would eat and how much, since he never indicated when he was hungry or full.
4 Pam Yogev-Paltek.
5 A sticker with a drawing, to mark the achievement.

Chapter 7

The autistic constitution and its impact on the disruption of parental functioning

Hilit Bechor Cohen and Hadas Benari Livny

Introduction

The development of a normal baby depends on its congenital constitution and its experience of the world. This development gradually matures through the baby's relationship with its mother, in combination with several capacities: curiosity about exploring external objects, movement, sensation, affect, cognition, and, naturally, relatedness. Each of its world-experiences requires the integration of psycho-physical capacities that are utterly indistinguishable in early life. Consider breastfeeding, for example, breastfeeding requires the baby to integrate capacities such as healthy phantasmatic relatedness to the breast, healthy sensory perception, motor planning and skills, organizational skills, integration of the various sensory modalities, and the like. The actual mother and her capacities are equally significant: she must hold the baby, be ready to present the breast when it is hungry, help it find the nipple, make sure that the rate of suckling matches the flow of milk, regulate sensory stimuli while gradually exposing the baby to moderate amounts of it and so on. Breastfeeding is a prototype for the synchrony between mother and baby. Through the feeding experience, the baby acquires the distinction between hard and soft, inside, and outside, and gradually begins to acknowledge separateness. Phantasies and non-verbal communication, followed by shared enjoyment with the mother, mutual play, symbols and language, emerge. The various capacities thus outlined serve as the foundation for the facilitation of the baby's subjectivity within the context of its relationship with its parents, as well as its capacity for healthy relatedness to its mother and subsequently to others. In autistic children, these innate organic abilities are impaired to various degrees, in a way which inevitably disrupts the development of the mother-baby relationship and the potential for mutual adaptation.

The object relations paradigm offers a rich platform for exploring and understanding normal development as well as the mother-baby relationship. The theories of Klein, Winnicott, and Bion focus on asking what kind of parental functions are needed for the baby's normal development. These theoreticians focus on parental conduct and argue that, in order to guarantee the baby's normal psychic development, the parent must fulfill certain behavioral and phantasized parental functions.

In our work with ASD children, object relations theory helps us understand and discuss the functioning, development, and inner world of our patients. The theories of Tustin, Meltzer, and Greenspan, which deal explicitly with autistic mental structure, provide an additional perspective to the one offered by our psychoanalytic fore-parents, by providing a profound portrayal of autistic mechanisms. In our work at the kindergarten, we have found that these theories supply us with significant answers, but are nonetheless lacking. Klein, Winnicott, and Bion described the normal conditions and parental functions required for normal development. Tustin, Meltzer, and Greenspan focused on the autistic baby or child[1] and defined its unique mental structure and object relations. The missing link is the connection between the inner world of the autistic child and the inner world and actual functioning of its parents. We wish to ask *what happens to parental functions in the encounter with an autistic baby and child?* How will such a baby affect the development of parenting? We became especially aware of this theoretical lacuna when exploring the unique countertransference evoked in us as therapists. In the consultation room, we were often confronted with powerful feelings and intricate processes, which required intense working through and supervisory guidance. We came across concrete forms of thinking, we often felt a sense of emptiness or meaninglessness when engaging the children or aggression toward staff members with whom we disagreed. While these feelings were significantly formulated through the theories of Meltzer, Tustin, Alvarez, and their likes, our emotional and practical response to the deficiencies these children exhibited made us curious about *the emerging inner world of a parent to an autistic child, that is developing in the shadow of this unique disruption*. We have noticed various parental approaches in response to the child's deficiencies and have often found these to be aggressive, extreme, and sometimes even bizarre. As good therapists, we tried to refrain from judging these parents, but the intensity of our encounter did not leave us 'unstained': we were often bewildered by their conduct and critical of their choices. At the same time, through our own experiences in therapeutic transference/countertransference relations, we sometimes found ourselves over-identified with them. The unsettling shifts between these two positions made us realize that *the birth of parenting is the result of reciprocal interaction with the child* and cannot be taken for granted. We formulated an understanding that just as the baby needs good-enough conditions for its healthy development; good-enough parenting also requires good-enough conditions. We began wondering about the prerequisites for developing good-enough parenting – for the miracle of 'the birth of a parent'.

In this chapter, we will demonstrate how the child's developmental deficiencies disrupt parenting, in terms of both intra-psychic organization and actual functioning. We will describe Stern's understanding of the psychic transition into parenthood with a normal baby, outlining the views of key object relations theories regarding the baby's innate foundation, which is lacking in ASD children. We will also review various theories concerned with the organic and psychic deficiencies of the autistic child. We will then show how these two theoretical aspects provide an in-depth understanding of the experience of the autistic child and the maternal functions required to ensure his good-enough development, while refraining from exploring the ways in which the relationship between the autistic child and its parents is formed and disrupted. Finally, we will offer our conceptualization of how such innate deficiencies contribute to *the disruption of the normal development of parenting*.

The birth of a parent to a normal baby

In *The Birth of a Mother* (Stern and Bruschweile, 1998), Stern argues that when a new baby comes into this world, a new mother is born. He offers a rich and lively discussion of the vast and profound internal change that women undergo when they become mothers. His depiction of the psychological process by which this new maternal identity is formed traces a deep individual transformation that gradually begins to emerge during pregnancy and continues several months after birth. This transition entails significant changes in virtually every layer of experience, repositioning the mother in terms of both actual and psychic reality and altering her perception of herself and of those around her. This change does not merely involve developing a new emotional and behavioral repertoire but has a profound impact on the mother's mindset:

> 'When you have a baby, it will determine for a certain period of time what you think about, what you fear or hope for, and what your fantasies will be. It will influence your feelings and actions, and even heighten your basic sensory and information-processing systems. Having a child will redirect your preferences and pleasures, and most likely realign some of your values. In a most startling way, it will influence all of your previous relationships, and cause you to reevaluate your closest associations and redefine your role in your own family's history' (6).

Stern portrays the aspects and challenges that comprise this process of becoming a mother. One of these aspects involves the acknowledgement of the parents that they are actually responsible for the physical wellbeing of another person. This heavy responsibility gives rise to many questions and anxieties. The parent is not only charged with keeping the baby alive, but also with helping it grow and flourish. The act of childbirth, the first touch, the first cry, the look in the baby's eyes, the experience of breastfeeding – these are the building blocks that will eventually construct the new maternal identity. Later on, the parents will have to deal with the gap between the phantasized baby, as they had imagined it throughout the pregnancy, and the actual baby. The parents are expected to establish an intimate relationship with their baby. This process is shaped by their personal relational history and unique manner of experiencing intimacy. Some of the questions parents ask themselves include Will I love this child? Will it love me? Will I be able to understand it? How will I recognize its needs? This uncertainty may lead new parents to reflect on their relationship with their own parents and contemplate the attitudes they wish to repeat or avoid in their relationship with their baby. The 'maternal (or parental) mindset' emerges through successfully facing these challenges. When parents accomplish basic everyday tasks, such as soothing the baby in their lap or feeding it, and when they experience their baby as developing and thriving, they begin to feel a quiet yet profound affirmation of their ability to answer the baby's needs and their competence as parents. The daily preoccupation sets in motion a positive cycle of interaction, communication, intimacy, mutuality, identification, and love. As time goes by, this assortment of pleasure and satisfaction that are mixed in with worries, fears, and tiredness, give rise to an internal experience of emotional competence and worth. The actual relationships of parents with friends and relatives serve as a background of support and affirmation that are vital for the establishment of their new parental identity. Stern's discussion of the possible disruptions of this process of nascent motherhood mostly focuses on difficulties concerning the mother's personality and her internalized object-relations. But what happens when the baby is born with a developmental disorder? Stern devotes a chapter in his book to the development of the maternal mindset in situations where the baby is born prematurely or with a physical disability. In his view, these situations entail far greater obstacles for the birth of a mother, as parents must face exceptional difficulties not only in establishing the maternal mindset but also in successfully incorporating this mindset into their lives. While they encounter many of the situations that every parent has to deal with, they must cope with considerably greater intensity over much longer periods of time. Nevertheless, Stern does not go into any detail concerning the dynamics of parental disruption in relation to a child with special developmental needs and, in fact, refrains from describing 'the birth of a mother to an abnormal baby'. In this, he joins a long list of key theoreticians who discussed the special needs of babies with constitutional deficiencies, while only focusing on parental functions from the baby's point of view.

Object relation theories: insufficient understanding of the dynamics between the parent and the autistic child

Klein (1926/1950, 1946) postulated an innate tendency for 'object relations', which is realized in actual relationships as well as in the relationship between the internalized representations of self and object. She argued that a baby is born with a considerable degree of envy and aggression, as well as love and the capacity to create internal representations of the feelings and experiences evoked in it by the significant people around it. The primary relation established between mother and baby serves as the model and prototype for the adult's relation to their environment and to other people. Klein divided the baby's early mental development into two positions – the schizo-paranoid position and the depressive position. The schizo-paranoid position is an intense psychic state that the baby finds hard to bear. At this stage, the baby has several primitive defense mechanisms for dealing with anxiety: splitting, projection, projective identification, and introjection – which also serve to manifest its relation to the part-object. The depressive position entails the development of ego-functions and the capacity for emotional regulation as well as the capacity to perceive objects as integrated and whole. The baby now gains the painful understanding that the mother is the source of both frustration and satisfaction and must face feelings of aggression toward an object that is also good. This gives rise to real concern for the mother, to the desire for 'reparation' and the attempts at reparation through love (Klein, 1952).

These elements are absent when dealing with a baby with autistic mechanisms: first, the baby's innate drive for relatedness is considerably deficient. Second, Klein postulates that, right from the very beginning, the baby has an innate need to create order and organization, a primary intuition regarding separateness, a crude distinction between inside and outside and primitive, though effective primary coping mechanisms. An autistic baby may have severe difficulties with all these organizational capacities.

Winnicott (1971a) went beyond Klein's focus on the internal world, adding the crucial dimension involving the actual parent and environment, which assist the development of the baby's primary mechanisms. He views emotional development as a journey from absolute dependence on the object, through relative dependence, toward independence. This motion is made possible through the baby's dependence on the 'environment-mother'. In the first stage of absolute dependence, baby and mother are indistinguishable, they form a single unit and the baby is unaware of maternal care, which perfectly addresses its needs. Even though Winnicott (1956) writes of 'good-enough' mothering, in early life the mother is required to engage in a 'primary maternal preoccupation'[2] that would allow her to hold the baby's extreme anxieties, which involve annihilation and the threat of extinction, in order to allow it to experience 'going-on-being', when everything is in order.[3] The baby gradually learns to withstand less and less precise adaptation to its needs, thus making it possible for the mother to regain her separateness. In the next stage, that of relative dependence, the mother gradually allows failure and forgoes her perfect adaptation.

The transition from utter dependence to independence requires the successful application of several parental functions: holding, handling, and object presenting (Winnicott, 1960). *Holding* means the unspoken communication between mother and baby in whom she is saying, 'you can trust me because I know what you need, I care about you and I want to give you what you need'. Holding allows the disparate parts of the baby to come together and be experienced as a single, integrated unit. By *handling*, Winnicott is referring to the myriad aspects that involve caring for the baby and concern for its physical well-being. Repeated experiences of adapted physical care gradually amount to 'personalization', a process by which the psyche comes to dwell in the soma, creating an internal sense of selfhood. *Object presentation* means that the mother-environment presents the object in a way that facilitates the baby's illusion that it created the object.

The stage in which the mother allows the baby to find the phantasized object is a vital step on the way to achieving object-relatedness and to relating to reality as something that is separate from the self, what Winnicott (1945) would call 'realization'. These processes are the foundation for engaging in projective and introjective relations with objects residing in the world outside the self. The next milestone, the use of the object (Winnicott,1971b), is a state in which the mother's ability to deal with the baby's aggression and destructiveness enables the baby to acknowledge her as an independent being, which lies outside its omnipotent control. The transition from omnipotence and oneness to acknowledging external reality entails the development of a 'transitional space', which paradoxically combines both internal and external realities, both 'me' and 'not-me', and enables the emergence of a 'transitional object' (Winnicott, 1971a). When a baby looks into its mother's face, it sees itself in it, establishing its experience of being seen and therefore of existing (Winnicott, 1971c). This experience would later give rise to creativity, spontaneity, and the ability to interact with objects that are separate from the baby. Winnicott thus argues that the mother's subjective capacities are crucial for development.

The tendency of object relation theories to focus on the relationship with the mother assigns less importance to the role played by the father in the baby's emotional development. Winnicott refers to the father as mostly performing an auxiliary or supporting role – by turning 'outwards', the father allows the mother to turn 'inwards', in order to care for the baby. The role of the father is to provide a safe environment for the mother, so that she could offer the baby a 'good-enough' environment. Yet another function the father performs, one seldom mentioned by Winnicott but elaborated by other theoreticians (Abelin, 1975; Britton, 1989; Brickman, 1993; Chasseguet-Smirgel, 1986; Mahler, Pine, and Bergman, 1975) is that of the 'third': representing the reality principle and extracting the baby from its merger with the mother, thus facilitating the process of separation.

Winnicott suggests that if the mother properly applies her beneficial maternal functions, she will necessarily encounter a baby eager to use her and her abilities. He is relying, however, on various assumptions concerning the psychic capacities already present in the baby from birth, capacities which are deficient in the development of the autistic child, which lacks the ability to use maternal functions to facilitate its emotional regulation and its separateness. As we shall see, because of these deficiencies and lacks, the development of parenthood is severely impaired.

Bion (1962, 1967) also places considerable emphasis on the abilities of the actual mother and their role in the baby's normal development, attributing the Kleinian mechanism of 'projective identification' with a communicative function, in addition to splitting. By means of the mother's intuitive reverie, she is capable of transforming raw elements of experience into processed elements that are eventually introjected by the baby in a process of introjective identification. Bion (1962) makes a distinction between normal projective identification and pathological projective identification. In the normal kind, while the mother may be thrown off balance, she is able to 'contain' projected emotions and treat the baby in a way, which turns its unbearable feelings into a bearable and meaningful experience. Frustration is transformed into a situation that one can think and potentially resolve through transformation and actual change. Thinking and the capacity to bear frustration emerge. When the mother's capacity for reverie is deficient, for personal reasons or because the baby's fragmentation is too extreme and intense, learning from experience is precluded: the mother is unable to process and soften the baby's frustrations, fears, and dread, and it is left utterly exposed to its fears. Optimal mother-baby (container-contained) relations entail mutual and reciprocal adaptation and change, so that each shapes the other and is shaped by it in return and the two engage in a flexible relationship that is constantly growing and developing. In pathological projective identification, the baby's innate capacity to bear frustration is underdeveloped and its projections are so forceful that they 'destroy' the mother and hinder the containment process. The kind of relationship established through such container-contained relations is fragmentary and the experience is one of non-containment and even mutual destruction. Therefore, the baby's characteristics may disrupt the containment process and even make the mother feel that she is 'bombarded', establishing a relation conducive to mutual destruction (Bion, 1962, 1967a).

So far, we have briefly presented descriptions and conceptualizations of normal development offered by key theoreticians of the Object relations school. We will now review several attempts to portray the mental organization of the autistic child and examine its effects on the emergence of parenthood and its subsequent characteristics.

The disruption of parental experience and function with ASD children

What happens to a mother who faces a baby that attacks her intuitive ability to address its needs; that fails to make the transition from absolute dependence to gradual independence; that gives no indication of its needs and does not signal that it is capable of bearing a growing amount of frustration and separateness; that will not reward her with a smile, a glance or the ability to calm down; that will not enliven her when she is tired; that is constantly overwhelmed by annihilation anxiety? What happens to a mother when her baby sends out erratic messages – sometimes responding to her voice and sometimes ignoring it – that often excessively 'vomits' raw mental elements into her or never projects any elements that can be emotionally and cognitively processed and transformed? How does such a mother react to her own phantasized aggression and destructiveness? And what happens to the father? Through the understanding of the autistic experience and the autistic child's impaired organic substrate, we will explore the way all these factors shape parental capability.

The implications of organic deficiencies in processing, regulation and inter-sensory integration on the birth of motherhood

All our experiences of the world are based on the integration of sensory, motor, and mental capacities. In normal development, both mother and baby share a similar organic substrate for their experience of the world. Therefore, by drawing on her own experiences, the mother is usually able to understand and interpret the baby's primary responses and alleviate its distress. With an autistic child, the mother has difficulties understanding experiences that she herself has never had and may not even be able to imagine. This difficulty may hinder her identification with the baby's needs and distresses, amounting to a cumulative experience of failure. The baby may also lie awake in its bed for hours on end, without expressing any kind of distress, without 'calling out' to the mother or seeking her presence. The mother assumes that her baby shares the same instincts she is familiar with – if it is not crying, then nothing is troubling it – and so she simply lets it lie there unattended, awake and alone, for long periods of time. In this sense, the baby desensitizes the mother's natural tendency for relatedness, keeping her from 'calling' it to interact with her in ways that are vital for its development.

For example, *Shai*'s mother recalls that when he was a year old, his leg was caught between the bars of his bed. Shai did not provide any signals indicating that he was in distress. Shay's mother expected her baby to cry if it is in pain. This trying ordeal taught her that her expectations were irrelevant. This may not be a case of failed communication; however, it is possible that Shai refrained from crying because he suffered from hyposensitivity, causing him to feel what other babies would experience as painful, as a pleasant sensation or as neutral stimulation and feedback on his bodily position. Alternately, it is possible that the pain was so intense and overwhelming that Shai resorted to dissociation and regressed to self-holding. Either way, his lack of responsiveness made his mother unable to help him. When this kind of situation repeats itself again and again, the mother's basic experience of herself as benevolent and competent may become deeply impaired, disrupting the delicate processes of mutual mother-baby attachment.

Effect of the baby's merging tendencies on the birth of motherhood

Many researchers who conducted baby observations (Berry and Brazelton, 1970; Stern, 1985; Trevarthen, 1977) have disputed Winnicott's assumption regarding the original state of absolute dependence. Their observations have shown that, in normal development, moments of alert and lively awareness and active curiosity are present from the very beginning of life. They argue that it would be wrong to believe that in early infancy the healthy baby is completely unaware of being separate from its mother's body. Therefore, these developmental scholars, reassured by Tustin's clinical research (1991), claim that the difference between the autistic baby and the healthy baby is already present at this primary stage of development and already bears its influence on 'the birth of the mother'.

In 'The Theory of the Parent-Infant Relationship', Winnicott (1990) discusses the importance of the mother's gradual 'recovery' from the normal 'illness' that is primary maternal preoccupation, in which the mother meets the baby's needs as if they were still a single unit. According to Winnicott, the prematurely separated mother leaves the baby 'with two alternatives; either being in a permanent state of regression and of being merged with the mother, or else staging a total rejection of the mother, even of the seemingly good mother'. Furthermore, it is vital that the baby signals to the mother that he has matured enough to be able to tolerate a lesser degree of adaptation to its needs. Thus, even in the first weeks of its life, there are moments – that grow longer and longer – in which the baby provides the mother with the confidence that allows her to occasionally interrupt her perfect adaptation.

In autism, the baby's deficient constitution, which creates the desire to preserve the state of merger, causes it to offer inconsistent signals – or even none at all – regarding its ability to withstand those brief moments of imperfect maternal adaptation. The subtle messages designed to let the mother know what is suitable for her baby are either missing or so few, inconsistent and unintelligible that they lose all communicative value. The mother drifts further and further apart from communicating with her actual baby and eventually comes to rely only on herself and her projections, meeting the needs of the baby as if it was part of herself. The period of absolute dependence continues unabated. Absolute maternal devotion, which in normal development has a set time limit, retains its initial intensity and persists regardless of the baby's chronological age. The situation depicted here is an extreme one; in reality, the picture is not as clear-cut. Most of the children which are eventually diagnosed with ASD will not leave the mother in a permanent state of absolute commitment and merger. More often than not, the mother will 'find rest' in moments of emotional detachment, shifting between merger and detachment (which is profoundly different from separateness).

The effect of the intensity of the child's anxiety on the mother's ability to initiate normal separation processes

In normal development, primitive anxiety has a limited duration and is further moderated by the mother's physical and mental holding which the baby eventually internalizes. In autism, anxiety remains just as potent as the years go by and is not similarly moderated by the child's benign experience of the world. Despite the mother's protective organization and the child's rigid defenses, the autistic child inevitably encounters the gap between inside and outside due to random inescapable everyday experiences or to the active gestures of the mother or other caretakers. When the autistic child experiences frustration, followed by high levels of anxiety, the mother, who keeps experiencing it as highly fragile, is unable to confront him with frustrating demands that will challenge its functional capacities and encourage it to become more independent. Since the level of anxiety remains so high, the mother's efforts to apply her basic maternal functions are constantly under attack. The baby may respond to maternal holding and care with incessant crying and a substantial difficulty in calming down. At other times, the mother's care and soothing suddenly prove effective, for reasons that she cannot understand. The mother finds it difficult to anticipate her baby's reactions, to maintain an inner experience of sequence and to trust herself and others to be able to properly understand it.

We will briefly explore the case of *Doron,* who is just about to enter first grade. Doron's cognitive and verbal abilities are only slightly behind the age-appropriate norm but he still drinks juice from a baby-bottle. As soon as his mother notices that his bottle is empty, she refills it. She never waits for Doron to say that he is thirsty or indicate that he wishes to drink. The mother also expresses a great deal of anger toward the kindergarten staff whenever breakfast is delayed. In her distress, she demands that the staff treat Doron as if he were a baby: 'he has to eat by 8:30, 9:00 tops. This is impossible! Would you let your baby starve?' This example demonstrates how, through extensive projective identification, the mother adhesively identifies with the child's fundamental difficulty in bearing frustration, thus disrupting the normal function of maternal reality-testing. On the one hand, the child's levels of anxiety are so petrifying that it attacks the mother's capacity to think about her son, to phantasize what is happening to him and to find alternate ways to transform his anxiety into a more bearable experience. When the mother does momentarily succeed in understanding her son and moderating his terror, the autistic child may find it difficult to internalize this maternal function. As the next vignette will show, the child's intense anxiety sometimes disrupts paternal thinking processes to such a degree that parents exhibit primary, quasi-psychotic thinking processes.

The effect of the autistic mental structure on the mother's archaic emotional organization

The psychic space of withdrawn autistic children is dominated by an occluding auto-sensuality. When the defense mechanism of auto-sensuality is obstructed, we often witness outbursts of rage, despair, and dread without the relief provided by projection. When healthy projection and projective identification processes malfunction, the baby remains full of primary survival anxieties, which may also infect the mother. Instead of digestion, we sometimes see mothers who describe an inability to keep the child in mind, a complete concretization of anxiety and an impaired capacity for thinking and symbolization. At times, they even describe a self-state reminiscent of madness.

Uri's mother experienced him, in contrast with her first daughter, as a screaming baby that would not be calmed down. All her attempts to soothe him only made him scream louder. She simply could not help him. She describes talking to herself, trying to come to her senses and calm herself down, but being continually unsettled by the sheer force of his screams. She found that the one thing that made her calm down was concrete action: taking a shower. She would take showers, phantasizing that she is washing off the anxiety Uri evoked in her. She says that after showering, she would go to Uri, to try and sooth him again, and repeatedly fail. According to her, she would sometimes shower up to ten times a day.

This difficult vignette demonstrates the profound danger facing parents of autistic children in terms of their mental survival. It illustrates the collapse of thinking processes and the mental space, as well as the emergence of inklings of psychotic thinking. Every person, even those with well-integrated neurotic personalities, has primitive defenses that may be triggered under stressful conditions. The mother's intense and prolonged experience of not understanding her baby and being unable to soothe it might lead to protracted traumatic reactions in the form of concretization and excessive splitting and projection.

The baby's innate difficulty in using the object and the mother's difficulty in being born as a subject

We have learned from Winnicott that the birth of the child's subjectivity is closely related to its recognition of the mother as exterior to it and as having feelings, sensations and thoughts that are different from its own. The birth of the baby's subjectivity is the result of a long process that begins in absolute dependence on maternal holding, which evokes object-relatedness, continues in the emergence of transitional phenomena (Winnicott, 1971a) and finally matures through object-use as the foundation of subjectivity (Winnicott, 1971b).

As the autistic child has difficulties relinquishing his omnipotence and acknowledging an external reality that lies beyond his control, the entire domain of transitional phenomena fails to develop properly and he remains trapped in omnipotent illusion. Instead of subjective cohesion, the child is left with an assortment of particular experiences that will not accumulate into knowledge and understanding of self and other. When transitional space fails to develop and the child cannot make the transition to object use, some of the most significant processes concerning the development of relatedness and the birth of the mother as a subject are impaired. When a child is able to use his mother in a healthy manner, he may evoke anxiety in her and may sometimes almost 'destroy' her, but within a period of time that both find tolerable he will also actively enliven her – reward her, animate her when she is tired, look into her eyes, reach out to touch her mouth or hair, smile at her, and so on. In order to develop her subjectivity as a mother, she in turn must be in touch with her aggression and be willing to feel very difficult feelings: that she is sick and tired of her baby, that having a child was a mistake, and so on. She can make room for such feelings as long as she has a baby that can withstand her aggressive phantasies and recover from them along with her. This process is deficient in mothers to autistic babies and children, because the mother experiences her phantasized destructiveness as concrete. When the mother experiences her baby as fragile and unable to withstand her projections, her pent up aggression may eventually be turned against herself, against other family members or external objects, including therapy providers.

If we embrace Winnicott's notion of the mother's 'mirror-role' (Winnicott, 1971c), we find that the baby has its own mirroring role in the development of the mother, since the mother sees herself in her child's eyes as well. When the baby's organic foundation is deficient, it reflects nothing of the mother's maternal preoccupation. The baby remains affectless, minding its own business and not trying to catch her eye. The baby does not seem to enjoy playing 'peekaboo', or respond when she calls its name. Without the baby's mirroring, the mother' vitality and significant existence cannot be affirmed. She feels hollow, withdraws into herself, and fades – as if there is nothing in her that can be seen. When auto-sensuality takes over, the mother's sense of play and her curiosity to explore the baby are diminished and cannot be realized. The joy of maternal discovery is impaired, her care of the baby becomes technical, emotionally detached and devoid of developmental nourishment.

A normal eight-month-old baby will reach out to touch the mother's face, putting its finger in her mouth or nose. The mother will smile at it or say something and the baby will stop feeding for a moment in order to smile. At eight months, an autistic baby such as Uri can sit in his stroller, fully awake, for an entire hour, without doing anything and without seeking the attention of his parents. Suddenly, he shows signs of discomfort and his mother prepares a bottle for him. She holds him in her arms and while she is feeding him, he stares vaguely into space. The mother does not try to meet Uri's gaze, nor does she try to enliven him. She remains equally passive and detached in other situations as well. She seldom speaks or sings to him; she does not show him pictures of animals in order to teach him the kind of sound each animal makes. 'He has no interest in that', she tells herself. The child's withdrawal and detachment set in motion a vicious cycle in which the mother, whose baby offers no affirmation of her selfhood and motherhood, sinks into depression, withdraws into a passive position and finds it difficult to provide 'live company' (Alvarez, 1992) for her son.

Disruptions in the child's experience of time and their implications for its parents

One of the most dramatic characteristics of autism involves the gaps formed by the fact that certain developmental processes are halted, while others go on uninterrupted. These often incomprehensible gaps between various functions have significant consequences for the parent's notion of sequence in a way that may even lead to a distorted notion of time. In parenting, time equals growth and development. The fact that the child keeps growing but does not develop inevitably disrupts the intuitive grasp of the flow of time. The distortion is sometimes so severe that it impairs parental judgment concerning the child's developmental stage. On the one hand, time 'stands still' and parents refrain from confronting the child with much needed age-appropriate developmental challenges, because he is 'still so young'. On the other hand, time keeps running forward and those same parents may expect their child to function in ways that would be premature even in the context of normal development.

The significance of the child's autistic constitution on familial relatedness patterns

As a result of the excessive autistic merger with the mother, the father's influence on the mental development of the autistic child is considerably lacking. These children do not face the consequences of having to share the mother with their father or their siblings and thus an essential component in restraining their typically exaggerated omnipotence is lacking. When the relationship with the mother is so intense, the father is often pushed out of the picture altogether. The baby, suffering from extreme anxieties, constantly turns to the mother, who is tempted to enter into an exclusive relationship with it. She does not encourage the father to become involved and the alarmed father often chooses to avoid any contact with the child. In addition, the urge to address the autistic child's needs often leads parents to neglect and ignore the needs of other family members. Parents might refrain from taking the child and his siblings out of the house, because they are afraid that he may embarrass them in public; they also refrain from going out without him, as it is hard for them to leave the child in someone else's care. The autistic child is allowed to sleep wherever and whenever he chooses, to eat off other people's plates and to touch his mother's breasts. This abnormal situation at home harms not only the development of the autistic child but also the physical and emotional wellbeing of the rest of the family.

Ronen is a second child; his brother is three years older than him. The mother entered a virtually symbiotic relationship with Ronen. Every time he wanted to tell her something he would turn her head to face him. He required her full attention. He rarely used his father to calm down and the father gradually gave up on his efforts to get through to Ronen. The family's everyday routine kept the father and the older brother locked away in their rooms with their computers, while the mother and Ronen stayed together in the living room. Nevertheless, the mother felt increasingly lonely and frustrated by having been abandoned by the father, who left her to care for Ronen and be the only one holding him in mind. Ronen's brother began exhibiting more and more reclusive behavior. At times, when Ronen was not at home, he would try reaching out to his mother, who was very much exhausted and often simply wanted to sleep, in order to have the energy to care for Ronen when he came back from kindergarten.

Case presentation

Orit and Yuval were in their mid-thirties and already had two children, a seven-year-old and a four-year-old, when they decided to have another child. They both felt accomplished in their careers and well rooted in the small community where they lived. Yuval's parents were holocaust survivors; he absorbed the anxious atmosphere that dominated their home and had always been a somewhat anxious man, who found his way into significant positions of power. Orit was the eldest of four children and always saw herself as responsible for her younger siblings. She never asked for help and always tended to rely on her own initiative and resourcefulness. *Amir* was born on time after a healthy pregnancy. He was a very sleepy baby and Orit felt that he was very 'low-maintenance'. Amir was breastfed and whenever there was a change in the flow of milk or when he gagged at the breast, he would fall asleep and Orit had trouble waking him up. He would always grip the little finger of her free hand and scream when she switched him between breasts. She thought he was just being spoiled. Amir was a quiet baby, but he responded when she spoke to him and occasionally made eye-contact. If he was in distress, he could only calm down next to her, by holding her pinkie in the fold of his hand, sometimes for a very long time. If she removed her finger, he would scream and 'fill up with a panic', that she found difficult to bear. For this reason, he would always sleep next to her, holding her pinkie. As her relationship with me – as Amir's psychotherapist – grew deeper, Orit told me that she sometimes enjoyed thinking that he needed her but at other times, especially as he started growing up, she felt that her baby was 'controlling her' and even that she wished that he would disappear. Amir had good cognitive skills but his communicational and linguistic development was delayed. He seldom initiated any kind of communication, knew few words and rarely made eye-contact or pointed. When he wanted something, he used his mother's hand to get it. Orit saw this as a creative way to overcome his linguistic impairment. At two, when Amir was diagnosed with ASD, Orit was reluctant to accept this diagnosis, claiming that he is responsive to her. She found it hard to leave him with other people, as she did not trust anyone else to care for his needs. She left her job, devoting all her time to caring for Amir.

Despite his diagnosis, Amir kept attending the same kindergarten as the other children in his small town and his parents had hoped that interacting with them would allow him to develop normally. At the kindergarten, it was clear that he was a highly intelligent child with a severe difficulty in coping with transition. He would often become detached, was unable to play with the other children – who were always too quick for him to join in – and avoided social interactions. When the other children went out to the yard, Amir would stay by himself, walking alone and mumbling songs or mimicking sword-fighting. Sometimes, he would crawl and hide under one of the tables, closing his eyes and detaching himself from his surroundings. At this kindergarten, Amir had a favorite caretaker, with whom he could calm down. He would try to hold her pinkie but she set a firm boundary about this, which he gradually came to respect. She also tried, with little success, to teach him how to express his feelings in words. Whenever he was upset, Amir would simply detach himself next to her.

Amir was transferred to our kindergarten around the age of four and a half. The transition to an ASD kindergarten was very hard on his parents; it was the first time they had to publicly face that Amir was different. The years-long delight of being part of a small, close-knit community now turned into a gilded cage, as the neighbors' stares became increasingly unbearable. They felt that people were drifting away from them. Yuval began avoiding other people and felt that he was 'losing his status'. He began working longer hours, left the local soccer team and became cynical about the people close to him. As the years went by, he turned into a 'walking pharmacy', trapped in his physical anxieties. He would come to our parent guidance sessions with a two-liter water bottle and a pile of pills.

While Orit maintained her relationships with her friends and kept trying to arrange for her son to spend time with local children that were his age, these meetings became more and more difficult. Orit had to acknowledge the fact that while her son yearns for the company of his peers, there were considerable gaps between him and them. She was caught in a vicious circle, in which all her strength and energy were devoted to her attempts to socialize her son. She eventually sank inwards, feeling utterly drained. She then spent four years in therapy, where she uncovered feelings concerning unresolved mourning for impossible things she had wished for. She also began taking anti-depressants. Therapy proved helpful and she began paying more attention to her own needs. Still, she did not feel that she could let go of trying to meet what she thought were Amir's needs and could not escape feeling that if she only did the right thing, Amir's symptoms would simply vanish.

After Amir began attending our kindergarten, he progressed considerably in his linguistic and communicational development. When he finished kindergarten, the pedagogic and therapeutic staff recommended that Amir start first grade at a regular school, with the help of a personal teaching aide. This recommendation evoked in his parents an anxiety that they found hard to handle and they chose to stay in the relatively sheltered haven of special-needs education. They felt that it was important to keep reinforcing Amir's sense of confidence and success and opted to have him integrated in a class that was part of a regular school but belonged to the special-needs system. When it was time to enroll him in second grade, the school staff recommended transferring Amir to a regular class, with a personal teaching aide. The parents were once again overwhelmed by anxiety, which affected their decision-making; they decided to integrate Amir into the regular education system, but have him repeat the first grade, despite his keen intellectual skills.

Even though Amir was never officially defined as a gifted child, he was repeatedly invited to attend the school's various enrichment programs for high-achieving students. His intellectual capacity for mathematical thinking and his physical abilities in basketball were clearly high. In second and third grade, he enjoyed playing with the other children during recess. When he was in fourth grade, his coach recommended Amir for the local junior basketball league. Orit was overjoyed, believing that Amir's achievements in school and in the basketball league were proof that his difficulties could be solved. She ignored the fact that she still had to coordinate his after-school meetings and that he was still struggling socially. While he was always enlivened by movement-based games, as soon as the game or the interaction switched over to speech or other non-physical communication, he gave up and faded away. It seems that his parents' difficulty in forming an actual and balanced notion of him in their minds also left a hole in Amir's notion of himself. Much like his mother, who tended to perceive relationships as 'doing things together', thinking that 'moving is what children do together', Amir could not understand the difference between playing basketball and engaging in mutual and meaningful social relations. Time was caught in a loop and Orit went back to coping patterns she had embraced when Amir was still a small child, using her acquaintance with local women to get Amir to meet with friends. Meanwhile, Yuval had stored up a lot of rage at his wife, feeling that she had become utterly immersed in caring for Amir in a way that was taking a heavy toll on their relationship and the entire family. Orit persisted in refusing to trust anyone else to take 'proper' care of Amir, so that she and Yuval never went on vacation together or even just out to watch a movie. Even when Amir was twelve and his older siblings were sixteen and nineteen, Orit refused to leave him alone with them. She could not bear the thought that he would be cooped up in his room with his computer. Feeling that Orit was neglecting their other children and her relationship with him, Yuval drifted away from Amir and had trouble engaging him in pleasant interactions. He would occasionally lash out in anger at him. The attitude he came to embrace was 'there's nothing more we can do for this kid, we're better off putting our effort into the ones who will pay us back with a sense of relatedness'. Once again, Orit felt that Yuval was leaving her to handle Amir on her own and was angry at him for giving up on his relationship with Amir. Orit herself felt that her career had been held back and that her care of and relationship with her older children had suffered. Their eldest daughter was starting to behave reclusively and their other son was falling in with some 'negative' kids.

As Amir grew older, when the other boys began showing interest in things other than basketball, his behavior became more and more withdrawn and Orit's heart was broken. She saw her son, who had been doing so well in special-needs education, withering away. Orit felt she had made a mistake in sending her son to a regular school; still, it was equally clear that he did not belong in the special-needs system. Amir also felt that he had no desire to 'regress'. He began exhibiting anxious behavior: refusing to leave the house for fear of dogs, walking around the house for hours on end swinging a sword from side to side and avoiding all contact with his peers. His parents sent him back to psychotherapy because he needed to make some kind of change.

It seems that both parents refused to acknowledge the fact that their psychic wellbeing and their parental capacities had been so diminished and distorted as to put Amir at risk. Amir felt utterly lost in the situation that emerged at home: his mother reacted with extreme anxiety to any social or personal experience he was involved in, while his father, who was also anxious, became more and more absorbed in his own physical and emotional distress and alienated himself from

Amir. With overwhelming intensity, Amir felt his parents' soaring levels of anxiety and despair had turned the family's home into a toxic environment that inhibited and precluded development. In order for Amir's individual therapy to be of any use, a massive change was required in the parents' ability to accept help in rehabilitating their parental functions.

Conclusion

In this chapter, we set out to explore object relations theories from a complementary perspective, considering not only how parental personality and phantasy affect the child's development but also how a baby with an impaired organic constitution affects the development of parenthood. Paraphrasing Winnicott's dictum that 'there is no such thing as a baby without a mother', we wanted to demonstrate that there is no such thing as a mother (or a parent), without a child that is relating to her. We have illustrated how many of the concepts put forward by object-relations theories – phantasy, aggression, container-contained, object-use, absolute dependence, the mirror-role – can also be observed from a complementary perspective. This complementary perspective is essential for completing the picture offered by these central thinkers – especially as far as ASD children are concerned.

Just as autism extensively impairs every area of the child's development and function, it is likely to cause an extensive disruption in the development of motherhood and parenthood – affecting unconscious phantasy, communication, thinking processes and actual parental functioning. Facing the inevitable disruption that is part and parcel of parenting an autistic child, while drawing on their own internal resources, parents often need our help in stabilizing the relation between personal and familial hopes and their actual available resources, their adaptive and non-adaptive defense mechanisms and the functional and developmental tasks facing the child itself and the family as a whole.

Notes

1 In the present chapter, the term 'autistic baby' or 'autistic child' serves as useful shorthand in referring to 'a baby or child with autistic mechanisms'. It goes without saying that the autistic baby or child also exhibits mechanisms and complexities that go beyond the framework of their autistic mechanisms and that there is great diversity among individual autistic babies and children.

2 A state that the mother enters during pregnancy and which lasts several weeks following childbirth. The pregnant mother is preoccupied with the changes she is undergoing, diverting some of her sense of self to include the baby that is growing inside her. She identifies with the baby, becoming attuned to its needs and acquiring a profound knowledge of these. This maternal position is a 'normal illness', from which the mother gradually 'recovers', as the baby grows and becomes more and more able to bear less perfect adaptation.

3 According to Winnicott, the baby is occasionally on the verge of feeling 'unthinkable anxiety', of 'going to pieces [. . .] falling forever [. . .] having no relationship to the body [. . .] having no orientation' (Winnicott, 1980).

A non-verbal 5-year-old ASD child draws and writes ‘imprisoned’.

Chapter 8

In spite of and because of words

Tamar Assal and Pazit Gur

Discussion group:

Tamar Assal – clinical social worker; Pazit Gur – speech therapist; Tali Yelin Shental – clinical psychology intern; Irit Pollak – speech therapist; Gali Cohen – occupational therapist

Anyone stepping into a kindergarten for autistic children will often encounter much chatter. Quite a few of the children attending our kindergartens, especially during the past several years, have already developed a certain vocabulary and some use of syntax, amounting to language-like speech. The nature of this chatter is not necessarily symbolic or communicative, nor does it function as a language in the full sense of the word. The present chapter discusses the intriguing and challenging presentation of patients whose acquired speech does not add up to a linguistic network per se, while still serving them as a way for establishing separateness and probing after their fragile sense of self. The development of language is an intricate process, which stems from physical, cognitive, emotional, and communicational maturation. Aided by various clinical vignettes, research, and theoretical thinking, we will hereby ponder the contribution of the therapeutic fabric, the multi-professional approach, and the psychoanalytic-developmental prism to the acceleration of integration and separation processes, as the foundation for transforming the children's use of spoken words.

In normal development, the acquisition of language as a creative communicative dimension that is both lively and meaningful is based on the accumulation of experiences of one's encounter with the world and one's relationships with the surrounding human environment. The acquisition of words is subordinate to the process by which their meanings are acquired. Psychoanalytic theory informs us that meaning emerges through the ongoing feedback loop of the baby's communication with its mother, which gradually enables it to digest its accumulation of raw experiences, turning these into thoughts. Later on, these thoughts grow clearer, more stable and more substantial as the capacity for verbal representation matures.[1]

Working with ASD children brings us face to face with a different picture altogether. We meet children who often utter words and sentences only as a quasi-linguistic performance, which they use to avoid communication rather than to interact. Very frequently, the contact these children have with the experience of the Other's existence as well as with any notion of shared meaning seems loose and meager. But nevertheless, there they are, using words, syntax, idioms, occasionally even what might seem like concepts. We assume that the process of language acquisition evident in these children is essentially different from that found in normal development. Throughout the years, we realized that the kind of speech these children employ manifests a struggle between the tendency to void words of meaning and turn them into shapes, which preclude relatedness and communication and a certain wish to use words to link form and meaning and be in contact with the world and with themselves. Therefore, we asked ourselves if the verbal performance we are witnessing is utterly uncommunicative, serving as an autistic shape (Tustin, 1984), which obstructs the normal acquisition process, or whether these words, although they were acquired partially and in a highly patterned way, may under the right conditions serve the child as a tool for communicative learning. By reviewing theory and research and through clinical vignettes featuring kindergarten children and alumni, we will discuss this unique linguistic performance. We will address the disruption of psycho-physical integration processes and the essential difficulty with separation processes characteristic of ASD children. We will describe and explore linguistic performances ranging between empty shapes and the search for communication and try to see how our multi-professional and developmental thinking, the everyday kindergarten environment and the therapeutic relationship offered by psychotherapy create a space where the use of language can be transformed.

Intolerance to separateness or un-integration?

Language appears at a relatively early stage of sensory-motor, cognitive, communicative, and emotional development, when the infant has already acknowledged that it is not entirely omnipotent and allowed basic separation processes to commence. This gradual, non-linear maturation, which depends on the accumulation of physical and emotional experiences, is the foundation for the potential for mental representation, an advanced expression of which is spoken language. In discussing symbolization and linguistic and cognitive creativity, we turn our gaze to mental capacities that develop through physical functioning, while remaining distinct from it. One might say that speech is the most abstract function characteristic of movement between inside and outside – other manifestations of which include ingestion of food, bodily secretions, and breathing. However, language is not a substance but an intention – a successful action that expresses a mental movement, which presupposes the potential existence of knowledge that is shared with external others. In cases of severe deficiency, such as acute dyspraxia, deafness, muteness, laryngeal impairment, or paralysis, one meets children who find ways to bypass the damaged physical mechanism and develop a communicative language. It appears that in such cases the physical disability does not disrupt the human desire for communication and the tendency to engage in outward movement, from thought to expression. The children in our care have difficulties with precisely this kind of movement. Anyone who has ever treated ASD patients knows this sense of emotional void, the motion between being astounded by the patient and merged with him and collapsing into nothingness. This motion is most probably a reenactment of the intolerable experience Tustin termed 'precocious separateness', an experience she believes occurs as a result of the innate tendency to excessive fusion with the object (Tustin, 1986).

Nine-year-old *Alon* is a kindergarten alumnus. In psychotherapy, he plays an intense game with various characters. The emerging material touches upon death and the transformation of the characters from kind ones to dark ones. The material appears to be a combination of bits and pieces from various television shows and mythological tales. Alon begins every sentence with the phrase 'now let's pretend': 'now let's pretend that Mozart dies and comes back to life as his own shadow'. At first, it is fascinating, an invitation to a shared imaginary adventure. Reflecting on the play material, the therapist asks herself what is Alon attempting to communicate to her or to understand about himself? Is he exploring the somberness and deadness within himself in relation to his more vital tendencies? As time goes by, the one thing that becomes especially prominent in his play is the endless repetition of the phrase 'now let's pretend', which accompanies Alon's absolute need to tell his therapist exactly which words to use in their game. She is ordered to play only the predetermined parts he assigns her. Loss, moments of joy, disasters and triumphs are all described with a uniform affect. The wondrous words 'let's pretend', imbued with all the joy and richness of the imagination, of the playful movement between inside and outside, words designed to be so communicative – as they presuppose that one has an inner world, that one knows that his interlocutor knows this and that both are able to distinguish this inner world from reality – become an intolerable utterance. Alon's use makes these very words obscure the distinction between imagination and reality, self and other.

When it develops on a foundation of communication, language is a complex system of symbols that is acquired naturally and informally by any infant in a human environment. Creative and communicative use of language relies on symbolization and abstraction. Symbols are arbitrary and abstract signs that represent something in the world or an idea in one's mind and that are different and distinct from what they stand for. Symbolization depends on the ability to bear a certain amount of frustration, which arises due to the gap or the discrepancy between the general symbol and the actual object. It entails the capacity to feel separate from the external world as well as the desire to communicate one's experiences. The kind of language Alon uses does not fully match this definition. His words are indeed shared signs, but their use evokes a sense that inside and outside, notion and action, therapist and patient have been glued together. ASD children commonly resort to such adhesion as a solution for their difficulties in withstanding the frustration inherent in the symbolic gap and the loss inherent in the very recognition of separateness. Nevertheless, in therapy, Alon uses language as an available medium for expressing an experience that wishes to exceed the bounds of his dictatorship of merger, a language that resonates the sharing of thoughts, ideas, and conflicts.

Wright (1991, 129) argues that a necessary precondition for the 'leap towards language' is the need to give up the '*doing*' attitude in relation to the object, in order to make room for an *idea* of the object, so that it could be contemplated. For this to happen, a 'mind space' must be formed between object and subject. Wright represents a widespread approach which identifies a linear and causal relation between the processes of separation and the capacity for symbolic representation. It posits the assumption that the difference or the gap between object and subject is a precondition for the formation of symbols. Wright describes how development toward the capacity for representation entails the infant giving up his constant contact with the physical world of actual inanimate and human objects in favor of a virtual space of meanings. In his view, once the child achieves tolerable separateness from the mother and once separation processes have matured, a space of symbols opens up which ranges from the initial recreation of the object to the full representation attained in the Oedipal stage. This approach may account for the frustrating adhesive experience encountered in treating children such as Alon, whose separation processes are disrupted and who thus try to deny the gap and preclude the emergence of an 'idea about the object'. As Amir (2014) describes it:

> The autistic relation to words much resembles the special use of autistic objects. It is not only non-conventional but also devoid of meaning. Autistic children add the word to themselves as though it were a hard 'piece', thus treating it as a concrete object: not as a signifier of a live part of the body but as an artificial body part. This is the reason for words' immobility as well as their repetitive and rigid use, which yields no new associative movement. [. . .] Autistic language does not allow one to linger within or with something, nor does it afford a place to be in (80–81).

Although the words used by our patients massively function as shapes, as sensory substances, as sources of sensory-auditory pleasure and as instruments of detachment, at times they also seem to be manifestations of transitional phenomena, attempts at contact and even symbolic expressions.

Meltzer *et al.* (1975) describe the autistic dismantling of the sensory mechanism to its primary components, in a way which creates repetition and meaninglessness:

> *rendering an incipient experience meaningless by dismantling it to a state of simplicity below the level of 'common sense' so that it cannot function as a 'symbolic form to contain' (Bion) emotional significance, but can only, in its various parts, find articulations of a random and mechanical sort* (217; emphasis in original).

Alvarez (1997, 236–237) suggests viewing linguistic repetitiveness and rituality in terms of a deficiency or frailty of the innate tendency for mentalization. She emphasizes that the autistic child does not always attack relatedness and meaning through his linguistic or other rituals. Even if the therapist experiences these as attacking the thinking mind and as empty, perverse, fetishistic or masturbatory, this may stem from the fact that these components were never unified in the child's experience. This implies that adhesive, non-communicative language is not an attack but a manifestation of the inherent frailty of the capacity for integration. In fact, difficulties in the formation of language may merely indicate that child's psychic components are still unintegrated. While this fragmentation is not natural, one can assume that by expressing these isolated and repetitive verbal fragments within a relationship, the child is doing more than simply attack. Even though the therapist may experience severe boredom at hearing the same chatter for the thousandth time, the child is exhibiting an attempt at integration and understanding.

Four-year-old *Ofer* is less stable or capable of orienting himself than a baby who is taking its first steps. He has no primary bodily defense responses, such as reaching his arms out. He still wears a diaper, cannot eat by himself and one has no doubt that he still does not experience himself as a distinct unit. He does not speak in any fluent or communicative manner and cannot engage in mutual conversation. Instead of saying 'good morning', he asks 'how to write good morning?' Throughout the day, Ofer usually fills up several pages with words and letters. We believe that he is taking pleasure in these sounds and letters as a form of auto-sensuality, but we gradually realize that his use of words manifests more than that. His speech therapist notes that Ofer takes longer than usual in processing sensory information and thus often seems detached, repetitive or very late in responding. His occupational therapist notes that Ofer has an impaired body-schema. Ofer exists in a space of inconsistent fragments of sensation and tries to pick up threads of experiential consistency in tunes, letters and written words. Every morning, when he asks his parents how to write 'good morning', his question is not completely out of context, it is both appropriate and inappropriate. However, before elaborating about the various ways in which language is acquired and about the unique uses our patients make of it, we will briefly depict the development of normal language.

Language acquisition: a research perspective

Recent studies have shown that the auditory acquisition of language begins before birth and later relies on many diverse tracks of development, such as the cognitive base and the emotional-communicative base, whose overlap, interaction, and integration are a prerequisite for development. Therefore, the widespread contemporary approach is a socio-linguistic one, emphasizing the baby's interaction with its environment and its motivation in initiating communicative intentions and sending messages to its environment in the very first year of life, while it is still pre-verbal. Such developmental approaches do not necessarily equate speech and the production of words with normal language, because the latter is both creative and grounded in the accumulation of experiences in the emotional, social and cognitive domains. Later on, we will elaborate on the notion of psychic spaces in psychoanalytic theory – as a sphere in which imagination, creativity and the capacity for symbolization develop. It appears that the most significant impediment to language acquisition in autistic children stems from their difficulty in integrating and experiencing these domains.

The per-verbal stage lasts from the moment of birth to the emergence of the first spoken word. The baby is born with the ability to scout its surroundings and make sounds, facial expressions and bodily gestures. These behaviors are interpreted as communicative acts, and serve as signals to which surrounding adults respond (Bates, 1979). This period in the infant's life is one of total dependency on being interpreted: the adult is responsible for communicative initiative and his role is to 'symbolize' the infant's behaviors and respond to them as though they were intentional acts of communication. The baby cries before it has any knowledge of communication, but it soon becomes aware of this aspect, as its mother is trying to understand its crying verbally ('do you need a diaper change? No . . . Are you hungry, maybe?') The responsiveness of adults to the baby's unintentional signals and their tendency to interpret and symbolize these in verbal form, help the baby develop communication patterns and gradually link the signals it is producing to their effect on the behavior of surrounding adults. Bates stresses that the exchange of gestures and sounds between baby and mother takes place in turns, which already constitutes a pre-verbal structure.

Newson (1978) describes how, alongside its interest in the human face, the baby is initially preoccupied with the visual exploration of objects, especially those it can manipulate. It has separate, unintegrated schemas corresponding to an interest in objects and an interest in people. Later on, the baby develops the capacity to unite these schemas, which allows it to relate to objects and people at the same time. This integration of 'object-schemas' and 'people-schemas' is crucial and it enables the infant to use the adult as a means for its ends and as an address for sharing its interests and affects. Around the age of nine months, the baby begins to initiate communicative intentions, as he becomes aware of its effect on adults and their potential use as active agents; it employs various means to express its communicative intentions, such as more diverse vocalization and communicative gestures (including 'give', 'show', 'reach' and increasingly elaborate additional gestures). According to Bruner (1978), in this period the infant is able to perform actions together with the adult ('joint action') and can also turn the adult's attention to a third object ('joint attention') – two preconditions for the emergence of the first understood words in normal development.

Working with ASD children brings us in contact with children of various ages who are still pre-intentional. These children either have difficulties initiating communicative intentions or they initiate a limited scope of intentions which only refer to the fulfillment of primary needs (such as asking for or rejecting a certain object), in contrast with more 'social' intentions (such as sharing one's experience and seeking information), which are abundantly present in normal development. In addition, it is important to note that autistic children are less active in exploring and learning about their world and, due to difficulties in establishing joint attention, also engage in fewer communicative interactions. They are thus under-exposed to spoken language in these contexts.

During one of the kindergarten's routine activities, one of the children asks the speech therapist for a toy animal by saying 'elephant'. He initiates the request and she responds. Once he is handed the elephant, he begins a sensory game, which involves smelling and repetitive touch in the nose and mouth areas. During this time, he completely ignores the therapist's presence and is unable to share his interest in the object with her. As soon as he is finished, he asks for a different animal. On the one hand, we witness a capacity for naming the object and expressing a communicative intention in the form of a request; on the other hand, there is apparent difficulty in sharing and, furthermore, in playing with and exploring the object itself.

Various scholars from the fields of language development and developmental psychology have discussed the significance of the emotional dimension to promoting and preserving the child's joint engagement with the adult, emphasizing the importance of emotional mutuality. They argue that the stronger the emotional bond, the longer this triple link (baby-adult-object) can endure. Through interaction with the adult, the child becomes conscious of understanding the 'other' and the existence of different perspectives regarding the same object. Hobson (1993) claims that the capacity for symbolization develops through the child's capacity for interpersonal relatedness, which enhances the ability to contain several different options simultaneously. Greenspan and Wieder (1998) indicated the importance of the emotional aspect in relation to sensory-motor integration. They argue that it is affect which helps link together sensory and motor patterns at increasingly higher levels. At the very early stages of the infant's life, its sense-perceptions are linked to its actions through emotions. For example, when the baby moves its head to direct its gaze at where its mother's voice is coming from, it is because its mother's voice bears emotional significance for it. During the second year of its life, as the baby becomes more physically separate from the mother and as the range of independent exploration increases, alongside its active participation in interpersonal communication, the knowledge gained through its experiences of the world and the various objects, people, and events therein is gradually linked to the words, which represent these objects and events. Cognitively, the baby can now contemplate objects and events outside of its present context and use generalization and classification processes to create prototypes. The child who asked for the elephant, for example, has no regard for the elephant's particular qualities and does not play with it; before he learned to utter the word 'elephant', no matching concept had been established through the accumulation of elephant-related experiences.

At the one-word stage, which begins once the first spoken words have appeared, the child uses words to represent objects and actions in its close and familiar environment. In normal development, these first words are acquired horizontally, that is, they are spread across many semantic fields (people, food, clothing, toys, animals, etc.). Studies indicate that, at this initial stage, children prefer acquiring concepts, which represent objects that are at their disposal (such as 'cap' or 'shoes') or phenomena that are under their control. In ASD children, we tend to witness irregular vocabulary development, which is also evident in gaps between different categories, such as profound familiarity with certain categories – vehicles, for instance, but little to no use of words representing food or people. One often finds that they have acquired abstract and formal concepts – letters, colors, numbers – alongside little use of everyday nouns and verbs. This can be comprehended as a manifestation of the children's tendency to cling onto formal aspects that are divorced of any emotional depths.

The next stages of language acquisition already concern expressions – several words that are joined together to form sentences. In order to construct a creative sentence, the child must be familiar with the syntactic and the grammatical rules of his mother tongue. ASD children have difficulties in understanding and inferring such rules and applying them creatively; therefore, they tend to rely on patterned language which is based on their memorization and rote-learning capacities. The entire phrase is learned as a single unit, without any understanding of its constituent parts. For example, a child who wants to let his mother know he is hungry will not know how to say 'I'm hungry'; instead, he might say 'do you want to eat?' formally relying on another person's sentence or on a text he picked up from a book or a movie, without any connection to his personal perspective. Patterned language acts both as an empty shape, which perpetuates the child's detachment from subjectivity, and as an attempt at communication, which circumvents his innate language-related difficulties. Even echolalia, once considered meaningless sensual speech, is now viewed as expressing the child's desire to continue the conversation.

The following vignette portrays a child with highly patterned language. At one point during the session, the speech therapist suggested jointly 'reading' the books he already knew by heart. The therapist gradually changed the characters in the story to people from the child's own life. In response to this shift to familiar and significant characters, the child began exhibiting a little more creativity and it seemed that his pattern, which was exclusively repetitive at first, now served as an anchor which helped him elaborate his experience and his self-expression. All throughout the year he had trouble participating in the kindergarten dance session, especially in free dance. Many months later, when he was finally able to take part, he said: 'once there was a duck who wanted to dance in the dance session'. He used the pattern from the story to say something about his own emotional experience. Nevertheless, it is important to note that patterned language is very limiting in terms of communication and limited in its capacity to serve as an actual instrument for understanding and expressing new events, experiences, or ideas. Patterned language also acts as a sort of trap, luring us to speak to the child at a level of speech that is somewhat higher than his actual linguistic stage, thus leaving him unable to understand, unprepared for what is about to happen and therefore anxious. This reliance on quoted patterns also makes it difficult for these children to acquire pronouns. Many children talk about themselves in the third or second person, or resort to names to indicate who they are talking about. In normal development, pronouns are deictic concepts, which depend on the perspective of the person who utters them. Both abstract and dynamic, they are acquired during the early grammatical stage, in which one learns to *creatively* form simple sentences, making their acquisition more difficult.

Signals, symbols, dimensions

The question of symbolic representation and symbol formation is at the root of the discussion of psychic development as a shift from relating to material objects to relating to meanings. Throughout history, the fields of literature, philosophy, linguistics, and anthropology have all been preoccupied with the distinction between things, signals, signs and symbols. Signals precede symbols: for a young baby, the approaching voice of the mother may signal the milk that is about to enter its mouth; when it is undressed at sundown, the murmur of flowing water signals the coming bath. The ability to be attentive and make use of signals entails the first inklings of separateness – the acknowledgment that something external to me is affecting my emotional/physical experience. When the capacity for processing sensory information or performing efficient motor-planning is deficient, this also impairs the ability to explore the world and establish a system of signs. These difficulties have both functional and emotional ramifications.

In some of the babies who will eventually be diagnosed with ASD, the ability to recognize signs, which seems so self-evident, will not develop as expected. The anamnesis later recounted by the parents describes a grumpy baby that will not calm down, a baby who – day after day – has trouble bearing the transitions from one activity to the next, who may have picked up no signs from the recurring experiences of its routine and of being interpreted/contained by its significant objects, and thus has difficulties developing a safe rhythm for its existence in its environment. Due to its essential difficulty in sensory/emotional regulation, such a baby may prove more difficult to interpret or contain, initiating a process that may further disrupt the developmental journey toward separateness, which is a precondition for the development of language. Whereas signals exist in the world, informing our consciousness that something is about to happen outside, symbols exist only inside consciousness. They represent occurrences in a separate domain, one of meaning, that is, within a network of links and contexts, which create a dimension of depth.

Eliahu, a five-year-old autistic patient from an ultra-orthodox family, looks out the window of the therapy room into the street and says: 'the redeemed lamp'. The therapist's imagination soars as she wonders what meaning redemption could hold for this boy. Talking to his mother, the therapist learns that every night, as he is lying in bed, she recites this blessing: 'the angel who has redeemed me from all evil, bless the boys . . .' (Genesis, 48, 16). His bed is right under a window which faces a street lamp. The window of the consultation room also faces a street lamp. It seems that Eliahu thinks that 'redeemed' is a name for a street lamp. Does the lamp outside his window give rise to a transitional experience of hazily drifting between wakefulness and sleep, inside and outside, being with a mother/caretaker and being alone? Or is Eliahu simply gluing signals together, because of his difficulty or his refusal to acknowledge their potential for creating meaning? It seems that Eliahu is at the seam between these possibilities: he does have a tendency to glue signals together and avoid dealing with gaps, but it also appears that he knows something about 'in between' experiences and maybe even something about redemption, even if his psyche still does not contain a world of whole, internalized representations.

According to Hanna Segal (1957), the 'transitional object' is developmentally situated between symbolic equation and the more mature capacity for symbol formation. Symbolic equation means that the symbol and the object are identical, serving as a way of dealing with the inability to bear the distinction between the actual object and its representation. The symbol, appearing once the capacity to experience and withstand separateness from the object is established, represents the object and helps maintain its significance even in its absence. The 'transitional object' links reality and illusion, real and represented, present and absent, operating as one of the means for gradually transitioning into the separateness afforded by symbolization. It seems that for the child to relate to the transitional object, it requires a combination of several developmental processes which are at their peak, such as the capacity for introjection, the ability to transfer meaning from one object to another and the ability to link together certain patterns whose relatedness holds a certain meaning for the baby (the softness of the mother and the softness of the blanket, for example). The baby is thus not confined to identifying and linking similarities in terms of objective qualities, rather, its process of identification also entails the subjective emotional experience of its relation to the object.

On the autistic spectrum, we often witness an over-attachment to the physical sensory world. Even when representations are supposedly used, one sometimes notices a certain quality of this use, which indicates the desire to recede back to materiality, to partial-objects and tactility. Bick (1986, 292–299) mentioned an adhesive quality she identified in patients who had difficulties with projective identification processes. Meltzer (1975, 289–310) coined the term 'adhesive identification', a process of identification with objects that entails impaired introjection capacities, as it is not processed in a three-dimensional psyche (there is no notion of space into which one can enter, as projective identification requires, nor is there an internal space in which one can put things, as introjective identification requires). Instead, the pattern governing relatedness and identification is one of two-dimensional surfaces, lacking any depth. The capacities for symbolization and language that develop under such conditions will have a different quality and we will encounter the use of patterned language and displays of playing, which are devoid of transformation.

We return to Alon, who recently began therapy. He is playing a game, which appears to be symbolic: it has characters and a chain of events and Alon is using language. But while the material that surfaces is quite rich, it brings no thoughts to mind. Words seem to be piling on top of each other and then sliding off and disappearing. The therapist finds herself looking at Alon, trying to study him – he is pale, his skin almost transparent, seemingly untouched. His mouth is slightly limp and drops of saliva frequently slide down his chin. Alon does not notice them. The therapist wonders whether he is aware of having an inside and an outside. She realizes that she is pressing her own fingernails into the flesh of her palm while watching him. No thoughts come to mind, only a bodily experience that emerges through skin sensation. The medium that slowly offers an understanding of Alon's experience is the physical one, especially his outermost regions – his skin, his lips.

Alon presents his therapist with an enormous challenge. When we talk about difficulties in communicating, we are not only talking about the ability to initiate the understanding that the Other exists and could be responded to. We are talking about the most essential components of the human encounter. The tendency toward a psychic space, which lacks depth means that pre-conceptions (Bion, 1967b) – the innate tendency to establish a three-dimensional psychic space into which one could project things in anticipation of meaning-generating transformations – are unavailable as the fuel for the most primary communication with the mother. Therefore, even if the mother is willing and able to enter a state of reverie, it is hard for her to intuitively recognize the elements projected into her, assuming that such projections do indeed occur. Thus, the infant's sensitive and sealed-off psyche does not expand and develop as it should. The mother and, later, the various caretakers, feel frustrated and disoriented by their *communication* with the child. The therapist is unable to think, but her emotions lead her to identify with the stifling and empty quality of Alon's experience. One cannot be certain that what one is thinking is correct, but the therapist knows that thinking is crucial, that it is like oxygen, and she will therefore keep searching for any kind of movement between her and the patient – through bodily experiences, through failures and misinterpretations and often through frustration and despair.

In the third year of therapy, Alon is already eleven years old. He is more lively now and his relationship with his therapist is richer and saturated with affect. There is less of a flatness about him and, seeing as he developed a capacity for emotional depth, he tends more and more toward invasiveness as a means for canceling out the gap and the difference between self and other.[2] He tells a story that is laden with characters, no longer resorting to his 'let's pretend'. It is impossible to overlook the immense gap between the extent of the factual knowledge he had amassed and his limited and rigid use of it. One of the characters Alon plays is the epitome of absolute evil, who takes revenge on everyone else. The therapist is ordered to play a variety of characters, including prototypes that are called 'the hoodlum', 'the feminist', 'the saluter' (a boy who obeys whatever he is told), 'the Arab king' and the 'Kibbutz people'. In the game, Alon in the role of absolute evil murders a little girl. He plays his part and then asks: 'what does the feminist say in the feminist language?' He wants the answer to be creative, but he also wants it to state that this vile act was one of male chauvinism. Session after session, for months on end, Alon uses this method to explore 'various languages'. He asks the therapist to sing the pioneer songs of the Kibbutz and to speak in a 'Kibbutz language' while the Kibbutz people are being attacked. When she says, 'okay', he warns her: 'you don't say okay on the Kibbutz, just "all right" '. Will the day ever come when Alon could let the therapist speak in her own language, from her own subjectivity? By dictating the various languages, Alon takes pleasure in the predictable familiarity of what she says at his command, thus avoiding the danger of separateness. Nevertheless, Alon uses the Other in his attempt to understand something else, something that is not under his complete control. Alon acquired speech, but not by developing a capacity for making generalizations, connections and distinctions. Words seem to have been imprinted onto him by his encounter with the world and now, by using them, he is trying – very cautiously – to explore, situate and structure himself in relation to external phenomena.

The therapeutic relationship: probing the gap

How then, can the use of language grow in a psychic organization that tends toward the two-dimensional? The patients we are discussing use a language which may sometimes seem perfectly normal, but lacks the crucial element of 'twoness'. What role is played by multi-professional therapy in transforming the child's use of words?

At four years old, it appears that *Ofer* has difficulties perceiving his body as part of him and as a system which is able to move and change its own condition as well as influence the external world. At six, Ofer is still rather inactive physically, but carries himself with a certain ease – he can comfortably eat and control his bowels. His parents report that at home he frolics about and jumps on his bed. He exhibits independence in his various daily activities and it is clear that he senses the boundaries of his body more clearly. During his first year at the kindergarten, we already noticed that the relationships he established in the various therapies were richer and more intimate than those he established in the kindergarten. We realized that Ofer needs maximal attunement in order to relate. His ability to express his feelings grew slowly and steadily stronger, by virtue of his human relationships and an environment that is constantly holding him and keeping him in mind. In a prolonged and fragile process, Ofer exhibited a tendency to devote considerable resources to deciphering the essence of language. Even before he turned five, Ofer was interested in other languages besides Hebrew. At first, he learned English with the help of programs he found online and wanted to translate everything from Hebrew into English. Some staff members found his preoccupation with English words to be repetitive and hollow, 'inauthentic' and undermining relatedness. Others were astounded and impressed by his abilities.

Many of us shifted between repulsion and astonishment. The staff discussion also revolved around the proper balance between the need to oppose this preoccupation and turn his attention to 'more communicative' activities and the need to try and be attentive to his translation efforts – as Ofer may be using them to try to share some aspect of his experience. While the staff agreed that this preoccupation had a formal quality that was detrimental to relatedness, we also noticed that the admiration of the staff as well as of the other children made Ofer proud of his achievement – an unquestionably communicative experience. In addition, after endlessly repeating words and the letters of the English alphabet, Ofer would suddenly change something, add a word as a personal association that had to do with something that happened at the kindergarten, with a holiday we celebrated around that time or some other event he experienced. In time, he learned several additional languages and his Hebrew became more and more prominent, with long and clear sentences that were sometimes patterned and sometimes creative. Toward the age of seven, he used many words to describe his numerous ailments. He expressed feelings of sorrow, loss and frustration at changes in the daily schedule and at the absence of staff members or friends, as well as longing for past happy occasions, such as a family wedding he attended. He would often repeat some sentence that described a sense of lack, such as 'Tom didn't come today'. We saw how the language he spoke told the story of his fragmentary psycho-physical experience, both in its contents and through the course of its development. It often seemed that he was confined to un-transformable repetition, but at the same time he was using language to try and bridge this gap.

In psychotherapy, following a cancelled session, Ofer was detached, minding his own business, sitting with his back to the therapist and neither initiating or responding to any kind of interaction. It had been a while since he exhibited such behavior in therapy. The therapist said that she felt that he was far away from her and asked him how he was feeling. Toward the end of the session, she expressed her frustration very emotionally and said that she did not know what was going on with him. He replied, 'the password is "oops, I forgot"'. It was a powerful response that immediately reminded her that she was absent from the previous session; he was telling her that he felt that she had forgotten him. She said, 'oh, Ofer, I'm sorry, I really did forget missing our last session'. Ofer moved, let out a laugh and then burst into tears. She shed a tear herself and from that moment to the end of the session there was a sense of communication and intimacy, a feeling that a new quality of being together has opened up.

One can see how the therapist allowed herself to experience the full intensity of her frustration at being detached and unable to think. In an almost desperate attempt at reclamation (Alvarez, 1992), she shared her frustration with Ofer. By this stage of the therapy (second year), their well established and gentle relationship allowed for a rapid reclamation, with Ofer's use of a supposedly patterned and adhesive sentence that he copied from the world of computers, but was actually saturated with emotional content and communication. Ofer is saying that his therapist forgot to come to the last session and even in the present one, she forgot to talk about having forgotten to come. In fact, he is saying that he feels as if he is slipping her mind. Ofer has no access to communicative language like other kids his age and, even though he tends to detach himself and avoid any action when encountering difficulties, he already bears the mark of interpersonal and mutual experiences and this enables him to respond to the therapist's attempt at reclamation and to offer her his emotional communication in its purest form.

At the foundation of our therapeutic-developmental-pedagogic work at the kindergarten lies the recognition that the children we treat need a multi-dimensional containing function, in order for the unthinkable to gradually become thinkable, in order for their copied and adhesive world-words to turn into symbols. Freud's notion of the psyche as a sense-organ (1911, 20) is significant to the emergence of movement toward integration. In many of these children, the capacity for sensory integration is just as impaired as their psychic sense organ, which fails to receive the hints that are the basis for the primary distinction between inside and outside and between sensation and its contemplation. Therefore, it is so important for us to have our therapists address both the distinctions and links in the sensory-motor system and the distinctions and links in the emotional and cognitive system, while deepening the bond between the two.

Four-year-old *Lior* will help us trace the transition from autistic representation, which dictates autistic communication to symbolic communicativeness which facilitates development: Lior sits on his therapist's knees next to the table, his back is pressed against her stomach. He cannot see the therapist, only her hand. He puts a marker in the therapist's hand and says, 'square'. She draws a square for him and he is very excited. In the same manner, the therapist draws a circle, a triangle and a trapezoid and, per his request, she write the words 'ketchup', 'cheese' and 'milk'. Afterward, Lior asks her to write down his name, 'Lior' and then 'my mom'. He looks at the words and for a moment everything is full of emotion and meaning. Then, his gaze suddenly changes and it appears that he is once more fascinated by form alone, by the straight and crooked lines that make up what we call the letter A.

The psychoanalytic exploration of symbolization processes is grounded in the assumption that the psychic growth that enables the emergence of a distinct, self-acknowledging self is related to the reality principle, to the capacity to bear psychic pain and the transition from the schizo-paranoid position to the depressive position. This process inevitably entails psychic turmoil. In Bion's terms (1965), this process involves the ability to transform this psychic turmoil, turning the two holes left behind after the breasts have disappeared into 'things' that can be thought and linked together – instead of being 'nothing', they become a 'no-thing'. De Cortiñas develops this notion and mentions the 'ghosts of no-thing' as the shadows of raw elements that remained in the psyche and had not been transformed into representations (2009, 103). For Lior, his therapist is an actual object that holds and collects him. The therapist's back serves as Lior's support and envelope. Lior is in dire need of these as his body is extremely over-flexible and lacks stability. He has trouble keeping himself seated for extended periods of time. His joints are very flexible and collapse under him like some circus contortionist and even a slight tugging at his leg or arm by an adult may dislocate his joints. In terms of his psychic experience within the relationship, it seems that the interaction enables certain moments of connection in a kind of imaginary electric circuit, with isolated elements developing into an image that is illuminated with meaning – an image of 'my mom', that one can subjectively contemplate. These are not 'ghosts of no-thing', but the potential for meaning is highly fragile and the psyche soon obscures it by withdrawing into meaninglessness and forms.

This motion between meaning and form is prominent toward the end of the therapeutic sessions. In one of the sessions, when Lior is told that the session is about to end, he says: 'sick crying hole'. Lior also says: 'we will say goodbye', 'it's time', 'say bye-bye'. He chooses words that are meaningful in an attempt to represent the pain of parting, but he joyfully repeats them again and again, until they are void of meaning and he seems to take pleasure in the sound and shape of each word. On one occasion, when the therapist informs him that it is time to conclude the session, he seemingly ignores her, lingering in the room for long moments. Finally, he reaches out his arms and she carries him back to the kindergarten. It feels as if he is glued to her body, his head tightly pressed against her breast and his eyes closed, he seems to be closing off all his openings. Stern (1985) mentions a feeling of oneness that is lost through the development of the 'verbal self'. It appears that Lior already knows something about the loss of this oneness, but he is on the verge, debating whether he will be able to bear the dread of separateness. It seems that in moments of crisis, the 'sick crying hole' that he articulated so clearly in the session, overwhelms him with intolerable dread, which impels him to void everything of its meaning, to dismantle and limit his experience of relatedness in favor of detached sensory stimulation.

Literature, poetry, and philosophy contemplate the inability of words to fully represent our experience and the loss inherent in using these modes of expression. The gap between experience and its representation implies an existential frustration that the children we treat seem to experience excessively. The mechanisms of transference and projective identification, which prevail in the therapeutic relationship, seem at times to allow this existential frustration to become somewhat more bearable to a child in psychotherapy. If we were to learn about our patients by using only language, our knowledge of them would have been narrow and limited. The gap between experience and its representation is such that the psyche, in its attempt to bridge it, is challenged to simultaneously bear the knowledge that it is insurmountable and inescapable. Painful as this gap is, the psyche knows that without it we would not be able to relate and/or communicate. De Cortiñas (2009) refers to Magritte's famous painting of a pipe, which features a text claiming 'this is not a pipe': the particular painted pipe is not identical to

The same non-verbal child writes 'not easy'.

the word 'pipe'. There will always be a gap between the concrete and its abstract representation. Normally, this space, this gap between concept and actuality is the foundation of play, creation and development. For our patients, it is unbearable. Nevertheless, these children keep surprising us with their courageous attempts to probe, touch and survive this gap, to explore it and despite everything, to choose words, life and development.

Notes

1 'We walked down the path to the well-house [. . .] Someone was drawing water and my teacher placed my hand under the spout. As the cool stream gushed over one hand she spelled into the other the word *water*, first slowly, then rapidly. I stood still, my whole attention fixed upon the motions of her fingers. Suddenly I felt a misty consciousness as of something forgotten – a thrill of returning thought; and somehow the mystery of language was revealed to me. I knew then that 'w-a-t-e-r' meant the wonderful cool something that was flowing over my hand. That living word awakened my soul, gave it light, hope, joy, set it free! [. . .] I left the well-house eager to learn. Everything had a name, and each name gave birth to a new thought' (Keller, 1954, 23–24). Helen Keller, who was born deaf, dumb and blind, needed professional mediation in order to set in motion a process that would have normally occurred both spontaneously and unconsciously. This is a vital and apt depiction of how the encounter between these raw materials – the sensory experience of the world, the emotional relation to the object and consciousness – weaves the matrix from which language can be born and opens up a space for thinking.

2 After developing his notion of dimensionality and adhesive identification, Meltzer sought a concept that could describe another form of projection-based communication, in which, despite having a three-dimensional view of the object's body, the patient's relation to the object is one vulgar penetration for the sake of dwelling inside it and robbing it of its goodness. He termed this process 'intrusive identification' (Meltzer, 1992).

Chapter 9

The consulting room – the structure, texture and beauty of the object as a path for the development of primal psycho-physical space

Tami Pollak

Autistic children often confront us with a layer of being that calls for a redefinition of 'clinical material' and 'therapeutic communication'. Such novel definitions are not meant to dwell peacefully in the realm of theory, but rather to open a wider range of clinical techniques. Spoken language is preceded by affective expressions and a syntax of gestures, as well as by the less conspicuous channel of projective identification. Nevertheless, autism often distorts even the most rudimentary channels of communication, such as these. In this context, it is important to be mindful of the body as the singular locus where the spontaneous and unconscious binding of physical and mental space occurs normally, motivated by relating and communicating with the Other.

The body is a unique entity that pre-reflectively binds together the material and the mental by being simultaneously both an object and a subject. In order to explore the possible meaning of physical activity as a channel for therapeutic communication, I will begin by defining both physical and psychic space. In due course, I will outline the ways in which autistic children make use of non-communicative actions in the consulting room, eventually constituting both the body and the room as psycho-physical entities that resonate and complement each other, as a basis for development.

While there are several paradigms for discussing the *physical space* of the world, I will retain, in this chapter, a measure of theoretical naivety and simply refer to it as the material world evident to sensory perception and therefore serving as the foundation of our Common Sense. *Psychic space* is defined, for the purposes of this discussion, as the totality of imaginary or conceptual forms we construct in order to organize our myriad signification activities and subjective representations.

In meta-psychology, there have been several different approaches to the body as the connecting link between materiality and psychic space. Klein and her followers assigned tremendous theoretical importance to physical functions as the fundamental link between the real and its representation. She viewed psychic space as 'internal', inhabited by 'internal objects'. Kleinian technique, ever interpretative and metaphorical, sees physical actions as a premature substitute for the associative processes designed to structure internal representations: materiality serves only as raw material for the psyche. Such an approach considers the physical concreteness of the consulting room as irrelevant to the therapeutic relationship, except as the stage for the reenactment of unconscious phantasies. Therefore, the room should preferably be clear and functional, save for the child's personal box, containing certain raw materials.

Winnicott, sensing the problematic nature of this reductive portrayal of psychic space as mere 'internality', shifted psychic space from *inner* to *transitional* space, which houses the paradoxical relatedness of psyche and soma (Winnicott, 1954a) the real and the represented, the objective and the subjective (Winnicott, 1971a).[1] This shift in the conceptual-imaginary location of psychic space also entailed a change in technique: playing came to be seen not just as a substitute for associations, but as an independent channel of subjective experience and self-expression. It integrates sensory-motor and interpersonal experiences through action, allowing the creation of meaning. The capacity for proto-playing such as playfully licking the mother's finger, depends on the infant's ability to bear a certain amount of frustration due to the unpredictable 'not-me' aspect, which lies outside the infant's control yet is not alien to it. This is the very heart of transitional space. Winnicott's contributions broadened developmental thinking in a manner that enabled us to interpret an act like throwing a ball not merely as a metaphor for something else, such as the child's phantasmatic relation to his mother, but as a vital and valuable experience that cannot and need not be reduced to representations. If the unfolding of primary maturational processes has been good-enough, the child comes to therapy already capable of communicating his activity as meaningful and unique, set apart from his everyday experience. In transitional space, each and every aspect of the room, from the door handle to the cluster of dust in the corner, might be colored by unconscious phantasy and transference relations, not necessarily as a projection but rather as the possibility for creative mutuality. Sometimes the walls grow soft or curved; the chair, like a capricious partner, varies in its sensation, and others. Both the structure and the texture of the room are under a paradoxical spell, midway between objective and subjective, material and representation. Since these capacities cannot be taken for granted in working with autistic children, I would like to focus on an additional potential of the consulting room's materiality for accessing a developmental path.

I will present both structure and texture of the consulting room's materiality as the supposedly a-personal channel for getting acquainted with the characteristics of 'space' as preconditioning the appearance of the subject and subjectivity. Structure refers to the room's envelope (walls), openings and holes. Texture refers to the availability of experiences in terms of perceptual parameters such as intensity, quality, and friction, as well as the adaptation of the child's needs to the experiential differentiation between animate/inanimate, permanent/changing, liquid/solid, cold/hot, light/dark, quiet/loud, hard/soft, far/near, in/out, and others. Much like the involvement typically found in the sphere of object relations, the body's involvement in physical space and its encounter with the materiality of the world always entails desire, effort, frustration, rage, surprise, wonder, intimacy, anxiety, strangeness, or any of the other emotions evoked by relatedness.

Lived experience always involves the mental and the physical, which are forever both distinct and intertwined, thus maintaining their potential for mutual enrichment.

A child whose primary development was good enough experiences the encounter with materiality by exhibiting an emerging ability to differentiate between various sensational aspects of materials. In therapy, a child might jump, climb, hold still, exert itself, throw things, be careful, be mindless, scatter about, try out different materials, choose a favorite object or place and much more. These actions, by their very nature, are meaningful as modes of being-in-the-world: through (1) unmediated channels for experiencing aliveness; (2) communication through object-relations; (3) an expression of the simple, yet necessary, need to 'experience' the essential features of physical space before 'knowing about' them; (4) a raw channel of pre-thinking, and so on.

The consulting room as a transitional space, experienced as both internal and external, is a very beneficial place to dwell in. For low-functioning autistic children, unfortunately, it is not so. In the one or two-dimensional autistic space (Meltzer *et al.*, 1975), the mental and physical are either unrecognizably fused into each other, or completely dissociated. My insights regarding the therapeutic potential of the consulting room are drawn from this kind of realization.

Physical action – as embodied therapeutic communication – might be analogically, metaphorically, or symbolically linked to its mental meaning. In order to illustrate the flexible movement between the various possible relations, I discuss the hypothetical activity of a child with the wash basin in therapy. The nature of the relation is not dependent on either the object (the sink, the plug, or the water) or on the child's activity in themselves, but on the subjective experience at a given moment, which may be classified in several ways:

1 *Non-relation*: in the one-dimensional autistic state, the child acts within an experience of 'nobody nowhere', without distinctions, associations or consequences. Acting randomly, the child may pay no mind to the water coming out of it, nor will he turn it back off.
2 *Identity*:[2] one senses a global correspondence between the homogeneous flow of water (strong, dripping, splashing.) and the child's utter sensory fusion with it. A regulation of the flow by the therapist is not meant to be didactic or to aspire to functionality, only to provoke the child's identification with a mental regulative function. Verbal-metaphorical interpretations such as: 'I can see that you feel just like the water' (Alvarez, 1992) are useless. Interpretations referring to one specific quality like 'pouring' or 'dripping', are more likely to be received. A rhythmic reference to the flow's indistinct sequentiality may leave a trace of familiarity in the sensorial matrix, as a kind of pre-understanding.
3 *Analogy*:[3] This state entails a budding experience of heterogeneity, encompassing several qualities or elements, without complete overlap between the self and what is present to the senses. There is some distinction between the

various body parts and a certain inclination to acknowledge 'not-me' aspects. The child gains a primal capacity to feel – 'water in the hole is like milk in the mouth'.

4 *Metonymy*:[4] as the water vanishes into the sinkhole, the child does not identify the mouth and the sinkhole but opens himself to possible variations in their existence as 'holes'.
5 *Metaphor*:[5] this form of organization requires a capacity for subjective association which is dependent not upon sensory likeness but on emotional significance. Opening the tap all the way presents, rather than represents, an experience of 'just like the water, I am bursting every-which-way'. This formation may relate to various layers of experience: desire, anxiety, rage, envy, and others.
6 *Symbol*:[6] Placing and removing the plug may symbolize the emerging ability to control the lower orifices during toilet training.
7 *Concept*:[7] The plugged sink serves as a model for the abstraction of container/contained. At such moments, one may refer to the reciprocity between the sink and the water in terms of general and abstract object relations qualities such as 'overflowing', 'holding', 'empty', and others.

The binding of the physical and the psychic attains different significance through each particular action, varying from child to child and from moment to moment. One parameter of development is the capacity for benign, spontaneous alternation between the different kinds of relations. This flexibility, mediated by the mother, is what engenders a kind of unconscious relational map, which allows spontaneous orientation in space.

To this we may add the fact that the body – the baby's as well as the mother's – is our primary basis for the experience of motion. We shall proceed to examine the body's role by discussing the normal relation between actual materiality and psychic space in the consulting room.

Normal relations between physical and psychic spaces in the consulting room

I would like to delve into the relationship between physical and psychic spaces through the entry-point traced by Winnicott in his paper on primitive emotional development (1945). According to Winnicott, we usually assume that our patient has already adequately acquired the three primary processes of integration, personalization, and realization, set in motion by the mother's concrete handling of the infant's body in the mother-environment (Winnicott, 1962/1965).[8] These processes serve as the underpinnings of psychic development, organizing the relationship between body and psyche, inside and outside, self and object in space in a spontaneous and unconscious manner (Winnicott, 1945).

Winnicott advised us not to take these integrations for granted and they are often the crux of our work with autistic children. He further describes 'abnormal' states where these processes are almost absent or where spontaneous motion between the various kinds of relations mentioned above is barred. Low-functioning autistic children will exhibit utterly mindless randomness and merger, employing adhesive sensory identification. In such cases, the consulting room is reduced to a concrete environment and the therapist must perform miracles in order to turn it into a subjective actuality in which integration, personalization, and realization may take place. How do such miracles happen? By definition, we may never truly know. However, occasionally, the consulting room comes to life for the autistic child as an animistic world where the qualities of physical space and its objects evince strange gravitational pulls, due to the singular encounter between materiality and the child's bodily functions. The notion of therapy is embodied in the language of touch, weight, texture, temperature, smell, sound, solidity, color, etc. This sensory language may then serve as an entryway into the experienced environment, both in terms of object relations and regarding the structure and texture of the world at large. I believe that such miracles are occasionally made possible by the therapist's ability to mind a non-spontaneous long-labored process, potentially associating three elements echoing each other within the consulting room: (1) the child's orifices and (2) the room's openings, as maintained by (3) the therapist's body. The metonymic, metaphoric, symbolic or conceptual relations between eyes, ears, nose, mouth and lower sphincters on the one hand, and window, door, sewage drain, keyhole on the other, enable the deep and meaningful resonance between the inside-outside aspect of the body-container[9] and transferential space. In its endless variations, this triple analogy is characteristic of the manner in which children investigate the actual aspects of the containing function.

I will first consider the room as a 'place' in which all three components resonate with each other, as a basis for therapeutic communication. Later, I will refer to several special objects, such as a blow-up tire, a sink and a hammock, that we have chosen for our consulting room, provoking pre-symbolic experiences and communication.

A place for dwelling

In the first stages of therapy with children with pervasive autism, it makes little sense to consider the room as a distinct place. It is located in physical space and in our mind, but not in the child's experience, whose tendency for undifferentiated globalism precludes any distinctions along the infinite continuum of space, motion, time, and so on. The child walks into the room not even noticing the door as a spatial signifier, wandering mindlessly about as part of his general spatial disorientation, leaving as mindlessly as he came in. One therapeutic and developmental goal would be to provide the suitable conditions for an initial emergence of 'a sense of place'. But what is it that endows a given location in shared space with the quality of being a 'place', laden with the potential for intimacy and belonging?

The developmental importance of finding a 'place' can be imagined in light of the fundamental significance of primal dwelling. Bion (1962) conceptualized the importance of the link between the mouth and the breast, a link which is both vital for the infant's survival and the prototype of the container/contained relationship. We should keep in mind that this link is realized not only through the encounter between intra-bodily functions such as the baby's digestive system and the maternal intra-psychic alpha-function; it is also completely dependent upon the capacity for orientation in external space: upon the good enough primary positioning of the infant body in the mother's lap.[10]

The mother's lap, as a particular location with its own texture, touch, temperature, motion, odor, and so on, is the primary locus in which sensory elements become associated with holding and transformation. It is the prototype of the profound significance the notion of a 'place for dwelling' can achieve through the correspondence between physical sensations and the inception of phantasy and communication.

Therefore, finding a place as a meaningful existential experience facilitates the creation of the inseparable fabric composed of experiences in physical and communicative psychic space. For autistic children, in the initial stage of global experiencing, the room, like the world in general, is unraveled, laden with stimulation and far too heterogeneous. It evades any actual examination and subjective knowing. They often wander aimlessly or adhesively engage themselves with an isolated element, while the process of getting to know the real materiality and the formal structure of physical space remains detached from subjectivity. Still, while the thinking or interpreting subject cannot be cumulatively used by the child, the room, as a stable, predictable and regulated environment is available to him in a significant, albeit limited manner. As distinctions and associations begin to emerge alongside the experience of locating oneself and finding a 'place', the various attributes of that place become knowable.

Clinical vignette: From nowhere to somewhere

During the early stages of our relationship, *David* would wander about in space without any point of reference, living an infinite sequence which perpetuated his mindlessness. Whenever I came to the kindergarten to invite him to the consultation room, he would follow me blindly. But to my surprise, once inside the room, he immediately 'jammed' himself in a corner, refusing to move, staring at me with tremendous anxiety. Sitting lumped in a corner, he tried plugging his ears, but kept raising one hand toward the various noises he was hearing, hypnotized by them. This identical response prevented any distinction between the noises: far or near, inside the room or outside it, mechanical or human, recognizable or vague, external stimuli or internal hallucination. Auditory wandering replaced motor wandering and became just as 'placeless'. Alongside their similarities, these two channels of perception were essentially different: David was utterly mindless about moving in space, while developing an ecstatic sensory identification with auditory stimuli. This kind of overwhelming and isolated sensuality is one of the central mechanisms of autism (Meltzer *et al.*,

1975). The constant flooding of the auditory system led to the impoverishment of the perceptual system itself, hindering its ability to form cross-modal sensory integrations, which are the matrix of mental structure. The auditory intrusions precluded any form of spatial orientation.

Limiting myself to the world of isolated sounds, I point toward the sounds' origins in order to create directionality in our shared space; I mimic the voices I hear in order to signal to David that we share a common auditory world. The room's envelope (walls, windows and doors) had failed to delineate any particular space, or to filter stimuli (Freud, 1895). I try to perform a regulating function by closing the windows, but this merely evokes a sense of futility as auditory penetration remains unaffected. Later on, I use my body and some of the objects in the room to produce sounds, hoping to emphasize an experience of 'here'. Using my affect, I chart the various subjective affects these sounds evoke in me. Some excite me, some confound me and others are completely irrelevant. Through sound, I try to spoke the wheels of David's total auditory identification, trying to insert gaps into the undifferentiated continuum between auditor and auditory stimuli. As time goes by, I refrain from referring to the vague sounds coming from outside, marking them as 'not ours'. Unlike the mouth and the eyes, which may be physically closed in order to regulate perceptual input, auditory input may only be partially regulated through the faculty of attention. I concentrated my efforts on supporting his acquaintance with this function.

One day, David stepped beyond passive absorption and toward initiative – he set out to close the windows and started making his own sounds. Later, he placed his ear against the wall separating the consulting room and the kindergarten, listening to the sounds coming from behind the wall. His facial expression suggested that this is not just another random auditory stimulus but the foundation for a significant subjective perspective. The wall reminded me of the placental sac and a strong womb-phantasy arose in me as I recalled that David had a twin brother. It seemed like we managed to share a phantasy in a common universe, because after a few moments, David uttered his twin brother's nickname. I was excited by the emergence of a new possibility for metaphorical imaginative exploration. We could now avoid falling into the trap of auditory stimuli as a mindless manifestation and bring his intrauterine trauma[11] – which flooded his sensory channels and prevented orientation – into the sphere of meaning and preverbal communication. We slowly stepped away from the wall to find a place in the room, which could be felt as 'ours'. In time, the regulation of the auditory modality led to its integration with other perceptual tracks, helping David realize that he is 'here', in a particular place: in the corner between two walls, underneath a window, as far away from the door as possible. There were still several more steps to take before David could begin relating to the structure of the place he was in, so this aspect will be unfolded later on. I will now focus on the moment when David 'hatched' from his corner, by discovering the hammock that was, naturally, always there.

The hammock – a place and a function

For many years, I have witnessed many therapeutic interactions in which the hammock enables unique, developmentally significant experiences. There are different kinds of hammocks, each offering different kinds of experiences. However, all hammocks provide the potential link between dwelling, holding and motion. Unlike the objects we encounter through vision or hearing – long-distance modes of perception entailing spatial orientation – the hammock, much like the mother's lap, invites us to reside in it as an 'environment'. It invites us to constitute a certain 'being' that precedes not only language but also motion. The hammock in question is a net-hammock, hung from a single ceiling hook and thus more suitable for sitting than lying down. The net-hammock, lacking a shape of its own, traces the contours of the child's body with utmost adaptability. It offers a transition from stillness to motion and its pendulum swing enables the rhythmic amplification of the potential for multi-sensory convergence and sensory integration in terms of touch (both tactile and proprioceptive), vision, hearing, and balance (kinesthesia). Dwelling in this hammock is paradoxical by nature: detached from the ground, it echoes each of the body's motions while holding it, as well as simultaneously drawing attention to gravity as an impersonal element, whose permanence and indifference to human manipulation allow it to serve as a stable point of reference. Additionally, it creates a paradoxical tactile envelope: strong enough to provide an illusion of a persisting envelope while being full of openings, inviting existential openness to what's outside. The nature of this envelope is associated with some of the hammock's additional features, as illustrated in the following vignette.

Out of 'his' corner, David runs around the consultation room, caught in a compulsive continuum of motion, fluttering about like a butterfly. I can't get his attention and his wandering becomes disruptive to our togetherness. On one desperate occasion, I decided to put up the hammock, hoping it would lure David and provide him with a point of reference. David immediately rushes to the hammock, snuggles up silently and 'floats' perfectly limp between heaven and earth. I sit beside him, waiting. The sudden change in his movement, from frenzied to petrified, was alarming. At one point, I entered the space of the hammock to lay my hand on his chest, just to feel his elusive presence. Like a mother touching a sleeping baby to feel its stomach rise and fall as it breathes, I was trying to ward off my anxiety, evoked by feeling the fragility of the line separating between existence and non-existence. There is no communication between us, but as my anxiety gradually fades, I begin to feel sweet warmth. I phantasize that he is resting, nesting, even growing in the hammock, like the popular belief that children grow in their sleep. Why not linger in the stillness of absolute passivity, as if this is how the world presents itself to us prior to any intention or communication? I make no attempt to interact or summon him back to the human world.

During one session, however, for no apparent reason, I become anxious again, feeling that I must pry him from the claws of silence, that I mustn't let him vanish in his bottomless passivity. Unlike Alvarez's 'reclaiming' (1992), I am not offering any particular interaction. In absolute silence, I gently rock the hammock. The hammock provides its own motion, born of the encounter between human application, which forces movement, and gravity which compels every motion downward, toward vertical stillness. This motion thus portrays the dialectic of motor-muscular-active intention and passive-limp dependence. These aspects belong to the to-and-fro motion, taking place simultaneously in the sphere of object-relations and in physical space. So far, David had been avoiding this potential completely. He reacts to the hammock's movement with some gentle movements of his own. Naturally, I add an auditory dimension, accompanying the swing with two tones of the sound 'ahh' – one for the 'to' and one for the 'fro'. In this manner, I am hoping to establish myself as a point of reference, as motion swings away from me and back to me. On one of the runs, I grab hold of his legs, holding them for a minute, disrupting the rhythm, and then let go. This is another kind of common surprise in interacting with swinging children which, in the therapeutic context, takes on a status of 'interpretation in action'. My intervention creates a moment's pause in the hammock's endless pendular motion and David sits up and awards me with a glance.

In this posture, the movements of the therapeutic hammock nourish the potential linking of all three aspects of the body-container: it connects the experience of 'being enveloped' to the metaphorical-transferential movement on the horizontal axis, where the attraction is the relation to the object, and both of these to physical movement in space, whose reference point is gravity, as a force that creates verticality. The hammock is not an exclusive or inherent manifestation of this kind of combination, but it certainly provides an exhilarating opportunity for the convergence of the components of the body-container. This pre-reflective foundation is not dependent on representation or the structures of phantasy, but paves the way for these to emerge. Observing these few episodes from David's therapy sheds light on the hammock as a 'place' where one can existentially 'dwell'. The clinical importance of the hammock varies according to the child's developmental needs, as David's case demonstrates.

In the second year of therapy, while the hammock still served as the core of his experiences, David's activities took on an entirely different character. He still does not speak and rarely addresses me with a gaze or a gesture, but he vigorously swings the hammock, which takes him all throughout our little room, bumping into the walls, the dollhouse and the table, peeking at his image in the mirror as it swings in and out of view, and others. I saw his actions at this stage as an active effort to gain subjective knowledge of the room's materiality, to map it as 'my place'. Action was his only available medium for acknowledging the inklings of structure in his psychic space. On my part, I pointed out with a gesture or a single word the various kinds of relationships I recognized between his body, the therapeutic space, and our communication.

I will now describe *Dan*'s treatment, depicting another aspect of 'dwelling'. In his case, the architectural structure of the room, which first served as an autistic medium for getting acquainted with the formal signifiers of space, is transformed into the grounds on which one may experience object relations in multi-dimensional space.

Dan was a captivating child, despite his impossible behavior that made him very difficult, both for his family and for the kindergarten's staff. He always carried a soft furry doll that was 'stuck' to his hand as if it was part of it, looking into its button-eyes with heart-wrenching hope. While the doll functioned as an autistic object, his desperate attempts to maintain eye-contact with it were reminiscent of a menacing encounter with a dead object, whose lack of vitality cannot be acknowledged. Whenever I invited him to step into the consulting room, he gazed at me enamored, a smile lighting up his face, reaching out his free hand to mine. Except for these isolated moments, he exhibited no desire or ability to adapt to his human surroundings. He had an extremely limited and non-functional vocabulary, which he rarely used, and there was nothing he wanted 'to know'. As soon as he would step into the room, he would tumble himself into a truck's tire tube located at one corner of the room.

A truck's tire tube

The tire tube is another one of the objects we keep in the consultation room, because their physical qualities invite one to dwell and form primary psycho-physical integrations. Its inner cavity is large enough to fit a child and it contains a pillow, a blanket and several shawls of varying translucency. This is a significant variation of the 'soft corner' (a carpet with pillows), common in consulting rooms adapted for children, as it offers an enveloping environment. Made of soft rubber, the tire tube creates an explicit and stable sensory envelope, while being flexible and malleable. In this sense, it is similar to the hammock, yet fundamentally different as it is grounded and stationary. In addition, the child may use it unaided, without experiencing dependence. Like the hammock, many children dwell inside the tube for considerable periods of time and so did Dan.

Dan would tumble into the tire with his back to me. He was alone with his doll: looking into its eyes, rocking it desperately, paying no mind to me as I sat on the floor next to him. Unlike other autistic children, it was evident to every staff member who met Dan that he was engaged in an intense phantasy of object relations. However, his inability to realize it with a living object was staggering. The whole span of his relatedness was rigidly and repetitively confined to the doll, the inanimate object that captured his attention far more than the potential functions of living people. Clutching the doll tightly, Dan would lie down in various positions, pushing against the tube's inner wall with his feet. I accept that physical materiality is his only medium for fanning the flames of his relatedness and bringing forth phantasy from mere matter. I withhold my presence and give him time, but at a certain moment the sensory-motor situation ignites my imagination. It appears that the gap between the lack of actual communication and the intensity of my phantasy evoke an association of being pregnant. Even though I sit behind him, outside his field of vision, I associate the wall of the tube with my stomach by placing my hands on it. As expected, Dan shows no sign of noticing. Throughout many sessions, his actions remain practically the same while I phantasize his pregnancy. I occasionally come up with new conjectures about his intrauterine trauma.[12] As an 'interpretation in action', I perform various movements in relation to my stomach. I try to become a magnetizing force, drawing his isolated activity toward an acknowledgement of my presence. At one point, without any clear reason, I flap the edge of my shirt to the same rhythm to which he is waving his doll around. I get a rare glimpse of his lit gaze. I take this split-second as confirmation of that very basic, yet almost unimaginable, hope: that my actions are perceived. Is this the emergence of a sense of time and space where motion opens up rhythmic spatiality, which in turn invites a depth of meaning? And what kind of meaning would this be – metonymic, metaphoric, or symbolic? Can this space house two people together, or does the extent of his autism preclude the co-existence of two living, unpredictably changing subjects?

Dan is expanding his activities: he licks the tire's rubber wall, scratching it hard with his fingernails, positioning himself differently in relation to the metallic valve, which protrudes like an umbilical cord. At times, I join in from a similar yet different position: I also scratch at the rubber, but unlike him, I run my finger over the 'scars' he left on it,[13] studying them through touch and sight, emphasizing my interest in the traces of this encounter. At a certain point, I feel that it is time to approach the sphere of relating. I scratch the skin[14] on my arm and Dan turns his head. I express pain. The rhythm of Dan's interaction with the wall of the tire changes and becomes livelier. Yes . . . A life-giving longing has surfaced. During one session, he turns his gaze to me. It is already apparent that the tire exists in an animistic world, imbued with transference that is drawing him closer to me. Our mute gestures carry on a significant, profound conversation.

One day, as Dan habitually slumped down into the inner space of the tire, to my astonishment, he pronounced the first word I ever heard him say – 'hole'.[15] He rolled his tongue over his teeth, gums, lips and cheeks and soon added another word: 'Pe' (Hebrew for 'mouth'). At times, his pronunciation confuses me, sounding like the word 'Po' ('here'). Soon, however, it became clear to me that he was deliberately and playfully alternating between 'Pe' and 'Po'. Much has been written about the vital role of the mouth in object relating and in establishing a body-schema. The validity of the essential coordinates of up/down, right/left and front/back is provided by stabilizing the sense of the body as a primary spatial coordinate signifying 'here' as the foundation of spatial perception.

Alongside the joy evoked by a child's first words – let alone a five-year-old autistic child – I want to share with you the unique bliss of these first words (hole, mouth, here). They cannot be reduced to mere naming, but rather testify to the establishment of a subjective experience endowed with depth. Every now and again, Dan drops his eternal doll and turns to examine the eyes and mouths of the plastic animals he finds in the room (i.e., objects that are associated with him but came from me). He is ready to imagine the primary integration between the mouth and the eyes as a basis for the realization of object-relatedness (Rhode, 1977).

This link is also vital for establishing spatial perception since the tactility of the mouth enables the experience of 'here', while the gaze is a long-distance mode of perception, enabling a 'there'. Is Dan ready to replace his adhesive, inanimate gaze, which seizes the doll's eyes in omnipotent possessiveness, with a perception of 'there' as 'not-me'? He bears this 'there' for no more than a few seconds before space collapses. He now watches while I warm and nourish the plastic animals in my lap.

Dan keeps searching for a way to become familiar with his mouth. This kind of pre-reflective experience is still unavailable to him directly. He turns to the *sink drain*, where he finds a flow vanishing inside an invisible darkness. The sink is not a 'place for dwelling' but a potential for the motion of the manifold of relations indicated earlier. If the most primitive experiences are fluid (Tustin, 1981), it is quite natural that children often experience this undifferentiated form of organization through their preoccupation with the flow of water, the sink and the drain hole, while relying on the regulating, organizing and thinking functions of the therapist.

I will not elaborate on Dan's interaction with the water and the sink. Instead, I will continue examining the process of salvaging the consulting room from the tyranny of autistic mechanisms, which preclude the creation of psycho-physical space and its realization in object relating.

Deeper in therapy, Dan took to using the *dollhouse*. For him, this was not a space for a functional or symbolic play, which echoes the domestic sphere. He has no interest in the house's open front. He heads for the side wall, a thin surface with one rectangular opening at the bottom and two symmetrical squares above it. This structure, meant as a door and two windows, serves Dan as a flat face with a gaping mouth and hollow eye-sockets. He endlessly takes his doll in and out through every hole, leading it from one to the other. This activity arouses in him a tremendous and ecstatic desire, which avoids any signification. What potential is lost here? The integration of eyes and mouth, which potentially provides primary perceptual depth, is reciprocally and simultaneously emptied from both perceptual and relational significance. Dan's repetitive, rigid and limited action eventually leads to an unnerving swing, racing from nowhere to nowhere. While it seems that this activity is motivated by its potential for providing a significant psycho-physical organization in the context of object-relatedness, this potential remains unrealized. The tactile and the perceptual fail to resonate, adding up to a zero-sum activity, void and barren of any transformation. At this point, the sense of tragedy that arises in working with Dan becomes extremely intense, resulting from the terrible gaping abyss separating his so apparent desire and drive and his utter inability to grasp the complex web enabling mental or physical depth, crucial for relating and communicating. As long as his relatedness manifested itself through the tactile modality, like his use of the tire, his experience could be directed toward object-relatedness. However, when depth was available, Dan became lost in a boundless space, exiled from his body, his world and my presence. Dan's autistic failure at this stage precludes any resonance between his body, the space of our room, object relations and the sphere of meaning. He will lead us forward in the study of autistic development as it progresses from concrete and isolated sensory elements toward an emergent psycho-physical structure enabling subjective depth.

Structure – envelope, holes, and openings

Just as the body includes a complementary relationship between the skin as an envelope and the orifices as its inherent existential openness, the room, besides the distinctness enabled by the envelope of the walls, also needs the openness provided by structural openings (door, windows) and holes (sink drain, toilet drain and keyhole). All these elements are given considerable attention by children. I will now focus on their significance for the establishment of space in autistic children.

1 *The body envelope and the room envelope – The skin and the walls*: the walls create an inner space that is normally intuitively present. When laden with transference, the walls may be experienced as projections of certain human functions: as a shield against stimuli (Freud, 1965); as a manifestation of the container function (Bion, 1962); as a projection of the gathering function of the skin (Bick, 1968); or as an acknowledgment of the shared therapeutic envelope (Anzieu, 1989) and more. In accordance with these functions, they may also be experienced as exhibiting certain qualities, felt as too thin or too thick, indifferent, rigid, dirty, dissolving, laden with goodness, and so on, they may thus be associatively experienced as identical, analogous, or in metaphorical relation to the physical function of the skin. The walls provide an envelope not through the direct presence of touch, like the tire, or through a tactile-vestibular-proprioceptive convergence like the hammock, but by means of an ontological pre-conception of depth. In the autistic world, walls are first of all an object of formal-tactile inquiry – through licking, hitting, peeling, clinging, and so on. Each quality is sensed separately, dissociated from all others. The therapeutic effort is then focused on producing inter-sensory links, facilitating subjective structure, relatedness and communication. I will now depict another scene from Dan's therapy in order to illustrate the fervent and diverse relatedness-patterns to the consulting room's wall as a flat and stationary element which is transformed into a three-dimensional space, imbued with relational meaning.

   One day, Dan noticed the shadow his hand cast on the wall next to the dollhouse. He was absolutely fascinated by it. He spent dozens of sessions enchanted by this silhouette-show. At first, he was astounded by the very projection of various objects seemingly under his absolute control. In this context, it is important to note that a cast shadow is not a representation, but a presence. At this point, Dan had several words at his disposal and he named some of the objects whose shadows he produced, but it was clear that naming was not the focus of his attention. His eternal doll provided the most riveting shadow. Sitting on the carpet behind him, I reached my hand into casting range in order to be present, even only as a shadow on the wall. In time, a certain relationship developed between our shadows, moving toward and away from each other. The shadow of my hand, which was farther away from the wall, was blurred and I tried to find the right distance for making its contours clearer. This action was supposed to vanish into the rigid repetitiveness of Dan's routine, but instead, it set the space ablaze. In a very crude manner, Dan was now ready to use me as a 'transformational object' (Bollas, 1979) and my movement as a transformational function. Dan was giddy, mesmerized by the effect of distance on the appearance of a shadow. With wondering curiosity, he explored the formation and unraveling of the shadow's clear cut outline, using motion as his instrument. He understood that the range of motion spread between his eyes and the wall and moved his chosen objects like a scientist in his lab. When he brought the doll all the way to his eyes, he lost sight of it; when he pushed it against the wall, he lost its shadow. Being able to produce varying degrees of vagueness in a manner which suited his capacity to bear frustration was his major achievement. Dan was now ready to withstand the tension between the doll's dead eyes, his physical perception which enabled his particular perspective and his mental perspective. He was searching for an attunement that would enable visibility as the basis for relatedness.

'Being' within a space that encompassed a dimension of depth was a startling discovery for him and he kept reaffirming it. I, too, began to incorporate depth in my motion, so that our communication stepped out of the two-dimensional to-and-fro on the wall and into the depth of a space enriched with perspective – both his and mine. At those moments, our communication did not rely on my ability to signify and assign symbolic meaning, but rather on my role as an 'object of perspective' – the active function which enables the spatial integration of the totality of meanings associated with the experience. The shadow, as a manifestation of depth-endowed space, opened up the possibility for metaphorical signification: the formation and unraveling of the shadows became analogous to the formation and unraveling of the experience engendered by the motion of living objects in general and Dan-Tami in particular.

Not long afterward, he dragged the shadow of his doll all along the wall and then sat down in the adjacent corner, with his back to the wall. He curved his back so as to lean on the point where the two walls meet, as they stretched out from behind him, like two arms, long enough to embrace the entire space of the room. From this corner, he turned to me, looking at my face with a bright gaze. I was suddenly charmed by his beauty, wondering if he was also open to mine – the beauty of sharing a world where the miraculous ability to see and be seen (hear and be heard, feel and be felt, etc.) exists.[16] Dan reached out his hands, beckoning me to sit down next to him. It was a moment of radical change. As if in some 'concerto for four eyes', we were creating our meaningful shared space by looking out from two near, yet not identical, perspectives. Joined, but not engulfed in each other, we discovered the depth in which usable objects are born. We gazed at our room, as it spread before us from one horizon-like wall to the other. The flat shadow-kingdom we have been wandering for many months gave way to the appearance of the beauty of the common everyday objects inhabiting the room. The hole was now analogously experienced as a mouth, a sensory junction which became a 'here', a spatial signifier in a shared universe. The establishment of directionality and the structuring of perspective, two prerequisites for subjectivity, allowed us to keep exploring motion as a way of establishing the proper distance for communication that unveils us as mutually discoverable subjects.

2 *Regarding openings*: Windows and doors form two utterly different experiences. While the door invites actual motion between inside and outside, the window invites a perceptual rather than spatial transition. The window faces a 'not-me' outside, evoking a reflective and existential openness to what lies beyond subjectivity. As the clinical material suggests, the autistic child does not necessarily experience the door as a spatial signifier or as part and parcel of the inside/outside distinction inherent in the clinical setting. It becomes noticeable only with the establishment of a three-dimensional organization which grounds the container-contained relationship. The transition to a post-autistic organization finds many children preoccupied with the door, astounded by the distinction made by closing it, repeatedly opening and closing it, locking it, running outside, and so on. These actions are meant to establish the paradoxical nature of the boundaries of the container as closed yet open. It demands the therapist's flexible judgment regarding the child's dominant developmental need at each particular moment, in terms of the container-contained relationship. On the one hand, we must keep the child inside the room, protect the clinical setting, preserve the frail distinction between inside and outside and cultivate the significance of 'being inside'. This will support the formation of inner space, potentially containing representations of absence and introjected objects. On the other hand, at times, only bursting out could produce an experience capable of engendering 'exteriority'. The autistic child cannot become acquainted with the benign movement between interiority and exteriority or between closeness and openness without the help of the therapist. Once this movement has been grounded in phantasy and the anxiety evoked by 'inside' and 'outside' has been worked through, it is likely that the child will lose his special interest in the door. He might peek through the crack under the door or into the keyhole, manifesting limited directionality and perspective, i.e., tolerating the structural frustration located at the heart of perception and the nature of space. These aspects of physical space would, in turn, lead to more highly developed aspects related to the structure of phantasy, which are beyond the scope of the current discussion.

It is important to note the symbolic relation between the perception of spatial organization and the embodied aspect of speech. Before verbal communication becomes central, the rhythm of speech and the manner of vocalization may create a resonating structure, linking physical and psychic space (Maiello, 1997). As an example, I would like to briefly describe an autistic child who was 'wasting' our therapeutic mutuality by placing animals on the carpet in a repetitive and detached manner. At one point, I realized his placement is starting to exhibit a certain structure: a grouping of several animals, a space, another group, another space . . . I soon sensed that this is a pre-linguistic structure. I tap on the tire, next to the animals – two taps, pause, one tap, pause, etc. This establishes a connection between the visual and the auditory, between space and time (as each sound has both rhythm and temporal continuity). Afterward, I sing a song, putting his actions into words, matching the rhythm of my words to the placement of the animals. Language is thereby introduced to the child as a potential form of communication located between the concrete and the represented, between the material and the meaningful.

Summary

This chapter is based on the assumption that a pre-reflective grasp of spatiality, intuitively endowed with depth, is not a synthetic by-product of the self, but rather the a-priori existential condition for the emergence of the self and the creation of meaning. Autistic children exhibit a structural deformation in the intuitive acquaintance with both physical and mental spatial depth, thereby disrupting the potential for realizing even the most basic manifestations of the container-contained relationship. This chapter joins the effort of the last decades to elaborate the description and the conceptualization of the therapeutic setting and the communication these require. Clinically, it focuses on the embodied aspects of the therapeutic communication from a developmental point of view. The consulting room often serves autistic children as the sole space in which the necessary conditions are met for them to start realizing subjective spatiality. Depth is initially realized through dissociated formal actions, casting the fundamental structures of embodied experience and its potential for metallization. When psychic space is unavailable, the physical space and the use of materiality are the child's sole potential for delineating the primary coordinates of psycho-physical spatial structure. The autistic child's perception of the body and the consulting room as psycho-physical subjective spaces does not occur spontaneously and requires the therapist's extensive mediation. This approach, which turns attention to action in the sphere of materiality, opens a doorway to a new understanding of the child's and therapist's actions. The clinical material illustrates the possibility that while being void of transference, it may be laden with meaning on the level of formal, depth-inducing signifiers. For instance, when a child is excited by a visual preoccupation with the line formed where the floor and carpet meet, the therapist must keep in mind that this might be a mere autistic sensory addiction (Tustin,

1981) but it might also be a crude signal, indicating the emergence of a distinct spatial structure in the child's mind, where two distinguished entities form one another (even if these are just floor and carpet). This distinction would remain insignificant unless properly addressed by the therapist, who could then link, through action (in terms of identity, analogy or metonymy), this organizational fragment to the child's subjective experience, which could later be realized in the context of object-relating as well. The therapist's actions – such as wrinkling paper, hitting the wall, softening play-dough, and so on – are often available to child-therapists as a medium for expressing and communicating their understanding of the child's phantasy. 'Interpretation in action' is described as an additional approach to communicating or understanding the child's experience. When mental representations and projective identification are unavailable, the therapist's 'interpretation in action' serves as a precious therapeutic tool, enabling physical presence to illuminate the psycho-physical depth.

This chapter marks the field in which we may sow, by concrete action, the seeds of communication and significance available to some autistic children, so that formal signifiers become the corridor leading to the world in which we live, a kind of prism capturing the refractions made by pre-container signifiers. Directionality, perspective, texture and motion are all mobilized to establish a shared psycho-physical space.

Notes

1 Philosophy saw the emergence of the phenomenological school, in which different thinkers such as Husserl, Heidegger, and Levinas, formulated an ontologically intermediary space.
2 A=B: The child *is* the flowing water.
3 A form of relating in which any member can stand for any other: A=B, B=C, C=D (and therefore A=D as well).
4 This form of relating emphasizes a particular element by replacing it with another in its temporal or spatial proximity. Associatively linked, one may represent the other.
5 An ambiguous relation between two vaguely distinguished elements, sustained by partial overlap. This form of organization requires a capacity for association and subjectivity, which relies not on sensory similarity but on emotional reality.
6 This is the big-bang of psychic space: it requires a certain distance from sensory aspects, as well as the capacity to bear the frustration involved in the disparity between the object and its expression (verbal or otherwise).
7 A form of relating, which requires the capacity for abstraction and generalization.
8 The notion of an environment-mother avoids the dichotomies of transference versus reality, subjectivity versus objectivity or material versus representation and constitutes an intermediary area centered around another subject, the mother. In autistic children, this capacity is very frail, as their sensory-motor experience does not join object-relatedness in the creation of psycho-physical actuality.
9 I have previously proposed the body-container as a primary psycho-physical schema, which describes a potential for experiencing pre-reflective presence, which is embodied in physical anatomy and enables an unmediated realization of psycho-somatic contact/exchange relations (incorporation-transformation-excretion)

between the subject and the world. In the body-container, ontological openness is concretely expressed in physical anatomy, which is a product of structural relations between three axes: 1) the envelope, which relies on the inside/outside distinction enabled by the skin; 2) the vertical axis, which I call the 'frontal spine', unravels this distinction by interconnecting the various body orifices (eyes, ears, nose, mouth, navel, lower sphincters). These invite the world to merge with the subject, while the subject is in turn pushed 'out of its skin'; 3) the horizontal axis of object relations, actualized first and foremost vis-à-vis the 'Mother', as the function which actively integrates various activities into a subjective experiential, communicative and meaningful wholeness. The establishment of the distinction between inside and outside, alongside its necessary and simultaneous unraveling, constitutes the body-container as a space of primal paradoxality. See Pollak (2009) and Chapter 5 in this volume.

10 Winnicott emphasizes the mother's holding the baby in her lap rather than feeding it.

11 During pregnancy, David faced a life-threatening condition and was born prematurely in an emergency procedure.

12 His parents had shared his prenatal history with me.

13 One of my supervisees recently told me of a child who rode his bicycle in the kindergarten's courtyard. At one point, he looked back and, having noticed the tracks left by the wheels of his bike, joyfully exclaimed: 'Sign!'

14 The role of the skin in psychic experience has been extensively explored in psychoanalysis. See Bick (1968) and Anzieu (1990).

15 Tustin described and conceptualized the developmental importance of the manner in which Autistic children experience their mouth as a hole. See Tustin (1981).

16 This ability with which we are endowed is far from evident in autistic space. It is related to an aesthetic dimension which precedes Meltzer's aesthetic conflict. See Meltzer and Williams (1988).

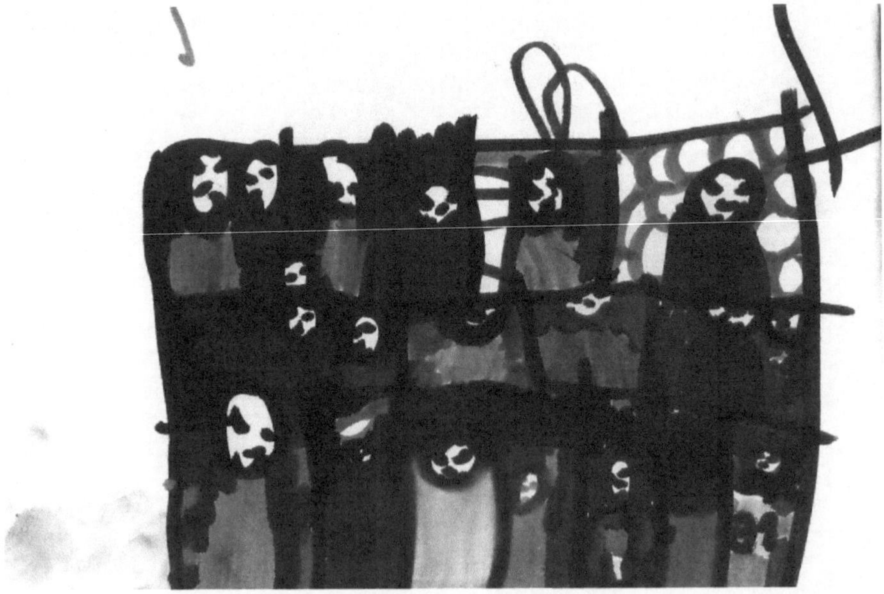

Chapter 10

Dimensions of (non-)space and the autistic state

Edna Lahav

In his novel, *The Map and the Territory* (2012), Houellebecq confesses that he is more or less finished with '*the world as narration*', in favor of '*the world as juxtaposition*' (201; emphasis in original). It seems to me that none are fitter to teach us something about the world as juxtaposition, as density and texture, than ASD patients. They are keenly aware of the sensuous qualities of the world, and are 'experts' in the subtlest characteristics of objects, in relations between different objects in space and in clarity-obscurity relations. I would like to dive into this heightened absorption of the physical aspects of the environment that characterizes autistic states and especially into the unique ways in which physical space is perceived. I will also examine the potential utilization of the room itself in attaining psychic transformation and establishing an internal psychic space.

Adam was a boy with a stiff and tense body, as if perpetually on guard, his face always expressing a kind of adult tension. He could not bear the sensation of clothing on his skin, and would walk around wearing only his underwear, which was stained with feces. He would shout garbled words, probably his mother's name, while hurling himself at the kindergarten fence repetitively and desperately. This Tarzan-child invoked in the staff intense distress.

Adam was in therapy four times a week. The window in the consultation room offered a clear view of the fence. Adam would use a large exercise ball to roll from the door toward the window, so that, in a repetitive linear journey, he would spread his body on the ball and slam into the wall underneath the window. I used simple terms to verbalize his intolerable pain of separation from his mother, how he was torn away from her and how much he wants and needs her. At the same time, I felt tremendous disintegration. In this manner, month after month, the room, the world and I were a sealed gate for Adam, closing in on him and blocking his deep connection to his mother. However, it seems that my continuous, long-term insistence on being with and understanding what was taking place, contributed to a surprising turnabout, which came as if out of nowhere. After many months, Adam stopped hurling himself against the wall. He approached me, leaned down and lay between my legs, curled up and relaxed. He glared at me for a long time and mumbled a few unclear words. The transition from the linear repetitive hurling around the room to a rounded existence of two souls enclosed in an interior, linked by a continuous gaze, was a powerful and astonishing moment for me. It engendered a different, more playful and flexible course for the therapy.

The question I wish to explore is how space is transformed from a confining interior or, alternatively, a boundless expanse to being experienced as a connective medium. For Adam, the wall that I had been at first, gradually became a space that retained, consolidated and even softened whatever was present in it. The inner experience was transformed from closure to a living interior, which included (the notion of) the Other. It became an experience of 'in between', of 'from . . . to . . .', of motion that included both time and space. A real change in transference took place: from an object experienced as an impenetrable wall – surrounding and closing in on him – I became a protective wall, then one with cavities and openings, with flexible mutable features and, eventually, a holistic space offering a place to be in, to become a subject.

In spatial terms, the autistic state has two opposing modalities. One is a petrifying contraction, a kind of gripping solidification that annihilates space, like a vacuum closing in from all directions. The other is an experience of scattering-shattering in a boundless space. These are extreme forms of claustrophobia or agoraphobia, which – whether by an overpowering grip or an intangible and disjointed breach – threaten to destroy psychic existence. Different patients are usually dominated by one modality, but sometimes they exhibit an irregular alteration between the two. Each modality entails different transference and countertransference relationships. The grip brings despair and pessimism, a sense of 'more of the same' and never ending asphyxiation. In its opposite form, the movement is of infinite disintegration, of hopelessness, of floating without focus, meaning or anchor, and an inability to assemble the fragments.

Amir (2013) describes the inverted manner in which a 'pedal point' is used in autistic syntax.[1] Instead of having a pedal point that anchors, supporting the polyphony and in close relation to it, in the autistic universe this becomes a repetitive motif which renders the diverse multiplicity obsolete. In analogy to the spatial conception, we can imagine how, as part of the rupture in autism, one feels immersed in an atmosphere too dense – analogous to a dominant pedal point – or alternatively, soaked in an atmosphere too thin, as in the scattering or evaporation of polyphony. I would argue, somewhat diverging from Amir, that these two modalities are central to autism, like two sides of the same coin.

I argue that we must clarify, in any therapy (not only with autistic states), which *space-object* we represent for the patient. By 'space-object' I mean the manner in which the object's spatial aspects are experienced, namely its measure of density or scarcity, the quality of its openings, its capacity to grant entry or exit, the range of movement it permits within it, and so on. In light of the massive effacement of the spatial potential for growth in autism, therapy and the therapist must become 'expansively crowded' spaces: a paradigm of optimal internal space, with clear boundaries as well as freedom of movement, coherence and focus, and openings for regulation and the encounter with Otherness.

The notion of the container function and the conceptualization of the psyche as an 'area', which things enter or are expelled from, are central to psychoanalytic thought. Klein (1946) contended that processes of projection and internalization are present from the first moments of life. In her view, the psychic mechanism is based on the baby's innate ability to internalize certain experiences and eject others. Bion (1963) adds the function of containment. The mother assembles, filters, removes the thorns and returns what can be returned in a measured manner, thus establishing the baby's capacity for mental processing.

Winnicott emphasizes the unique conditions of the parental environment required for emotional development. The mother's adaptation to the baby, her acceptance of its sometimes delusional world, enables the construction of a unique 'true' self and delineates for the baby a delicate back-and-forth transition from outside to inside. *Potential space* is a liminal space between territories, between self and other, where states of 'me' and 'not-me' co-exist. For the child, this space becomes a point of reference for his interiority and a source of well-being. It is a mental living space, situated 'in between'. Winnicott (1954b) describes states of regression in which the faculty of symbolization collapses. The patient may then experience the physical features of the room differently, to the extent that the couch and the pillows become the therapist's body.

The human body is perceived as a container for substances, with 'many orifices and many cavities' (Babylonian Talmud, Berachot, 60b). The body is a rich source of psychoanalytic imagery. It is an intersection that maintains the psychic matrix but is also separate from it (Pollak, 2009). Bick (1968) saw the baby's primitive psyche as containing components that are not initially connected to each other. The baby needs to have a 'psychic skin' that groups them and gives them shape. It must internalize the object, which protects it and creates a boundary with its exterior. If such protective 'skin' is not formed, a 'second-skin formation' develops – a rigid and impenetrable shield, which isolates the baby from external nourishment. Anzieu (1989) writes of the 'skin-ego' formation, which develops in the baby following the mother's containment function. The mother relaxes, comforts, and strengthens its stimulus barrier. She establishes the 'skin-ego' as a psycho-physical envelope, enabling a sense of security and an ability to withstand pain. The absence of such care gives rise to intense anxiety, an experience of rupture and fear of becoming empty.

It is widely accepted that ASD children have an impaired ability to experience the self – and the Other – as a living container. Meltzer (1975) argues that the impairment of dimensionality is fundamental in autism. He uses a geometric metaphor to argue that 'autism per se' is akin to one-dimensionality, in which it is impossible to separate self from Other, where there is no mental space and the self traverses a series of events that cannot be remembered or understood. Two-dimensionality is a form of mental functioning, which only acknowledges the surfaces of objects. The object is experienced as flat, as only significant in its sensory qualities, which can be adhered to or pushed away. In three-dimensional functioning, the object is felt as a container, and one has a desire to penetrate it and a capacity to project into it. The self too is experienced as containing an internal space and a potential for phantasy. The four-dimensional modality adds continuous development in time. In Meltzer's opinion, autistic children cannot perceive the three-dimensionality of objects. The identification that arises is strictly that of skin touching skin.

Ogden (1989) defined the *autistic-contiguous position* as a mode of demarcating sensory experience, an effort to erect definitions against the fragmentation of sensory integrity. Normally, this modality, which includes the sensory-tactile array, acts in addition to the two positions identified by Klein. In normal circumstances, it provides the demarcation of experience, the 'sensory floor' (Grotstein, 1987) or the 'place' (Ogden, 1991).

However, when sensory experience is unbounded, anxiety arises regarding the violation of bodily integrity. The internal threat is that of leaking, as well as of collapsing, either through auto-sensuousness (i.e., through autistic phenomena and objects [Tustin, 1981]) or through the paralysis of the process of knowledge formation and disruption of the capacity for assigning meaning. The two-dimensional world thus arises as a means of imposing a lost sense of cohesion. The 'sensory matrix' (Ogden, 1991) serves to replace the dependence on the object. Being predictable, fixed, and replicable, it creates a repetitive and sterile universe.

I would like to apply these concepts to the experiences of transference and countertransference in autism and especially to the typical states of annihilation of space or floating in an infinite space. The notion of the one-dimensional point is useful, I believe, for demonstrating these two conditions, bound together as a paradox contained within 'autism per se'. The point is the dispersion and shattering of a fragment in a vast space or, conversely, a confining and hermetic encirclement of a tiny, isolated point. In contrast, the two-dimensional line is an example of the mental functioning of being thrown off an impenetrable wall or adhering to it.

Thinking of Adam, we find that for a long time he experienced me as a sort of cold barrier between him and his emergent need to merge with his mother. Throwing himself repeatedly at the wall reflected feelings of impotence and anger at the intolerable separation from her. The experience is that of an unreachable object, opaque and impenetrable as a wall. The accumulation of projections by means of an Other, who simplifies and verbalizes experience, led to a shift in Adam's self-perception. Experiencing me as an accumulating container, three-dimensional and breathing, enabled the softening and rounding of his body towards the center of the room, into my lap.

Meltzer (1975) considered the experience of the world through one sense at a time, as a primal defense, which he called 'dismantling': mental organization is not integrated and falls into pieces, to the point of mindlessness. In autism, the experience is of a torrent of stimuli, which results in blockage and collapse into activity that is guided by one dominant sense alone. The disruption on the sensory level is indicated by Tustin (1984) who proposes touch as the dominant mode of experience: sight, sound, and even smell, are felt as tactile experiences.

When Adam gazes at me and mumbles continually, he experiences vision as a valid mode of sensing. Moreover, he is connecting various senses together through the simultaneous activation of sight and speech. Thus, he experiences a temporary integration of the frailty that engulfs him. It is not only the envelope that is more cohesive and consolidating; at that moment, my face is perceived as a magnet where everything converges, as an external function that integrates and unifies. Bruner (1968) argues that the baby acquires and learns the art of sensory integration with the help of the mother. Only after some time is it able to simultaneously suckle and look at the mother. She must first become a focal point of attention and containment. The intensity and duration of the reciprocal gaze between Adam and me, as a sign of transformation, lead me to reflect on its spatial significance. Resnik (1995) suggests the therapist's eye as a place for thought and reflection, a window overlooking an internal universe. The therapist looking at the patient is a testament to the creation of space, constituting introspection and insight ('in-sight', as Resnik puts it).

Meltzer and Williams (1988) describe the formation of spatial perception through the object as part of the aesthetic conflict. In this conflict, the mother is experienced as mysterious and out of reach, evoking in the baby a desire to know, as well as knowledge of what cannot be immediately perceived. The mother's interior, which the baby tries to imagine, is a focal point of interest and attraction.

The drive for development, knowledge and creativity, stems not only from the need to represent the absent desired object, but also from the need to explore the existing object. This is the seed from which psychic space sprouts. The beauty of the mother awakens the baby's senses, which are captivated by her appearance. Seeing her uplifts him, in times of exhilaration or inner pain. She is enigmatic and constantly changing and the baby tries to decipher her. While imagining the space inside her, which produces both beauty and obscurity, the baby feels it inside of itself, as a place to which it may withdraw and from which it may act. The baby is driven by a desire to find meaning and to know the mother's interior. The 'solution' to the conflict is the recognition that one can take in the beauty of the world, despite its threatening and mysterious aspect.

This process requires that the mother tolerate the child's desire, as well as the extent of its retreat from her. In the baby, the emergence of this internal space is disrupted if it has difficulties in perceiving or inscribing the mother's figure within itself or in being absorbed in her. However, the key to the internal sense of space is the feeling that the object contains space within it and is accessible and open for exploration. Thus, as long as I, as a therapist, am not experienced as a wall with some degree of flexibility, as a kind of breathing membrane, Adam cannot form the foundation of his psychic space.

The baby may remain without the ability to be interested in the mother, or to tolerate her beauty – and with a feeling of elusiveness, multiple meanings and pain. One possible collapse of such a process is the baby's withdrawal into itself. In that case, the baby will form an 'adhesive identification' with the object (Meltzer, 1975), by which it will have no interior and the object will be two-dimensional. Another possible collapse of this conflict is intrusive identification, or its result – the *claustrum*. Facing acute anxiety about separation from mother, massive parts of the self are projected into the object and become confused with it, the boundaries between self and object are blurred and separation is denied (Meltzer, 1992). Identification with the mother's interior, along with the massive penetration into it, results in a paralyzing and confining sense of space, in which parts of the self are trapped. This trap from which there is no escape exists alongside the threat of being ejected into a 'no-place'. The claustrum is the inside of the object that is confused with the self, which is attacked and breached through intrusive identification. Melzer emphasizes how precarious the process can be: when an autistic patient begins to experience space, he is far from capable of supporting interiority, thought and imagination. In fact, the patient is bound to feel constant dread of being pulled too far, by being dangerously trapped or hurled into a shapeless space.

Dor, who is thirteen and suffering from autism, has been under my care in bi-weekly meetings for seven years. Dor was born in an emergency procedure, due to fetal distress. As a baby, he was very quiet and exhibited motor precision. In time, it became evident that Dor had great difficulties with maintaining eye contact, with abstract understanding and with human reciprocity. His speech, once acquired, was repetitive and monotonous, saturated with verbal expressions of mechanistic preoccupations. When Dor started the treatment, he was drooling, and his body could barely withstand the constant need to use the bathroom. In the small first-grade classroom he had just recently entered, he would throw himself to the floor or jump repetitively. If he managed to remain in the classroom, it was at the cost of uncontrollable fits of laughter or endless burping spells. This constant state of bodily explosiveness and outburst reflected an experience of a porous and weak self, subjected to intense bombardment from the outside. At that time Dor seemed indifferent to me. The only thing that caught his attention was a tiny crack, hidden between the flat floor tiles in my room.

The meetings are filled with long, futile lists of bus numbers. A ball is kicked from one foot to the other for hours on end. Playing is private and confined. When he agrees to play with me, he merely pushes the ball away, never catching it with his hands. My words are similarly deflected as soon as they materialize, often by his own immediate overlapping verbiage. I must insist time and again on keeping him present in my mind; to assume, if only through faith, that my words reach a living and breathing recipient. We develop a routine game of football, whose only possible rules are for me to make minute adjustments and attune myself to him completely, as well as applaud his every success.

My pregnancy emerges. My body is taking up more space in the room. He seems entirely oblivious to the whole situation. When I return to work after giving birth, he fills his mouth with marbles and then hurls them at the floor, proceeding to put them in a container filled with water and scatter them again in the room. I imagine how painful the violence of being hurled must have felt for him in my absence. I also witness his tremendous effort to maintain integration. Dor makes a very basic connection between the soft – the water – and the hard – the marbles in his mouth. He struggles to make connections between painful facts and to hold his sensations together. He maintains an experience of an interior, using the mouth as a locus of consolidation, but it is breached and is scattered outside. Then he picks up a small bag and begins to fill it until it is completely full. He tries to squeeze together my body and his. He clings to me, notices one of my pockets and tries to shove a huge cushion into it. I am shaken, wondering about the transition to this new arena – my body, but I continue to search for meaning. I am excited by his acceptance of this new possibility of containment, even if its expressions are still primal. Further working through the idea of birth (mine, from which he was absent, as well as his own) he talks of Rob, his 'baby', who is 'a child like himself'. He says in broken words, 'every year is one day'. Rob seems to be without any needs, abandoned, incapable of growth and almost outside of time, more inanimate than alive.

These things appear in a massive, strictly ordered configuration, but beyond it, as if through cracks in a wall, I witness short utterances of a different, creative quality. Dor says: 'I am made of iron. I have an engine inside'. He puts a small engine into a soft doll's tiny pocket, turns it on and holds it close, as if finding reassurance in the fixed frequency of uninterrupted existence. Dor is informing me of his mechanical and impaired sense of self. He later describes himself as filled with stench, snot, disease, eruption. I am overwhelmed and shaken by these images. At the same time, I am aware that Dor's ability to express them is indicative of a gaze directed both inward and out, toward a recipient.

Dor oscillated between a ceaseless attack on his senses and precarious mental apparatus and his wish to be impenetrable, undisturbed, machine-like. His body container is damaged, ruptured and he experiences the world as threatening. He is 'made of iron' so as not to feel the painful absence of psycho-physical unity. But once he is able to express it in play and in plain words, he is no longer confined by it. It is then possible to hesitantly begin to recognize existing reality and to maintain, if only fleetingly, a creative relationship with it.

Dor, like many autistic babies, exhibits massive impairment of eye contact, disrupting the prolonged quiet observation of the mother's face, typical of other babies. The mother's face as a mirror that reflects and signifies the child to himself, as a means to the basic formation of the self (Winnicott), as an anchor for regulation and orientation (Stern), as the key to involvement with the world and the aesthetic field (Meltzer) or as the path to the fundamental recognition of Otherness (Benjamin) – of all these the autistic child is deprived. However, I believe that treating ASD children with a psychoanalytic approach restores the centrality of the gaze to their world. The therapist makes herself present in various creative ways, so that the patient can perceive her, take an interest in her and even become immersed in her. Dor's look, completely oblivious to my face, slowly appeared and found its way to me. While it initially felt mechanical and functional, like some object just hanging in the room, it slowly came to reveal a different, somewhat shy quality.

Another factor that allowed Dor to recognize my centrality as an Other, was my pregnancy. My body steadily got bigger, occupying more space in the room. Its motion changed. The additional space within me took a concrete form through my physical changes, through Dor's flickers of understanding that there is a baby in there, my baby – and perhaps, in his phantasy, ours – as well as through his awareness that the impending birth will bring with it parting and absence. Investigating the body and its possibilities of moving in the room became a key factor after returning from child-birth. Dor became aware of my pocket – a tiny space, in close proximity to my body, that had an opening. He stuffed a pillow into it, as if owning this body of mine, that kept changing, while demonstrating an emerging awareness of an interior that can be filled.

In one session, Dor's gaze is caught for a moment in the window and he agrees to tell me that over there, beyond the window, a speeding train is exploding, with people coming out of it. He invites me to watch this through the window, which overlooks a serene garden. I am amazed at this explosive delusion. It is a moment of unfolding catastrophe, but, it is also an extraordinary spatial arrangement that Dor creates, in which the two of us are present together in a shared protected space, watching the horrors outside through the window. Later, Dor decides that we should 'monkey around'. Each of us in turn must choose an object in the room and do something with it. Dor explores the experience of flinging various objects at different parts of his face and looks with interest at me repeating his gestures. He is fascinated by throwing things to different places in the room, watching their flight through the air and their contact with the walls, the floor and the corner where these meet. I become a colleague and a partner, although under restrictive terms, to the exploration of space and the possibilities of movement in it. I become aware of the emergence of flexibility in the rigid pattern, which can now accommodate reciprocity and tenderly welcome novelty and surprise.

In one remarkable moment, Dor discovers a toy drill and embarks on a joyful journey of repairing the walls. He approaches the walls, touching them and examining them closely. He enjoys the phallic drill held in his hand and his ownership of that interiority. It is a constitutive moment in the discovery of the room itself as three-dimensional and in recognizing himself as capable of repairing and mending, of exerting a positive influence on the outside.

Dor's preoccupation with spaces becomes increasingly complex. He has long been preoccupied with elevators: which company produces them? In which buildings are they installed? I try to understand his fascination: while elevators are mechanical and linear in their vertical motion, they are also a space with an opening, located inside another, larger space. Dor vividly imagines himself entering this space, lingering in it, taking pictures and leaving it. The phantasy expands and he is eager for us to leave the room, walk down the street and enter one desired elevator, which is 'locked up' inside a specific building not far from the clinic.

His plan of action is detailed: the 'elevator gang' includes Dor himself, the 'elevator watcher'; whereas I, his 'assistant', am supposed to accompany him in silence, along with a soft doll that he had carefully chosen. We must outwit the hostile 'king of the building', who denies us entry. We need to force open the front door, using various pieces of equipment, all in order to gain entrance and 'obtain information'.

I enable this planning and elaboration of phantasy. A new and exciting Oedipal quality emerges by way of this coveted experiencing of an inside that can be pursued and penetrated. The equipment we need for this operation is inspected and collected in sacks. We are going to throw explosives at the front door, in order to create an opening and allow access to the coveted elevator. We test them on the room's door. Dor covers his stomach and mouth with hard toy bricks, as if turning himself into a wall. Like life collapsing, everything soon becomes tediously constricted and repetitive. Dor demands again and again, uncompromisingly, that we set out. He wants 'outside meetings' and is perplexed by my refusal: 'you have to respect my wish . . . I want to show you . . . I want to see the elevator from inside and out'. Nothing I say is acceptable to him and he is furious at me.

Dor banishes me to a 'ship of fools', condemning me as 'a traitor and a coward', but he keeps seeking my approval. Otherwise, he covers himself in a blanket, holding hard weapons close to his body under the fabric and remains dead silent, as if life suddenly left him. I feel weary and depleted. Meltzer likens autism to a tower without cement. In those moments, I imagine a foundation that has been breached and is now crumbling. Sometimes, when Dor moves away and covers himself in disappointment, a sort of struggle takes place under the blanket. He simulates, quite faithfully, an experience of being trapped, with no escape, and seems to be gagging or laughing wildly. I recognize the creative value of his game, yet I feel genuine concern for his well-being. The space that was once fruitful and refreshing has become petrifying, stifling and claustrophobic for us both.

Facing my repeated refusal to partake in concrete activity, Dor collapses in despair and covers-seals himself against me. I feel drained. We run into a therapeutic dead end, which is, metaphorically speaking, narrow and confining for us both. The presence and avoidance of 'dead ends' in working with ASD patients merits elaboration. I believe that, with these patients, there is a hint of dead end in every session. But the other side of the same coin is that even in situations that seem devoid of meaning, the therapist sometimes develops a vague sense of sluggish mobility. I will now outline the movement that became possible after some time in the same blocked and clogged stage.

I suggest to Dor that we start assigning 'homework'. Between sessions, I am tasked with observing the building where the coveted elevator is located and gathering information about it. I fulfill my obligation and in the following sessions I describe my findings as vividly as I can. I somewhat satisfy his intense desire to include me in his search (for a life-giving interior) and also symbolically mend the rupture experienced between our sessions.

Dor begins to talk about Mor, his friend who managed to blow up the Old City walls while all the 'bad guys' were asleep. Mor, the imaginary friend, appears to be a perfect copy of Dor, with idealized skills and desirable qualities. He succeeds where Dor has failed – in breaching the obstructing wall.

Dor recalls a tent he had at home and I offer him a real tent inside the room. My guiding thought is that this is an opportunity to establish an integrated shared interior, similar to the one he yearns for in the shape of the elevator. We share the actual construction of one interior inside another – a tent inside a room. The tent is built at the start of each session and folded away when it ends. The co-construction involves joining the folded poles, crossing them together and sliding them through the fabric. The sensory-motor effort that this activity requires is arduous for Dor. He fails repeatedly, but is determined to complete it. He is excited by the process, yet, once the tent stands erect, he examines its openings discontentedly and rushes to cover them with blankets before stepping inside. This reminds me of a grave, into which the child disappears. The routine of these sessions – three-dimensional construction, staying in the tent, getting back out and wrapping up – creates a different pace. Staying in the tent becomes less turbulent. Despite Dor's sparse communication with me, I ask him where he wants to put the tent: which direction will the (covered) openings face? where does he want me to sit? Does he want us to talk? Sometimes I get a reply and sometimes a deadly silence. Yet Dor is gradually becoming a subject, capable of making choices and shaping his environment. Paradoxically, it is with a solid physical barrier between us – precluding a direct view – that our conversations become more free. Sometimes I sit quietly and sometimes I describe the room as I see it, asking him about what he sees from inside, what colors, brightness and senses are felt from within.

During these sessions, Dor describes the basement of a house next door to his. He pictures a naked, murderous monkey in there, knives flying through the air, ghosts. The basement door is full of holes and 'you can't see what's inside'. I think about our consultation room, which is located on a lower floor and feels like a basement, and of the intense anxiety that arises now. I ask, 'maybe the basement is just empty?' and Dor answers, 'empty is a trap'.

In light of the heightened sense of vulnerability and invasion, I decide to create a more secure sense of continuity. For the next few sessions, when Dor arrives the tent is already waiting for him, with its openings in the same positions he left it. After anxiety subsides, my room goes back to being a protected and deplorable space. It is again possible to build and dismantle the tent together.

Very gradually Dor lets go, out of his own free will, of the covers that block the tent's windows. He becomes more aware of the openings in the space of the tent, checking to see what is outside by inquisitively peeking through them. He is interested in the differences between hard and soft materials. He is also intrigued by the seams that connect the tent sheets, familiarizing himself with the different surfaces of the tent-object and creating a basic integration of opposites.

In subsequent sessions, Dor begins to perform 'exercises', which he lets me repeat. After some time, he also accepts my suggestion that we repeat each other's 'exercises'. He moves his body in a vital and coordinated manner, inside and outside of the tent, using the door, the windows and the space between the tent and the walls. He also routinely carries around a soft doll, which he bounces from one opening to another, in and out. The movements of his body, as well as of his chosen transitional object, become an important part of the investigation of space.

During one exercise, the tent collapses under too much weight and vigorous activity. For a while, we are left tent-less and we mourn. Later, I bring another, more spacious tent. After some time, Dor invites me in. Our moments together in the tent are very quiet and intimate. The soft doll, using my voice, sometimes wants to join us inside and sometimes prefers to stay outside.

Dor wants me to stay in the old, broken tent, while he dwells in the new one. I agree, shouldering the burden of the broken and damaged, tasting the strangeness of staying inside of it. Later on, he asks me to bring the two tents closer together, while maintaining a dividing barrier between us. Then he wants us to switch tents. My compliance, while avoiding interpretation of any kind, is crucial at this stage. Being contained in an interior with a distinct boundary, beyond which life can be felt, as well as departing from it at a specific moment, evokes images of birth in me. Only after some time, I decide to share these thoughts with Dor. He becomes curious, asking a few questions about birth in general and about his own birth. I answer honestly, thrilled by his multi-layered working through of not only his own birth, but also of the birth of my baby, from which he was excluded. Dor recalls someone who died, and asks with great interest: 'when will you die?' He demonstrates an awareness of finitude.

In one extraordinary moment, Dor narrates dream in an indifferent tone: he is with a friend inside a tent, on the stands surrounded by fans, in a stadium where an intense soccer game is underway. He tells of a goal through which the friends pass. I am thrilled by the dream and by Dor sharing his inner world with me. In his dream, the tent becomes an island of serenity, a refuge from the match. The tent enables the two friends to be together as well as part of the game, in proximity to that masculine environment. It is an inside that provides protection against the outside, but also allows one to be 'within'; an inside that embodies a friendship between two. It leads to (an experience of) the goal, a symbol of transition and growth into an open, infinite, new, and knowable space.

Discussion

For many years, I had been for Dor a deadening 'space-object', a tomb closing in on him or a dangerous trap, a paralyzing claustrum. In the transference relations, I was experienced as an impenetrable concrete wall, preventing access to the faintly discernible world far away. I was a barrier to be breached at all costs. It took a long therapeutic process for Dor to be able to experience me, and my room, as an interior with openings, capable of regulation and containing movement and life. I became for him as that which negotiates inside and outside, allowing both as a function of mediation and transformation.

Resnik (1995) describes one of his patients, Mr. Duval, who would move from interior to interior as if 'bottled' from one body to another. Mr. Duval moved from his mother's house to a train car, to therapist's clinic, unaware of the possibility of moving between outside and inside. At first glance, Dor seems very different from Mr. Duval: he longs to burst open the door – and the entire therapeutic space – and break through into a real external space, which leads to the other, coveted inner space of the elevator. He appears to be able to perceive the transitions between inside and outside, yet these do not seem to bring growth. The creation of a phantasmatic space in the room and its recurring collapse, make me doubt the value of the therapy. Dor decrees that I am to be exiled if I do not surrender to the 'elevator force', if I do not comply silently, and I feel as if I have been exiled from my own capacity for thinking.

I use the spatial images that Tustin (1972) employs in her attempt to understand the nature of autism: the 'black hole' versus the 'incubator'. At the root of Tustin's thought is the elucidation of the meaning of the autistic child's experience of premature separation. For that child, separation from the mother is extreme pain. Tustin likens it to a breast being pulled away from a baby's mouth without warning, leaving in him a 'black hole' (as John, her patient, put it). The hole is an unbearable absence, sucking in and annihilating by nature, which eliminates the possibility of a nurturing connection between baby and mother.

Tustin (1981) writes: 'as therapists, we need to be aware that it is a serious responsibility to lift the autistic covering to disclose the open hole or the unhealed 'wound' beneath' (239). This responsibility means that therapy needs to be a kind of incubation, a psychological 'aid' for basic integrations. The incubator is an enclosed protected space, with stable warmth and a minimal number of openings, allowing careful safeguarding of the life at risk inside of it. Similarly, psychotherapy, under carefully crafted terms, is intended to collect the faint signs of that shaky vitality trapped under the 'ice-cap of autism' (240) and to enable its affirmation.

In Dor's case, I tried to maintain the therapeutic environment by staying in the room and refusing his demand to leave, but this created the bitterness of a confining life-threatening space. Time and again, it felt as if the room turned from a living space into an oxygen-deprived environment for both of us, similar to Dor's primal intra-uterine situation at birth. Finding revival and purpose *within* therapy had a truly rectifying and healing effect.

Dor experienced me as a door on which he bangs ceaselessly. The experience of a two-dimensional wall, from which Dor is forcibly pushed away, is eventually replaced by the possibility of a soft interior. Ghent (1992) suggests 'object probing' as an attempt to penetrate to, arrive at and recognize that 'the metaphorical wall, the other, is a human being' (141). The object might not survive the destruction in a wide range of ways. Ghent illustrates the paradox rooted in the process in the sense that one must destroy the object in order to find it is there: 'you have to knock and knock, try and try, to work at penetrating the other, only to discover that there was no door. The object was always there' (141). This is a discovery, the lifting of the veil. The experience of endless knocking gives birth to the tent inside the room – a space both real and phantasmatic, with an inside and an outside that nourish each other. At first, we build the tent together, but then I am asked to place myself outside of it, while maintaining awareness of and connection to what I cannot see. Ogden (1991) notes that the extent to which the mother tolerates her child's isolation is what enables its transition to states of dialogue. He remarks that when the patient is so massively isolated, the therapist must be very confident in order to become a source of meaningful assistance to the patient. She has to constantly refine and restore her ability to reflect on the patient.

The covers are removed from the tent and it becomes an inside, which Dor is excited to explore. He experiences several points of view simultaneously and thus acquires a sense of depth. Through 'exercising', Dor adds the presence of a doll as well as myself. Three entities are there to experience, each in turn, different angles and rhythms of the room and of 'togetherness'. We share the tent and discover it. Dor 'uses' me, in the Winnicottian sense: I become for him someone with a past (pregnancy) and a future (death), someone who has a world that can be explored and shared.

It is during this period, however, that Dor's anxiety of the void reawakens. The empty next-door basement is perceived as a source of terror and bestial murderousness. This sense of void requires a process of mourning (Klein, 1946). Dor perceives the void as a hole in a densely woven fabric. For him, the void is a 'trap'. In his world, the hole must be filled immediately and so it becomes a dangerous, imprisoning and annihilating claustrum-like space. It is up to me to sew or tighten the holes in our therapeutic framework. I prepare the tent for him in advance. The absence slowly turns from a source of horror into an experience of quiet presence. It is an emptiness from which something new may sprout. In this sense, what takes place not only sets the stage for working through the traumatic experience of birth, but engenders a psychic birth in itself. In Dor's dream, the goal is a means of moving '(in)to', a marker of the transition from one state to another, of the possibility of transformation itself.

The transition is from flatness to depth, from infinite hardness to a potential softness. A psycho-physical space seems to grow more rounded in a process of healing. In describing the 'pulsing room', Levy (2012) remarks: 'as we let go of the visual control of space, as the gaze wanders from focused to scattered attention, so the room grows rounder' (155). In the autistic world, hard objects block and plug the leaky interior, providing it with an elementary sense of cohesion. The hardness is an existential necessity. However, experiencing the outside (in the form of the therapist), so threatening at first, as (also) holding more than hardness, is fundamentally transformative.

Bollas (1978) emphasizes that the perception of form is fundamentally different from that of content. The baby experiences the mother's movements and different facial expressions as a whole. Her aesthetic appearance is before him, alongside its increasingly refined capacity to understand her words. The baby is gripped by his mother's appearance and is embedded in her. The mother is a *transformational object*, which changes the baby's internal and external reality. She is the cause for the baby's transition from one state to another. Therefore, it is not just the object that is introjected, but an entire process. There lies the seed of transformation and the baby's developing sense of self. Accordingly, the therapist's manner of speech, tone, rhythm of breath, pauses, body language, as well as the overall look, warmth, colors and lighting of the room – all of these are of great importance in therapy. Bollas speaks of psychoanalysis as an 'aesthetics of care'. The overall aesthetic layout besides, in front of and outside the level of contents has a decisive impact on the patient.

But what does aesthetic experience have to do with the autistic state? In these patients, the fundamental embedment-immersion of the child in its mother, whether through its steady gaze at her or through its need for sensory regulation, is disrupted. The disruption of eye contact, which anchors and guides relationships, lies at the crux of the autistic disorder. I believe that devoted long-term psychotherapy can put this process of immersion, which allows a fine-tuned working through of the aesthetic conflict, back on course. The process is lengthy and elusive, but may engender a fundamental structural change. It involves a deep acceptance of a space that is external, but also includes the self, as well as deep acceptance of transformation. This means that the self (as well as the Other) has different expressions and exists in a number of different, sometimes contradictory, ways; but it is still coherent enough to be perceived as one, as an agent of its actions.

For ASD patients, the difficulty to think or feel is structural and the therapist's eye can be used as an intermediate zone of reflection. The therapist holds the function of contemplation, acting as a window into the patient's inner world and validating it. When Dor shows interest, first in the crack in the floor, then in scoring a goal and later in my body, even in my death, he signals that he is ready for transformation. It is a structural shift of consciousness toward accepting a world that features time and space.

In *The Mind's Eye* (2010), Sacks tells the story of Sue Berry, who following a medical intervention, suddenly gained stereoscopic vision – three-dimensional vision – for the first time in her life. She recounts:

> One winter day, I was racing [. . .] After taking only a few steps from the classroom building, I stopped short. The snow was falling lazily around me in large, wet flakes. I could see the space between each flake, and all the flakes together produced a beautiful three-dimensional dance. In the past, the snow would have appeared to fall in a flat sheet in one plane slightly in front of me. I would have felt like I was looking in on the snowfall. But now, I felt myself within the snowfall, among the snowflakes. Lunch forgotten, I watched the snow fall for several minutes, and, as I watched, I was overcome with a deep sense of joy (142).

In psychotherapy, I believe that we may witness a sensation of exhilaration similar to Sue's in our patients, as they transition into this new modality. They discover the possibility of existing in deep affinity and connectedness to their environment, as part of it, immersed and thriving in their surroundings.

Note

1 A 'pedal point' refers in musicology to a long continuous bass tone, serving as a substrate for other tones or as a carrier of melody.

Chapter 11

The multi-aged child

Nechama Faber Ben Pazi

Discussion group:

Nechama Faber Ben Pazi – Clinical Psychologist, Meital Ben-Meir – Teacher

The task facing the ASD adolescent or child is to develop in spite of this disorder, and to grow in spite of the gaps in their intellectual and emotional development. The concept of the *multi-aged child* has evolved throughout many years of engaging and observing the complexity of the developmental process by which these infants turn into boys, from boys into adolescents and from adolescents into young men. Several different developmental layers that may reflect different chronological ages may be observed in the multi-aged child. In the first part of this chapter, I will present the *multi-age* theory, which is based on developmental psychoanalytic theories. In the second part, I will illustrate the unique therapeutic practice derived from this understanding of multi-agedness in clinical practice. In the third part, I will demonstrate the application of this clinical understanding to pedagogic-educational work in a high school.[1]

Developmental theories predict the possible and likely changes occurring over time in a human being's physiological, functional, cognitive, emotional and social faculties, as these constantly become more complex, organized and integrated. Such theories describe how change and growth progress in an ordered and relatively cumulative sequence, stage by stage, so that emerging capabilities, skills and future knowledge are grounded in those already acquired. The normal pace of development differs from child to child and from one developmental task to another in the same child, but it always remains within a certain predictable spectrum of difference. Each developmental stage is, to some extent, built on achievements from previous stages and early experiences have a cumulative effect on each child's overall development. Each stage in the developmental process is characterized mainly by a range of events that are typical to that stage, alongside fewer instances of events characteristic of other stages.

At the same time, the transition from stage to stage rests not only on attaining certain milestones of psychic development, but also on a process of maturation, which occurs independently as part of spontaneous human growth. These are universal human maturation processes, which provide optimal windows of opportunity for various types of development. Accordingly, one may say that each chronological age has a range of what can be defined as *age-appropriate* developmental, physiological, cognitive, emotional and social tasks – tasks that are expected and predictable at a certain age.

Since this chapter relies on the premise that development is comprised of an endless number of experiences, any reference to a developmental level as a distinct category is only for the sake of clarification. Maturation processes are at work in ASD children and adolescents and may pull them along the axis of their chronological age. Alongside the developmental forces pushing them forward, their difficulties are always present and so are occasional failures. Development undergoes many twists and turns and its schedule may be disrupted in various ways: age-appropriate development may appear alongside development that is not age-appropriate.

The development of ASD children exhibits difference in a variety of aspects. Sometimes, the rate of maturation is delayed. Sometimes, there is a different starting point, which steers development off its normal course and is already apparent at birth. More often than not, these two factors are closely interrelated. Therefore, at every new developmental stage the child reaches, he is likely to suffer from deficiencies due to congenital factors, inadequate achievements in previous stages and experiential deprivation. Thus, the delays affecting subsequent stages of development simply keep accumulating.

In addition, another aspect of the developmental divergence of these children is the impairment of emotional motivation for change and development. Successful development means having the emotional capacity to endure the change inherent in maturational processes, a change that is not yet integrated into the existing psychic organization. In their deepest sense, normal development processes involve having access to parts of the psyche which are developed enough to allow experiences of separation and mourning for what has passed – which is the very essence of change – as well as including a desire for novelty and a love for discovery and renewal. A weaning baby may mourn the loss of its actual and material connection to the mother, but in exchange it gains an intimacy which exposes it to new experiences: as it leaves the breast behind, it gains access to different kinds of food and can explore new eating experiences with its mouth, discovering new tastes, smells, and eating positions. It can be fed by different people, enriching its world of relatedness. In a 'normally' developing child, the capacity to separate from what is and the capacity to desire and relish what is new are available through very little effort – they are 'self-evident', a part of the life instinct.

For the ASD child, this is not necessarily the case. Some children suffer from impaired motivation for development, while others have motivation but their impaired capacities for working through and adapting to change hinders their ability to use change as an engine of growth. One may even say that the developmental mechanism itself is disrupted in various ways. In some children, these difficulties are at times too much to bear and their impaired motivation turns into acute withdrawal, detachment and disrupted progress. It is often painfully evident that the experience of life, which is supposed to facilitate growth, only deepens their impairment. In many situations, the child or adolescent has to muster up exceptional forces in order to be able to say 'yes' to life and growth.

Since development occurs over time, I would like to briefly outline Meltzer's notion of psychic space in relation to the axis of time and the perception of reality. Let us examine his description of the transition from a 'two-dimensional' to a 'three-dimensional' organization, and from there to the ability to incorporate the fourth dimension as well. In *Explorations in Autism* (Meltzer *et al.*, 1975), Meltzer states that every form of organization entails a notion of space, which informs a distinct relation to the dimension of time. For the purposes of this chapter, we may say that Meltzer ranks the level of this notion of time in relation to the level of development and vice versa.

In the 'two-dimensional' organization of psychic space, perception of self and objects occurs exclusively through the sensory modality, lacking any notion of depth. Objects have no independent existence and thus external reality is precluded. In this kind of organization, time is experienced as circular and closed and there is no capacity for sensing change. There is no historical dimension, only a continuous and Sisyphean present. The 'three-dimensional' organization entails a sufficient sense of separateness for allowing a notion of inside and outside, thus enabling a notion of depth as well as a certain understanding that processes of change occur in time: that events begin, end and evolve over time. In the three-dimensional organization, events that occur in the external world are perceived as dependent on one's inner world. The object can be experienced as 'good' or 'bad', without the person being aware of the projective element of this experience and without them looking for a permanent element in the object, which is independent of their projections. Therefore, the person has notions of time and reality, yet time is perceived as reversible, not as continuous and one-directional, and reality is not independent.

The next step is the relinquishment of narcissistic omnipotence. This relinquishment, which is actualized in post-autistic development, enables the discovery of time as a one-directional element, which accompanies and facilitates hope for change, an understanding of constancy and change and the development of will. This allows the autistic child to experience time as passing independently of his actions and reality as real and actual, regardless of him and his desire for change. He can now accept that changes may occur outside of his control (Meltzer *et al.*, 1975, 227). The three-dimensional organization allows one to begin extricating oneself from timelessness and the reality of autistic presence. This is the post-autistic stage. Attaining the four-dimensional experience is a universal human struggle and is not limited to autistic states.

People with autism do attain (post-autistic) developmental achievements that enable depth understanding, but they keep fluctuating between the less and more developed parts of their personality. At times, the psychic space available to them lacks a notion of time and reality, leaving the person filled with the dread of any process of change, to the point of complete denial of psychic space. At other times, one sees the impact of the emergence of increasingly intricate levels of separateness, of the capacity to understand and bear change and, accordingly, of the capacity to have significant notions of time and reality. In conclusion, development is not uniform and is dependent on the level of anxiety at any point in time, on the attending human environment and the nature of the task.

Let us now return to natural maturation processes. As mentioned above, even children with developmental delays continue to advance in line with the expected schedule, but their progress from stage to stage is anomalous. They reach developmental achievements, but these are incomplete. They tackle age-appropriate tasks, but can only rely on partial previous achievements. Sometimes, due to their resistance to change, they refuse to take part in activities expected of children their age. Sometimes, their profound resistance to life and change makes them distort the developmental task at hand, resulting in functioning that seems age-appropriate but is, in fact, distorted. If we attempt to offer a developmental map of these children, we will find that even at a relatively young age, ASD children (and later adolescents) function at several age-levels simultaneously and with great internal disparity within each developmental layer.

Several developmental levels may be simultaneously active in each of us – this is characteristic of normal development. However, in the course of normal development, we find that the developmental tasks with which one is preoccupied and the developmental achievements one has already attained are clustered around a core of tasks and achievements that match that person's chronological age. Maturation serves as the central axis, uniting the key aspects of the normal person's development. Like a magnet, this axis attracts the various dispositions scattered throughout the different levels and adapts them to its own level. This organizing axis joins maturation processes and developmental motivation around the 'magnet' of chronological age. One might say that once a normal and sufficiently strong motivation for development merges with the natural maturation process, the two jointly create an axis that is organized around the emerging person's chronological age.

One of the significant expressions of chronological age lies in the social sphere. Impaired motivation and social adaptability in autistic children, which causes profound experiential deprivation, also disrupts developmental integration in relation to time. Meltzer's theory of psychic space illustrates how the way time is perceived both reflects a certain level of development and dictates certain development maneuvers in one's psychic world. Meltzer's theory also implies that the intra-psychic attitude towards development is not only a catalyst or an auxiliary for development, but may also act as an impediment.

A person's developmental level is not a mere diagnostic factor which aides our understanding of that person. At any given moment, the developmental level determines how a person experiences what is happening to them and the level at which experience is organized in their being. Later on, the cumulative organization of events in the psychic world will also dictate the capacity to work through anxiety and the capacity to embrace change and development. In *The Interpersonal World of the Infant*, Stern (1985) describes the various stages in the emergence of subjective experience. The first stage, 'the sense of an emergent self', expresses the idea that there is a very early internal notion that is focused on the experience of development itself, independent of its contents. The sense of an 'emergent self' marks the beginning of an awareness of the movement necessary for development and it includes extremely primary and sensitive subjective impressions of the encounter between the 'physical' and 'time'. One source of enjoyment for the infant is the very experience of development and change. This enjoyment is constantly intensified throughout life, regardless of content. This ability to take pleasure in change and thus to aspire to it, is part of the engine of growth that drives one to develop beyond one's current abilities. Any disruption, as partial as it may be, in the development of the sense of the 'emergent self', will affect a person's development throughout life.

As mentioned above, it was this insight that, several years ago, inspired me to coin the term *multi-aged child*: a child situated in various developmental levels in different parts of its being (in terms of personality and functioning) and equipped with varying capacities for coping with the tasks prescribed by its chronological age. This child may keep progressing along the developmental axis, but he carries with him, in an obsessive and encapsulated way, certain incomplete developmental tasks, which still expect change. It is important to distinguish between the kind of encapsulation, which preserves the event until the opportunity arises for transformative emotional interaction and that which is designed to keep out any live or transformative elements – as when a child endlessly repeats the same story or action. Sometimes, this repetition expresses the hope (however faint) of gaining an understanding that would transform the 'event' (which is devoid of time and subjectivity) into an 'experience' (which is embedded in time as a singular occurrence and involves subjective processing). At other times, such repetition serves to block anything new, to avoid any contact with time and forgetfulness. The therapist is often able to touch upon developmental tasks that are 'stuck' in the patient through memory or, more precisely, through an 'event' that had occurred but was not worked through, thus becoming endlessly repetitive. Working through is the developmental task. The experience of working through an external 'event' and transforming it into a represented inner experience, which enables remembrance and forgetfulness, is the developmental task whose completion enables psychic change. I believe that every ASD child carries experiences – or, rather, events – which are preserved, concealed on different levels of mental functioning. However, unlike psychoanalytic theories that speak of the autistic core of the personality or describe the damage caused by such concealed states, these events are indeed concealed, but not necessarily destructively so.[2] In Meltzer's terms, these are parts of the personality that are confined within more primitive (or more fragmentary, depending on interpretation) levels of psychic space and that function in the way that level of development (to which they are confined) allows. Experiences stored in two-dimensional organization can make use of the developmental mental tools appropriate to this organization; however, such tools do not enable the kind of processing required for the transformation to higher levels of organization.

The repetition of a repetitive event with a 'healthy potential' entails a desire for change – some notion of a future that bears some potential for growth. The realization of this growth potential depends on the therapist. In order to extract these parts of the personality from their confinement, the therapist must identify the active mental level and respond with the tools appropriate to it. This is my expansion of sorts of Anne Alvarez's concept of 'reclamation' (1992, ch. 4). The therapist's living function is necessary not only for those states of extreme passivity found in regressive patients, but also for neglected personality parts that became 'stuck' and motionless during development. At the *Frances Tustin Memorial Trust* convention in Venice in 2006, Alvarez spoke of the need to identify the active, healthy mental level in the autistic child and to address it. As I see it, we must take another step further. We must be very precise about the healthy developmental level and offer emotional-existential care at that developmental level while retaining responsive tools that are appropriate to the patient's chronological age.

Some reference to this can be found in Tustin's last article, 'The Perpetuation of an Error' (1994). Tustin strongly criticizes the therapeutic approaches, which engage these parts of the autistic child's psyche through 'regression therapy' – and which means 'let them behave as infants so that they could continue growing from there' (17). Tustin goes on to state that this approach is harmful to children, because allowing regression ignores the fact that in such regressive states, children have no access to the mature tools required for turning this experience into growth. She goes on to state that:

> it makes a difference as to how we handle such material whether we see it dynamically as happening in the 'here and now', alive with new possibilities for ongoing development, or merely as a repetition of past happenings. [. . .] It is not just the recapitulation of an old situation, but a re-enactment of the old situation with something new injected into it. This can bring hope (Tustin, 1994, 17).

Thinking about ASD children in the terms offered by the multi-age theory gives rise to a difficult and profound dilemma, one that has served as a recurrent wake-up call in my work: which of the many developmental levels that the child or adolescent presents to us should we respond to? Once this decision is made, a new dilemma arises regarding the manner of response: if a fifteen-year-old teenager is looking for intimacy as a three-year-old, should we address this need? Or should we instead strengthen his intellectual part, which is more appropriate to his chronological age? Perhaps addressing the early and primary needs, manifest in his search for intimacy, would only increase the incongruity and strengthen the destructive and seductive aspect of autism? And if we do choose to respond in this manner, should we do so with childlike affection, which truly meets his emotional needs, or with the kind of response appropriate for a fifteen-year-old teenager? And how does one respond in a way that is appropriate at fifteen, while still developing those parts that remained 'stuck' at three? This is a constant dilemma, and I will now try to elucidate the reasons that make it so difficult in a twofold manner.

The first reason lies in us, the therapists. It is extremely difficult to hold something so complex for a long period of time. One might almost say that it is contrary to human nature. In order to meet multi-aged needs without creating a common denominator or compromise for a single isolated level of function, the therapist must devote conscious thought and maximal attention. I must confess that, during my work with school teams, I am impressed and even moved to see how the teachers are able to make use of the supervision and embrace complexity and the search for complexity. In doing so, they let go of natural methods, which are closer to the natural intuition that accompanies them in all other life situations. This concession is courageous and not a simple matter.

The second reason lies in the strength of the seductive element of the autistic disorder – the temptation to annihilate the psychic turmoil inherent in any process of change, growth and development in order to attain the peace, calm and emptiness of the inanimate world (Meltzer *et al.*, 1975, 27–28). This 'contagious' temptation leads us as therapists to repeatedly resort to providing care that fails to pinpoint the exact location of the healthy wish for development, making us respond in a way, which is inappropriate to the patient's chronological age.

A nineteen-year-old patient, with whom I have been working for the past nine years, spent many years in a state in which I had to protect him, and myself as well, from being repeatedly pulled into emotional states of disintegration, annihilation, withdrawal; states which tempted me to treat him as a small child. Again and again, I ended up rebuking myself for talking to him as if he were a small child and vowing to stop. The autistic attraction to psychic zones devoid of movement or development, which 'drags' the therapist along with it, is in my view one of the most difficult experiences in working with ASD patients. During the last four years, more and more parts of this young man's psyche were divested of seduction, alongside parts in which seduction has become increasingly hidden and deceptive. He no longer feels 'obliged' to eradicate his own will and is willing to say 'yes' to life. However, it took some time for me to realize that this significant shift had occurred and that I no longer had to be constantly on guard. In certain situations, he would scold and correct me, indicating that he was no longer trying to destroy our relationship and his contact with reality. This adolescent now matches his chronological age in many ways. He is not 'cured', but the main axis connecting chronological age-appropriate maturation with his developmental motivation is now a little more independent, and not only due to my efforts and those of other external caretakers. This increases his chances of becoming independent in the future. This is a huge difference and internalizing, stabilizing and preserving it as an active and readily accessible factor still requires continued daily effort, for me as well as him.

I find that encouraging therapists to identify the healthy parts in these children, while addressing these in an age-appropriate manner, is extremely important. It is the foundation of my clinical practice as well as my work as head of the 'In School' Support System for ASD children and youth at the Association for Children at Risk. For the sake of precision, I would like to stress that I am not saying that we should ignore the underdeveloped and delayed parts. Far from it. We should be more precise, holding this complexity and trying to locate age-appropriate parts as focal points in our work. We should proceed with yet another version of Alvarez's reclamation, which would enable us to invite lost personality parts back to the axis of life through accurate understanding and identification.

In the following section, I will present case studies that feature years of clinical accompaniment of developmental processes; I will then present the applications of the insights described above to the pedagogic work done at the school. It is important for me to demonstrate that the theory that accounts for the cognitive and psychic state of these children is not limited to clinical work or psychotherapy sessions. This is the state in which these children are in and the pedagogic and therapeutic staff they encounter are charged with supporting their efforts to grow successfully, despite the difficulties that are so ingrained in their mechanisms of development and change.

Case study A: Assaf

I began seeing *Assaf* when he was three and have been treating him for the past ten years. Assaf was born at thirty weeks due to non-syndromic Intrauterine Growth Restriction (IUGR), but with massive difficulties. He suffered from indigestion and constipation since birth, refused to eat as an infant and wore thick glasses since he was one. When Assaf came to therapy, he was very weak physically and had difficulty climbing stairs. He seemed smiling and sweet, but would not speak at all when addressed. He uttered no sounds, except for feeble shrieks. He refused to offer any imitations whatsoever.[3] He was treated by several speech therapists, with little progress.

I saw him for preliminary consultation, to determine whether I would be able to help him. For most of the meeting he was preoccupied with arranging toy animals in a line, in a way that gave no impression of any intention. I deliberated whether Assaf might be suffering from mental retardation. Following two minor events, I decided to take him in for therapy. The first event happened when the session ended and we put the animals back in place. Assaf handled all the animals quite indifferently, but saved a family of giraffes for last. He deliberately took his time putting them back in the box and it was clear that he was mentally associating them and considering them as a separate group. The second incident took place during the session, when I was physically close to him. I bent down, more or less to his height, and said something to him. In response, he lowered his thick eyeglasses and stared at me over them. For a moment, I was filled with immense anger and surprise. I felt that he was canceling me out, that he was annihilating my actual existence in his sensory perception. I bent lower to enter the field of vision of his glasses, and said: 'forget it – I'm here'. These two events indicated to me that a thinking person was alive somewhere in there.

Assaf's level of resistance to development was one of the most severe I had ever met. My own diagnosis included a post-traumatic reaction to the IUGR, cumulative trauma due to the protracted developmental difficulties, as well as major tightfistedness. . . . The world was holding Assaf back and, in response, he annihilated any willingness to partake in life. He wanted nothing, asked for nothing, ate nothing and excreted nothing. His lips and anus were both constantly clenched.

During the first six months of therapy, one of the parents was always present during the sessions. I felt that they needed to witness Assaf's first gestures of readiness for psychic movement. The parents, the primary and most important human figures in a child's life, must be present at his 'birth'. The therapist should and must see herself as a mediator between the child and his parents, rather than someone who precedes or replaces them. Only when I felt that Assaf was beginning to develop a tentative distinction between me and his parents, as well as between the two of them, only when I felt that he was able to draw an outline (however loose and feeble) of a distinct human object, did I begin seeing him alone. After a year of therapy, he began to utter sounds, which I patiently collected and which painstakingly slowly turned into words.

At that time, I began to realize that Assaf needed a womb-like environment. He found it very difficult to want to enter, know and conquer the Other. He remained limp and repetitive. I felt that he was yet to fully experience being in a womb – being inside of a mother who offers protection, nourishment and everything that is necessary in order to dare to exist.

But I had neither the ability nor the means to hold him close to my lap, either metaphorically or physically. Assaf would never come within touching distance (and it was only years later that he suddenly jumped at me for a hug). I could not create a musical envelope for him,[4] because Assaf could not even hold a melody. I could barely hold a verbal envelope, because words created such great difference between us and so intensely reminded him of what he did not have, so that he could not rejoice in anything. Assaf needed age-appropriate care that addresses the primal needs characteristic of intra-uterine development. Still, I had trouble identifying age-appropriate behavior in him, to enable me to begin addressing his primary needs from a higher developmental level.

During that time, all Assaf did in therapy amounted to moving objects around the room, to various distances. He would do this again and again, unable to remember what he did in the previous session. I decided to use his attempts to change his environment and to organize things (this disposition for organization later became a positive and useful force in his life) as a stepping stone. It took some effort to define the 'order' he was creating in the room as an attempt to influence the world and me, but that was all I had. At the end of each session, I began meticulously recording the location of the objects he had moved. Twice a week, for eighteen months, he would find the room just as he had left it. I relied on his activity, translating it into attempts to establish continuity, and created a state of consistency which enabled an 'absolute' connection between the different sessions. In that way, we started to create a foundation for experiencing sequence, an experience that requires the capacity to hold the illusion of sequence. Assaf did not possess the tools for holding illusion, nor could he trust another person enough for me to be able to hold it for him. Instead, I relied on my trust in myself and in therapy and thus held it for him.

For Assaf, this was a salvation. His joy was immense. He did not have the strength to re-create my image in his mind in every session and this created the sense that I was renewing for him conditions which no longer existed. The trauma of developmental arrest constantly returned, since he lacked the right tools for development. Time after time, Assaf was pushed forward unprepared, with his efforts coming immediately to a cruel ending. The conditions I created in the room enabled him to register a new possibility for development.

Naturally, after eighteen months, Assaf no longer needed this external enveloping sequence – namely, my arranging the room just as he had left it at the end of each session. I found myself forgetting to record the room's arrangement after sessions ended; I sometimes rearranged the room but not very carefully and, eventually, one might say that it was a 'life-saving forgetfulness' that caused the dissolution of the artificial sequential conditions I had created.

Over the years, Assaf developed the ability to conceptualize and recreate in therapy the experience of developmental arrest, the experience of death and the anger and vengeance that had stifled all his joy and his desire to grow. During one session, as Assaf lay down and played dead, he managed to say that his mother was the one who saved him. Many sessions later, in the same death-like position, I told him that if he opened his eyes for a moment, he would discover that he was alive and he opened his eyes and laughed. Today, at the age of thirteen, his speech is highly developed and he is independent and extraordinarily talented in various manual tasks, but still suffers from learning disabilities, social difficulties and loneliness. The constipation has since disappeared and his cheeks have begun to blush with libido and desire. As years went by, it became evident that Assaf was suffering from significant developmental delay, but not autism, and when he reentered the developmental track, when he began saying 'yes' to life, in many ways he began being 'reintegrated' into the axis of his chronological age.

I have been Assaf's therapist for a long time, but the above vignette is taken from when he was a small boy, before his diagnosis was fully clear, when Assaf was actively refusing to grow and thus virtually avoiding any relation to the dimension of time. In an imaginary way, I could say that at the time Assaf was 'un-aged', that there was no chronological age to which we could relate or on which we could rely. In order to pull him toward development, I engaged those psychic and behavioral parts in him that did not exactly match his chronological age. The key quality that singled them out as a potential axis was that they contained tiny elements of psychic movement.

Compared with Assaf, Moshe is an example of a person who is constantly negotiating the existence of time in his life. Moshe preserves concealed parts of his experience, which render his psychic existence multi-aged. In order to witness the manifestation of multi-agedness, one must often observe the child, the adolescent or the adult after they have already lived through several years of life.

Case study B: Moshe

I first met Moshe (now twenty-three) when he was four and a half years old. I worked with him for three years in ASD kindergartens and later in my private practice. This year is our nineteenth year in therapy together. Only at the age of seven and a half was Moshe able to share with me the name he had given me in our first few years of therapy. During those years, he called me 'Ni-Nechama'. In our first session, I introduced myself by saying 'Ani Nechama' (Hebrew for 'I am Nechama') and he combined the two words into one, resulting in 'Ni-Nechama'. I do not wish to dwell on the reasons for this, but to focus instead on the fact that it took more than three years since this incident for Moshe to possess the sufficient tools to be able to observe it from without and tell me about it. Finally, I was there as Nechama, not 'Ni-Nechama', and he was able to introduce the historical dimension – the dimension of time – into our conversation.

Moshe witnessed most of my life history, events and changes. I met him shortly after getting married and he accompanied me throughout three pregnancies and births, as well as several office relocations. The following is an example that illustrates Moshe's experience of time: when he was ten, I moved my clinic from Tel Aviv to another city, no doubt a massive change. Then, during a session at the new clinic, Moshe asked: 'how is Nechama who stayed in Tel Aviv?'

In order to understand Moshe's response, we need to indicate several different levels of development, which are only distinct for the sake of discussion. At the most primitive level, that of the 'environment-mother': 'Nechama' is not a distinct object, she is part of the room, part of the environment. Therefore, there must be two 'Nechamas', since there are two rooms. Another developmental level is expressed here as the hallucinatory solution, which seeks to avoid the loss that change entails by splitting into two 'Nechamas': one that remains unchanged and one that represents separation, separateness and change.[5]

This mechanism was so massive that it was also manifest in his sensory apparatus. I found that at the end of each session, while I carefully practiced an actual separation (properly saying goodbye), Moshe would squint, creating two Nechamas and avoiding separation from a single Nechama, who exists independently outside of his inner world. When I realized what he was doing, I reacted by saying that he was 'very rude' – that he was trying to 'ruin me' in order to avoid having to say goodbye. In response, Moshe burst into an authentic laughter, came close to me and said, quite unexpectedly: 'I love you'.

The conclusion I want to draw from this story is that Moshe had a tendency to linger in several developmental layers simultaneously. He knew that the office had moved and was developmentally capable of understanding that I had a single, rather than a double, existence. In fact, many parts of Moshe's personality parts could be characterized as post-autistic. In previous years, when my clinic was in Tel Aviv, the level of change was tolerable and this double existence never came up. But leaving Tel Aviv emphasized separateness to the point of becoming a frightening sense of alienation, so that Moshe withdrew to a more primitive level of organization, a level that eliminated change through the triumph of apperception over perception, by eliminating external reality in favor of hallucination, even on the actual physiological level, as we have seen above.

If we examine Moshe's statement from the perspective of his capacity to internalize time and temporality, we find that he regressed to a circular conception of time in order to avoid recognizing any process of separation. However, one of the consequences of a circular notion of time is life without memory.[6] A circular notion of time prevents the transformation of a present 'event' into a memory and a past 'event'. Moshe belongs to that group of autistic children/adolescents/adults who preserve entire sections of their lives not as memories, but as present occurrences. The ability to remember depends on the ability to forget. Many post-autistic children carry with them parts that their autistic experience has sealed off as a continuous present and that have remained so even after they have moved to the post-autistic stage. Their abilities range from being able to process and transform experience into memory to states in which the event cannot be processed and continues to occur through endless repetition.

I will now describe a clinical example by which I will also address the dilemma of choosing a therapeutic path that addresses both the developmental and chronological ages. When Moshe was six years old and still in kindergarten, an extraordinary event happened one day. His regular escort in the taxi that drove him to the kindergarten was absent that day and Moshe had to sit out the ride next to an unfamiliar escort – a friend of the driver.

Thankfully,[7] I no longer remember what exactly happened that day, except that something took place. For the next few years, Moshe would repeatedly tell me of this event (to the best of my recollection, not immediately after it happened, but I am uncertain). He was very frightened by the change in his taxi ride and spent years describing (with far more detail than he usually gave) the driver's friend, who was lying in the back seat and 'really scared him'.

For several years, this event resurfaced. My interpretations were that this represented how Moshe's persecutory experience was created by a changed reality, the fact he was left unprotected and that I, too, was not there to protect him, etc. I have always treated this event and its experiential consequences at face value. Over time, however, I developed the ability to think about that situation more deeply and, as often happens when one is working through, external factors helped break through the circular organization of time and introduce a linear dimension.

Properly dealing with what is concealed, with an 'event' which was experienced years ago and was still governing the patient's attitude towards anything similar or anything in the same emotional category, requires us to interweave those 'events' into the patient's 'here-and-now'. Discussing what happened is not enough and may sometimes even be harmful. The patient is seducing me to discuss events that happened *in the past*, but speaks of them as happening *now*. When I naively responded to him and discussed those events, this very conversation confirmed his experience that these past events are still happening. This would nourish his psychosis, confirming his annihilation of time. For this reason, from a certain age, I made sure to occasionally break his direct speech and say, jokingly or with sarcastic bluntness, that what he was saying was impossible – I would 'ruin' or 'break up' his story.

Therefore, when Moshe mentioned a certain teacher, seducing me to fall for the illusion that he was describing a memory, even though he was living it as an ongoing present event, I would surprise him by saying: 'but she's retired already'. In response, he would simultaneously scream at me and burst out laughing. When he would inform me that he was going to marry some figure from his past, I would playfully reply that she was already married. In response, he would swear at me, throw a tantrum and laugh wildly. Moshe laughs because of the encounter that was created and he is grateful for having been rescued from his petrified capsulation. But he also screams because at the same time he is full of refusal and inability to cope with change. My role as a therapist is thus to add the wrinkles of time to his stories, as part of the attempt to make him conform to his current time and age.

When Moshe was about seventeen and a half, he moved into a hostel, which was a positive and most welcome change. It started with Moshe's impressive and age-appropriate request to move away from his parents' home and live with his peers: 'I am autistic and I want to be with people like me'. I will not discuss the move itself, which was traumatic, but it did provide us with the opportunity to work through the taxi incident on a new level. After some time there, Moshe told me that a new tenant was going to join the hostel. In his repetitive and unregulated manner, he shared with me his plans, his imaginings and his anticipation. That is to say, he repeated sentence fragments from which I was able to derive an experience and conceptualize it in words, which he then used to continue with the story. He eagerly anticipated the imminent arrival of the new tenant, which indicated to me that he had already internalized the possibility that change could be an opportunity.

In the next session, Moshe came and laid down on the couch, as he often did when he was in distress, and said that the guy had not come. However, that was a thought he could not hold. His massive instability and inability to hold the experience of absence were the focus of our work during that period.[8] Moshe is unable to hold the absence of this new tenant as a thought and it lingers as a physical wound. However, he has a surprise for me: as if out of nowhere, he tells me that some stranger came to the house and lay down on a bench at the entrance. I was astonished, because of the resemblance to that mythological story about the driver's friend, who lay on the back seat of the taxi. Daringly, I decided to say that in my opinion there was no such person at the hostel. I told him that the fact that the new tenant never came created a hole in the picture Moshe imagined.

He imagined a new friend arriving, a picture was created and the world was supposed to match his thought. Regression to two-dimensionality means that there is no correspondence between a person's mind and reality; it entails the profound expectation for complete agreement between the external reality and the internal image. The man who never came created a hole in that picture. In response, Moshe goes 'crazy'. He laughs wildly and shouts: 'there is a hole in the picture! There is a hole in the picture!' It takes him a few minutes to calm down, but he still insists: 'there was someone there'. Explaining, I reply that we have plugged the hole in the picture, the hole that turned into a thought.

Two or three more sessions revolved around this subject – whose recurrence attested to Moshe's wish for growth and development – allowing us to return to the story of the ride from age six: once again, Moshe is talking about what happened during the ride as if it was happening now. But I mention the possibility that perhaps the incident never happened: maybe the escort really failed to come, creating a scary *hole*, but no scary *man* was actually there. I was glad that I had an opportunity to link these two events. Linking different periods of time enables the kind of internal work that includes memory and desire. Memory – because there was work and internal working through, and desire – because there was a wish for growth and development, for the inner world to become the center of experience which examines and discovers the world of actual reality.[9]

We then went through a long period in which this experience was worked through and only after a few months was Moshe able to let go of his hallucination. At that point, I could safely say that I believed no one was there and he would burst into laughter, able to share his distinction between events where someone was actually there and those where there was 'just a hole'. Today, he is already clever enough to be able to tell me when he experiences something as a 'hole in the picture'.

To me, the beauty of this story is that the presented events, provide an age-appropriate coping mechanism that suits the capacities of the child's mental and emotional age, and can be used to cure events that have remained concealed in early developmental levels and in frozen age layers. Hallucination has become a manipulation of reality, which already entails a higher level of organization and the ability to hold communication as well as the anxiety caused by absence – in other words, to hold separateness alongside a desire for development.

This case illustrates working on those parts that have remained concealed and stuck in earlier levels of development, as well relying on present forces in order to extricate them from their confinement. My insistence on age-appropriate functioning and tools[10] is manifest in my demand that Moshe commit to the level of integration required by a notion of reality appropriate to later ages as well as in the humor, directness and bluntness I applied in confronting Moshe with psychic processes. If we do not insist on age-appropriate thinking, we will be placing these children and adolescents at the mercy of time-annihilating mechanisms, which essentially hinder any development.

The multi-aged child, who continues to live on several age levels at once, requires us to apply *contemporary* treatment to the child he once was and whom he continues to live out in endless repetition. In Moshe, the old wound is alive right now and demands healing and development. This wish is a healthy one, but it corresponds to an earlier developmental stage and remains concealed. For years, it only emerged destructively. Now, after the intra-psychic conditions have slowly changed (and maybe after the therapist has sufficiently matured as well) and healthier contact could be made with the wound – which now appears in its contemporary guise – we see the potential for healthy engagement with this wound from the past.

Case study C: dealing with multi-agedness in school

Special-needs classes for ASD children within mainstream schools in Holon span from the first to the twelfth grade across five schools. The case presented takes place during high school years, a time when multi-agedness manifests itself in full force. The students in the special-needs classrooms exhibit considerable diversity, which makes working with them extremely complicated. This diversity is expressed in many areas, including learning disabilities, difficulties in communication and gaps in emotional development levels, in functional capacities and organization. The school strives to strike a balance between tailoring a personal program, which emphasizes the singular way of helping each adolescent, and focusing on the group's common denominator.

As part of our emphasis on age-appropriate tasks, we encourage those behaviors and tendencies in our students that are 'normative' for their age group. These include regarding their age group as a point of reference for proper, permissible and even smart conduct; independence, even rebelliousness; developing personal opinions; and beginning to detach from their dependence on adults.

The attempt to stimulate independence, personal opinions and even rebelliousness is extremely complex with these adolescents, who are often unmotivated, infantile or in need of such intense prodding, that one hardly remembers that they have the energy of teenagers. The staff faces the difficult challenge of engaging them, encouraging their growth and maintaining their dignity in an age-appropriate way.

Ido, sixteen-years-old, is a handsome boy who looks just like any other boy his age. He is endowed with exceptional charm and his longing for relatedness is moving and evokes empathy in others. He is often interested in others, sometimes even from a thoughtful and friendly position; he is alert to changes and ready to compliment others and applaud their achievements. Ido appeared to possess good communication skills, but a closer look revealed that he was making maladjusted use of these: he would repeat the same mantras and questions for many months, often eager for the answers and reactions of his interlocutors. Sometimes it seemed that he was simply clinging to the speaker's voice, completely inattentive to the contents of the conversation. Ido usually smiles during any communication and conversation, regardless of content. He even smiles when he is scolded (sometimes it seems as if he is unaware of his smile and sometimes it appears that he simply enjoys hearing the admonishing voice and becoming addicted to its sound). Ido uses repulsive behaviors as means of communication; he has bad hygiene and suffers from severe body odor. He does not shower and refuses to change clothes. In addition, he often picks his nose or reaches his hand down to his groin and then smells it, etc.

Ido has many learning difficulties, some of which stem from fundamental difficulties in remembering and being able to maintain a sequence of organized bits of information. His memory is mainly applied to social contexts. Ido has a personal study plan, which allows him to express his abilities and experience success through a variety of memory aids.

Phenomenologically, he presents delayed development of age-appropriate experiences of sequence, rhythm and continuity. Unsurprisingly, alongside this delay, he has many difficulties with separateness and relatedness. It sometimes seems that his inner world is not sufficiently inhabited and that he reacts with tremendous panic to the void he experiences every time separateness emerges. As a result of this panic, he interprets separateness as a loss of the self and the other. Separateness means not only rejection, but even mortal danger. This understating is a direct extension of his learning disabilities and developmental deficiencies.

Over the years, Ido adopted several methods for creating the experience of a continuous self, in order to be able to feel that he exists: using his own body movements, intentionally provoking reactions, imitating the movements and tone of voice of a powerful other and clinging. Ido always finds someone to cling to. Usually, this kind of relatedness is unsuccessful, and he is in fact desperately glued to someone – someone he hates, someone whose attention he craves and someone whose disappearance he dreads. In class, we saw that once he acted unacceptably and provoked the teacher's reaction he often relished her admonishing tone and secretly started mimicking her. This mimicking enables him to secretly cancel the differences between them. In a joint staff discussion, we realized that Ido needs the response of the Other in order to feel that he exists. This, however, posed a serious problem, because Ido mostly knew how to provoke angry responses, which made him feel extremely anxious and detached. To overcome this detachment, he would cancel his own existence and merge with the Other. While needing another person in order to feel that he exists is a positive thing, Ido's communication difficulties and developmental delays distorted the expression of this need.

Ido needs a lot of positive reinforcement in order to be able to feel safe, welcome and loved – feelings that motivate and facilitate both his academic and behavioral achievements. At the same time, however, his destructive parts, the parts that make him cling to others and cancel his own abilities – that hinder his development and learning – must be met with clear and unwavering boundaries.

We realized that we had to find an age-appropriate way to meet his earlier developmental needs. We elected a response pattern that would enable us to set boundaries for his destructiveness without pushing him toward the kind of reaction that eliminates separateness and enjoys being admonished with a drugged smile. Whenever Ido did something that merited a scolding, when we knew that his reaction would be to eliminate separateness, the teacher would put him in his place and then immediately attend to him and calmly remind him of who she was and ask him who he was. She would then offer him a choice of several small temporary assignments. The emphasis is on *choice* and on providing Ido with a task to *perform*. Our sense was that at such moments what we needed to do was reinforce his sense of self, through choice and performance, thus not complying with his elimination of the self and the other.

This is an example of an immediate intervention, which we complemented with a personal work program that included starting various collections. In our view, constructing personal sequences would reinforce the experience of sequence. Ido responded wonderfully to activities such as joining many links to create a single chain. In time, he was able to hold more complex processes of collecting and grouping, as well as communicatively sharing his successes with others. The scope and significance of these projects grew steadily: the first involved collecting and 'publishing' the family recipes of the school's special education students; the last – the pinnacle – was creating a booklet of methods for dealing with stressful situations. In order to compile and put together this booklet, Ido collected and documented his own stressful experiences, as well as those of other special education students, and came up with various solutions for these all by himself.

During the three years Ido spent at the school, he made significant progress and overcame many emotionally complex challenges. Although his progress is still incomplete, one can certainly state that he is capable of enjoying the good things that happen to him and even to partly trust certain friends. It seems that he also has a little more faith in himself and in his right to be happy.

Gladly, we can trace a direct relation between these changes and his learning processes and abilities. We have also witnessed their impact on his willingness to learn, as well as on his increasing ability to understand and remember. Ido is motivated to develop and progress in both the academic and social spheres. He is able to listen to the staff and learn from his conversations with them and, gradually, to feel safe and welcome as well.

In conclusion, this chapter began with the 'task' facing the child or adolescent who grows up with a developmental disorder. It went on to describe the 'task' facing the therapist and the teacher, who try to mobilize age-appropriate capabilities in the child or adolescent in order to overcome archaic difficulties that remain locked up, devoid of time and place. Alongside this 'task', I believe that we can also note the 'gift' received by all those who work with these children and adolescents over the years. It is a gift that provides an opportunity to explore the numerous and simultaneous layers of human psychic development; a gift that enables us to trace and retrace the notion of hope in the various layers of time.

Notes

1 This chapter is based on a workshop given at the Shaked Kindergartens conference. Meital Ben-Meir contributed to the conceptualization of these issues and their presentation at the workshop.
2 An exception to this rule is offered by Rosenfeld (1997, ch. 9), who describes 'autistic capsulation' in Holocaust survivors as a means of self-preservation and suspension, pending the recovery which enables new enlivenment.
3 An intensive and relatively rare phenomenon.
4 It is sometimes possible to use music to create an enveloping environment, which lightly touches the patient's experience without over-emphasizing its 'not-me' aspect.
5 I have refrained from making do with 'separateness' for two reasons: first, because in the world of psychoanalysis this word is highly saturated and must be used with caution; second, because it is critically important that we understand just how catastrophic and significant actual separation is for ASD patients.
6 Living without memory is both a result and a cause of a circular notion of time.
7 As Moshe now allows the space of forgetfulness.
8 This task of leaving home and moving to a hostel is age-appropriate (since eighteen is when young people usually leave home – and so did Moshe, in his own way).
9 Bion's (1970) recommendation to conduct therapy without memory or desire is extremely important, but it is only relevant to the developmental layer in which memory and desire already exist as a given foundation. Autistic children avoid 'catastrophic change' (Bion, 1965) by eliminating the various dimensions of depth, which are at the core of the distinction between perception and apperception.
10 It must be taken into account that, at twenty, this gap is far more serious in those who have remained in lower developmental levels and with fewer age-appropriate parts.

Bibliography

Abelin, E. L. (1975) 'Some further observations and comments on the earliest role of the father', *International Journal of Psychoanalysis*, *56*: 293–302.

Abraham, K. (1923) 'Contributions to the theory of the anal character', *International Journal of Psychoanalysis*, *4*: 400–418.

Alvarez, A. (1992) *Live Company*, London: Routledge.

Alvarez, A. (1997) 'Verbal rituals in autism: The concept of autistic object and the countertransference', in T. Mitrani and J. L. Mitrani (eds), *Encounters With Autistic States*, London: Jason Aronson.

Alvarez, A. (2012) *The Thinking Heart. Three Levels of Psychoanalytic Therapy With Disabled Children*, London: Routledge.

Amir, D. (2013) 'The psychic organ point of Autistic syntax', *Journal of Child Psychotherapy*, *39*: 3–21.

Amir, D. (2014) *Cleft Tongue: The Language of Psychic Structures*, New York and London: Karnac Books.

Anderson, R. (1992) (ed.) *Clinical Lectures on Klien and Bion*, London: published in association with the Institute of Psychoanalysis.

Anzieu, D. (1989) *The Skin Ego*, New Haven, CT: Yale University Press.

Anzieu, D. (1990) (ed.) *Psychic Envelopes*, London: Karnac Books.

Ayres, A. J. (1970) *Sensory Integration and the Child*, Los Angeles, CA: Western Psychological Services.

Bates, E. (1979) 'The emergence of symbols: Ontogeny and phylogeny', in W. A. Collins (ed.), *Children's Language and Communication: The Minnesota Symposia on Child Psychology*, *12*: 121–155.

Beebe, B., and Cohn, J. (1998) *Faster Sampling Rates Reveal Mother-Infant 'split-Second' Facial-Visual Contingencies*, New York: New York State Psychiatric Institute.

Beebe, B., Jaffe, J., and Lachmann, F. (1993) 'A dyadic system view of communication', in N. Skolnick and S. Warshaw (eds), *Relational Views of Psychoanalysis*, Hillsdale, NJ: Analytic Press, *23*: 61–81.

Beebe, B., Jaffe, J., and Lachmann, F. (1994) 'Representation and internalization in infancy: Three principles of salience', *Psychoanalytic Psychology*, *11*(2): 127–165.

Beebe, B., Jaffe, J., and Lachmann, F. (1997) 'Mother-infant interaction structures and presymbolic self and object representations', *Psychoanalytic Dialogues*, *7*(2): 133–182.

Ben Bassat, S. (2017) *Prenatal immune cell relations as a prototype of object relations*. Paper read at the annual EPF conference 'The familiar and the unfamiliar', The Hague, Netherlands, April 2017.

Berry, T., and Brazelton M. D. (1970) *Infants and Mothers*, New York: Delacorte Press.

Bettelheim, B. (1967) *The Empty Fortress*, London: Collier-Macmillan.

Bick, E. (1968) 'The experience of the skin in early object-relation', *International Journal of Psychoanalysis*, *49*: 484–486.

Bick, E. (1986) 'Further considerations on the function of the skin in early object relations', *British Journal of Psychotherapy*, *2*(4): 291–301.

Bion, W. R. (1962) *Learning From Experience*, London: Maresfield Library.

Bion, W. R. (1963) *Elements of Psycho-Analysis*, New York: Aronson.

Bion, W. R. (1965) *Transformations*, London: Heinemann.

Bion, W. R. (1967) Second Thoughts: Selected Papers on Psycho-analysis. London: Karnac Books.

Bion, W. R. (1967a) Attack on linking, in: *Second Thoughts: Selected Papers on Psycho-Analysis*, London: Karnac Books, p. 93–110.

Bion, W. R. (1967b) A theory of thinking, in: *Second Thoughts: Selected Papers on Psycho-Analysis*, London: Karnac Books, p. 110–120.

Bion, W. R. (1970) *Attention and Interpretation*, London: Tavistock Publications.

Bloom, L., and Tinker, E. (2001) 'The intentionality model of language acquisition', *Monographs of the Society for Research in child Development*, *66*(4): 1–101.

Bohleber, W. (2002) 'The development of trauma theory in psychoanalysis', in S. Varvin and T. Stajner-Popovic (eds), *Upheaval: Psychoanalytic Perspectives on Trauma*, Belgrade, Serbia: IAN, pp. 207–234.

Bollas, C. (1978) 'The aesthetic moment and the search for transformation', *Annual of Psychoanalysis*, *6*: 385–394.

Bollas, C. (1979) 'The transformational object', *International Journal of Psychoanalysis*, *60*: 97–107.

Bollas, C. (1987) *The Shadow of the Object: Psychoanalysis of the Unthought Known*, New York: Columbia University Press.

Brickman, H. R. (1993) 'Between the devil and the deep blue sea: The dyad and the triad in psychoanalytic thought', *International Journal of Psychoanalysis*, *74*: 905–915.

Britton R. (1989) 'The missing link: Parental sexuality in the Oedipus complex', in R. Btitton, M. Feldman, and E. Oshonosy (eds), *The Oedipus Complex Today: Clinical Implications*, London: Karnac Books.

Bruner, J. S. (1968) *Processes of Cognitive Growth: Infancy*, Worcester, UK: Clark University Press.

Bruner, J. S. (1978) 'On prelinguistic prerequisites of speech', in R. N. Compbell and P. T. Smith (eds), *Recent Advances in the Psychology of Language: Formal and Experimental Approach*, New York: Plenum Press.

Chasseguet-Smirgel, J. (1986) *Sexuality and Mind: The Role of the Father and the Mother in the Psyche*, New York: New York University Press.

Cohen, J. (1985) 'Trauma and Repression', *Psychoanalytic Inquiry*, *5*: 163–189.

De Cortiñas L.P (2009) *The Aesthetic Dimension of the Mind: Variations on a Theme of Bion*. Translated by P. Slotkin *et al.* London: Karnak Books.

Dromi, A., and Ringwald, P. (1996) *Speech and Language Therapy Intervention for Hearing Impaired Children, Pre-verbal Phase*, Tel Aviv: Ramot.

Durban, J. (2011) 'Shadows, ghosts and chimaeras: On some early modes of handling psycho-genetic heritage', *International Journal of Psychoanalysis*, *92*: 903–924.
Durban, J. (2012) 'Vergänglichkeit und die inneren Beziehungen zum Todes-object', in B. Nissen (ed.), *Wendepunkte: Zur Theorie und Klinik psychoanalytischer Veränderungsprozesse*, Geissen: Psychosozial Verlag, pp.107–135.
Durban, J. (2014) 'Despair and hope: On some varieties of countertransference and enactment in the psychoanalysis of ASD (autistic spectrum disorder) children', *Journal of Child Psychotherapy*, *40*(2): 187–200.
Erikson, E. (1950) *Childhood and Society*, New York: Norton.
Frenkel, A. (1979) *A Different Journey*, Tel Aviv, Israel: Masada.
Frankel, A. (1980) *Once Upon a Potty*, New York: Barron's Juveniles Educational Series.
Freud, A. (1965) *Normality and Pathology in Childhood: Assessments of Development*, Madison, CT: International Universities Press.
Freud, S. (1895) 'Project for a Scientific Psychology', *S.E. 1*: 355–417.
Freud, S. (1900) 'The interpretation of dreams', *S.E. 4*: 1–310.
Freud, S. (1905) 'Three essays on the theory of sexuality', *S.E. 7*: 125–171.
Freud, S. (1908) 'The character and erotisism', *S.E. 9*: 167–197.
Freud, S. (1911) 'Two principles of mental functioning', *S.E. 12*: 218–226.
Freud, S. (1919) 'The uncanny', *S.E. 17*: 217–256.
Freud, S. (1920) 'Beyond the pleasure principle', *S.E. 18*: 7–65.
Freud, S. (1923) 'The ego and the id', *S.E. 19*: 19–28.
Freud, S. (1926) 'Inhibitions, symptoms and anxiety', *20*: 87–175.
Gaddinni, E. (1992) *A Psychoanalytic Theory of Infantile Experience*. London: Routledge.
Gampel, G. (2005) 'Presence – developmental prespective', The Hebrew Introduction to Alvarez, A. *Live Company*, Tel Aviv, Israel: Tolaat Sefarim.
Ghent, E. (1992) 'Paradox and process', *Psychoanalytic Dialogue*, *2*: 135–159.
Green, A. (1998) 'The primordial mind and the work of the negative', *International Journal of Psychoanalysis*, *79*: 649–665.
Green, D., Charman, T., Pickles, A., Chandler, S., Loucas, T., Simonoff, E., and Baird, G. (2009) 'Impairment in movement skills of children with autistic spectrum disorders', *Developmental Medicine and Child Neurology*, *51*(4): 311–316.
Greenspan, S., and Wieder, S. (1998) *The Child With Special Needs: Encouraging Intellectual and Emotional Growth*, Boston, MA: De Capo Press.
Grotstein, J. S. (1987) 'Schizophrenia as a Disorder of Self-Regulation and Interactional Regulation', Presented at *The Regressed Patient*, Boyer House Foundation Conference, San Francisco, CA.
Haag, G., Tordjman, S., Duprat, A., Urwand, S., Jardin, F., Clement, M., and Dumont, A. (2005) 'Psychodynamic assessment of changes in children with autism under psychoanalytic treatment', *International Journal of Psychoanalysis*, *86*: 335–352.
Heidegger, M. (1962) *Being and Time*. New York: Harper and Row
Heimann, P. (1962) 'Notes on the Anal Stage', *International Journal of Psycho-Analysis*, *43*: 406–414.
Hobson, R. P. (1993) *Autism and the Development of Mind*, Hove: Lawrence Erlbaum Publishers.
Houellebecq, M. (2012) *The Map and the Territory*, New York: Vintage International.
Houzel, D. (2004) 'The psychoanalysis of infantile autism', *Journal of Child Psychotherapy*, *30*: 225–237.

Joseph, B. (1998) 'Thinking about a playroom', *Journal of Child Psychotherapy, 24*(3): 359–366.

Keller, H. (1954) *The Story of My Life*, New York: Garden City.

Klein, M. (1926) 'The psychological principles of infant analysis', in *Contributions to Psycho-Analysis, 1921–1945.* London: Hogarth Press, pp. 140–151, 1950.

Klein, M. (1946) 'Notes on some schizoid mechanisms', *International Journal of Psychoanalysis, 27*: 99–110.

Klein, M. (1952) Some theoretical conclusions regarding the emotional life of the infant. In J. Riviere, (ed.), *Developments in Psychoanalysis* (pp. 198–236). London: Hogarth Press.

Klein, M. (1963) 'The sense of loneliness', in *Envy and Gratitude and other Works 1946-1963*, London: Vintage Books, pp. 300–314.

Klein, M., Heimann, P., Isaacs, S., and Riviere, J. (1989) *Developments in Psychoanalysis*, London: Karnac Books.

Klein, M., Heimann, P., Isaacs, S., and Riviere, J. (1952) 'Some theoretical conclusions regarding the emotional life of the infant', in M. Klein, P. Heimann, S. Isaacs and J. Riviere (eds), *Envy and Gratitude and Other Works 1946–1963*, London: Vintage, 1989.

Langer, S. (1942) *Philosophy in a New Key*, 3rd edn, Cambridge, MA: Harvard University Press.

Lantz, J. (2002) 'Theory of mind in autism: Development, implications, and intervention', *The Reporter, 7*(3): 18–25.

Laplanche, J., and Pontalis, J. B. (1967) *Vocabulaire de la psychanalyse*, Paris: PUF.

Laplanche, J., and Pontalis J. B. (1988) *The Language of Psychoanalysis,* London: Karnac Books.

Levinas, E. (1978) *Existence and Existents*, Evanston, IL: Duquesne University Press, Northwestern University.

Levy, I. (1985) *Ethics and Infinity*, Pittsburgh, PA: Duquesne University Press.

Levy, I. (2012) *Home and Road, Reflections on the Psychoanalytic Imagination*, Tel Aviv, Israel: Resling.

Lewis, P., and Loman, S. (1990) *The Kestenberg Movement Profile – Its Past Present Applications and Future Directions*, Keene, New Hampshire: Antioch Institute Publication.

Mahler, M., Pine, F., and Bergman, A. (1975) *The Psychological Birth of the Human Infant Symbiosis and Individuation*, New York: Basic Books.

Maiello, S. (1997) 'The sound object: A hypothesis about pre-natal auditory experience and memory', *Journal of Child Psychotherapy, 21*(1): 23–24.

Maiello, S. (2001) 'Über das Fehlen rhythmischen Zeiterlebens im Autismus,' in J. Staigle, S. Maiello, P. Warsitz, C. Krüger, F. Nielebock, E. Ramminger, I. Petramer, M. Maas and H. Nonnenmann (Hg.) *Zeit ohne Ende? Aspekte der Zeitlichkeit in der psychoanalytischen Sozialarbeit.* Tübingen, Germany: edition diskord.

Meltzer, D. (1974) 'Adhesive identification', in A. Hahn (ed.), *Sincerity and Other Works: Collected Papers of Donald Meltzer*, London: Karnac Books, 1994.

Meltzer, D. (1975) 'Adhesive identification', *Contemporary Psycho-Analysis, 11*: 289–310.

Meltzer, D. (1992) *The Claustrum: An Investigation of Claustrophobic Phenomena*, Perth, UK: Clunie Press.

Meltzer, D., and Williams, M. H. (1988) 'The aesthetic conflict: Its place in the developmental process', in *The Apprehension of Beauty*, London: Karnac Books.

Meltzer, D., Bremner, J., Hoxter, S., Weddell, D., and Wittenberg, I. (1975) *Explorations in Autism: A Psycho-Analytical Study*, Perth, UK: Clunie Press.

Menninger, W. C. (1943) 'Characterologic and symptomatic expressions related to the anal phase of psychosexual development', *Psychoanalytic Quarterly, 12*: 161–193.

Ming, X., Brimacombe, M., and Wagner, G. C. (2007) 'Prevalence of motor impairment in autism spectrum disorders', *Brain and Development, 29*: 565–570.

Moore, B., and Fine, B. (1990) *Psychoanalytic Terms and Concepts*, New Haven, CT: The American Psychoanalytic Association, Yale University Press.

Neisser, U. (1991) 'Two perceptually given aspects of the self and their development', *Developmental Review, 11*: 209–197.

Newson, J. (1978) 'Dialogue and development', in A. Lock (ed.), *Action, Gesture and Symbol*, London: Academic Press.

Ogden, T. H. (1980) 'On the nature of schizophrenic conflict', *International Journal of Psychoanalysis, 61*: 357–373.

Ogden, T. H. (1989) *The Primitive Edge of Experience*, London: Jason Aronson.

Ogden, T. H. (1991) 'Some theoretical comments on personal isolation', *Psychoanalytic Dialogue, 1*: 377–390.

Peirce, C. S. (1992) *The Essential Peirce, vol 1: 1867–1893*, Bloomington, IN: Indiana UP.

Peirce, C. S. (1998) *The Essential Peirce, vol 2: 1893–1913*, Bloomington, IN: Indiana UP.

Piontelli, A. (1992) *From Fetus to Child: An Observational and Psychoanalytic Study*, London: Tavistock Publications.

Pollak, T. (2003) 'Image formation of a "Frontal Spine" in work with Autistic Children', *Israel Psychoanalytic Journal, 1*(4): 565–605.

Pollak, T. (2009) 'The "body-container": A new perspective on the "body-ego"', *International Journal of Psychoanalysis, 90*: 487–506.

Pollak, T. (2017) *The BodI – The Question of the Body Between Object Relations Theory and Perleau-Ponty Phenomenological Philosophy*, Tel Aviv, Israel: Carmel.

Provost, B., Lopez, B. R., and Heimerl, S. (2007) 'A comparison of motor delays in young children: Autism spectrum disorder, developmental delay, and developmental concerns', *Journal of Autism and Developmental Disorders, 37*: 321–328.

Resnik, S. (1995) *Mental Space*, London: Karnac Books.

Rhode, M. (1977) 'Psychosomatic integrations: eye and mouth in baby observation', in S. Reid (ed.), *Developments in Infant Observation: The Tavistock Model*, London: Routledge.

Rhode, M. (2012) 'Whose memories are they and where do they go? Problems surrounding internalization in children on the autistic spectrum', *International Journal of Psychoanalysis, 93*: 356–376.

Rosenfeld, D. (1997) 'Understanding varieties of autistic encapsulation: A homage to Frances Tustin', in T. Mitrani and J. L. Mitrani (eds), *Encounters With Autistic States*, Northvale: NJ: Jason Aronson, pp. 179–195.

Sacks, O. (2010) *The Mind's Eye*, New York: Knopf.

Salomonsson, B. (2006) 'The impact of words on neuropsychiatric children – consequences for psychoanalytic technique', *International Journal of Psychoanalysis, 87*: 1029–1047.

Salomonsson, B. (2007a) 'Semiotic transformations in psychoanalysis with infants and adults', *International Journal of Psychoanalysis, 87*: 1029–1047.

Salomonsson, B. (2007b) '"Talk to me baby, tell me what's the matter now". Semiotic and developmental perspectives on communication in psychoanalytic infant treatment', *International Journal of Psychoanalysis*, *88*: 127–146.

Salomonsson, B. (2007c) 'The Breast, the hole, and the ghost. The transition to verbal symbolic functioning', Paper presented in the Symposium *Psychoanalysis in Phases of Developmental Transition*, Berlin: IPA Congress.

Sandler, J. (1960) 'Background of safety', *International Journal of Psychoanalysis*, *41*: 352–356.

Segal, H. (1957) 'Notes on Symbol Formation', in *The Work of Hanna Segal*, New York: Aronson, 1981.

Shahar-Levi, Y. (2001) 'The function of the human motor system in processes of storing and retrieving of preverbal, primal experience', *Psychoanalytic Inquiry*, *21*(3).

Shahar-Levi, Y. (2004) *A Body-Movement-Mind Paradigm: For Movement Therapy and Psychophysical Analysis of Emotive Movement*, Tel Aviv, Israel: Y. Shahar-Levi.

Shannon, D. (1998) *No David!*, New York: Scholastic Inc.

Solan, R. (2007) *The Riddle of the Childhood,* Ben Shemen, Israel: Modan.

Steiner, J. (1993) *Psychic Retreats*, London: Routledge.

Stern, D. (1985) *The Interpersonal World of the Infant*, New York: Basic Books.

Stern, D. and Bruschweile, N. (1998) *The Birth of a Mother*, New York: Basic Books.

Trevarthen, C. (1977) 'Descriptive analyses of infant communicative behaviour', in H. R. Schaffer (ed.), *Studies in Mother-Infant Interaction*, London: Academic Press.

Tustin, F. (1972) *Autism and Childhood Psychosis*, London: Hogarth Press.

Tustin, F. (1981) *Autistic States in Children*, New York: Routledge.

Tustin, F. (1984) 'Autistic shapes', *International Journal of Psychoanalysis*, *11*: 279–290.

Tustin, F. (1986) *Autistic Barriers in Neurotic Patients*, London: Karnac Books.

Tustin, F. (1990) *The Protective Shell in Children and Adults*, London: Karnac Books.

Tustin, F. (1991) 'Revised understandings of psychogenic autism', *International Journal of Psychoanalysis*, *72*(4): 585–591.

Tustin, F. (1994) 'Perpetuation of an error', *Journal of Child Psychotherapy*, *20*: 3–23.

Winnicott, D. W. (1945) 'Primitive emotional development', *International Journal of Psychoanalysis*, *26*(3–4):137–143.

Winnicott, D. W. (1954a) 'Mind and it's relation to psyche-soma', *The British Journal of Medical Psychology*, *27*: 101–109

Winnicott, D. W. (1954b) 'Meta psychological and clinical aspects of regression within the psychoanalytical set-up', *International Journal of Psychoanalysis*, *36*: 16–26.

Winnicott, D. W. (1956) 'Primary maternal preoccupation', in *Through Paediatrics to Psycho-analysis*, London: Karnac Books.

Winnocott, D. W. (1958) 'The capacity to be alone'. *International Journal of Psychoanalysis*. *39*(5): 416-420.

Winnicott, D. W. (1960) 'The theory of the parent-infant relationship', *International Journal of Psychoanalysis*, *41*: 585–595.

Winnicott, D. W. (1962) 'Ego integration in child development', in *The Maturational Process and the Facilitating Environment*, London: Karnac Books, pp. 56–76.

Winnicott, D. W. (1963a) 'Communicating and not communicating leading to a study of certain opposites', in L. Caldwell and H. Taylor Robinson (eds), *The Collected Works of D. W. Winnicott* (2016) , *6*: 1960–1963, Oxford: Oxford University Press.

Winnicott, D. W. (1963b) 'From Dependence Towards Independence in the Development of the Individual', in *The Maturational Process and the Facilitating Environment*, London: Karnac Books, pp. 83–92.

Winnicott, D. W. (1965) 'The theory of the parent-infant relationship', in *The Maturational Process and the Facilitating Environment*, London: Karnac Books, pp. 37–55.

Winnicott, D. W. (1980) 'Fear of breakdown', *International Journal of Psychoanalysis*, *61*: 351–358.

Winnicott, D. W. (1971a) 'Transitional objects and transitional phenomena'. in *Playing and Reality*, London: Tavistock Publications, pp. 1–26.

Winnicott, D. W. (1971b) 'The use of an object and relating through identifications', in *Playing and Reality*, London: Tavistock Publications, pp. 86–94.

Winnicott, D. W. (1971c) 'Mirror-role of mother and family in child development', in *Playing and Reality*, London: Tavistock Publications, pp. 11–118.

Winnicott, D. W. (1982) 'Ego integration in child development', in *The Maturational Process and the Facilitating Environment*, London: Karnac Books.

Winnicott, D. W. (1990) *The Maturational Process and the Facilitating Environment*, London: Karnac Books.

Winnicott, D. W. (1992) *Through Pediatrics to Psyco-Analysis*, London: Karnac Books.

Wright, K. (1991) *Vision and Separation*, London: Jason Aronson.

Zur, B., Segal, M., and Rom, A. (2012) *So Says the Child, Language Acquisition and Communication in Childhood*, Tel Aviv, Israel: Mofe't.

Index

Locators in *italics* refer to figures.